Writing to Create Ourselves

Writing to Create Ourselves

New Approaches for Teachers, Students, and Writers

By T. D. Allen

Foreword by John F. Povey

University of Oklahoma Press : Norman

By T. D. ALLEN

Not Ordered by Man (Santa Fe, 1967)
Writing to Create Ourselves: New Approaches for Teachers, Students, and Writers (Norman, 1982)

EDITOR:

The Whispering Wind (New York, 1972)
Arrows Four (New York, 1974)

IN COLLABORATION WITH DON ALLEN:

Doctor in Buckskin (New York, 1951)
Troubled Border (New York, 1954)
Prisoners of the Polar Ice (Philadelphia, 1956)
Ambush at Buffalo Wallow (New York, 1956)
Tall as Great Standing Rock (Philadelphia, 1963)
Navahos Have Five Fingers (Norman, 1963)
Doctor, Lawyer, Merchant, Chief (Philadelphia, 1965)

IN COLLABORATION WITH EMERSON BLACKHORSE MITCHELL:

Miracle Hill: The Story of a Navaho Boy (Norman, 1967)

Library of Congress Cataloging in Publication Data

Writing to create ourselves.

Includes bibliographical references and index.
1. English language—Composition and exercises—Study and teaching—United States. 2. Creative writing. 3. Indians of North America—Education. 4. English language—Study and teaching—Foreign students. I. Title.
PE1405.U6A44   808'.042'07073   82-1878
                                      AACR2

Copyright © 1982 by the University of Oklahoma Press, Norman, Publishing Division of the University. Manufactured in the U.S.A. First edition.

Contents

Foreword — vii
Preface — xv
Introduction — 3

Book One: *Teaching English Upside Down*

Chapter 1. Why Try? — 11
2. Why Write? — 15
3. What Is It Possible for Us to Teach? — 17
4. The Five Doors — 20
5. Here and Now — 30
6. What Shall I Write? — 41
7. Now That You Have Something on Paper — 48
8. The Raw Material of the Writing Game — 63
9. Is It a Poem? — 70
10. Building Blocks for Prose Writing — 88
11. A Story Is a Structure — 103
12. Capsule Lessons in Writing — 110

Book Two: *Experiments That Worked or Didn't Work but Might*

Chapter 13. Teacher Exchange — 127
14. Writing Teachers Write — 132
15. Teacher-Student Experiments in Learning to Write — 142
16. Grading—That Required Abomination — 151
17. Let's Talk Pictures — 159
18. We Write to Be Read — 172
19. Letters Are Not Dead Yet — 183
20. The Identity Thing — 188

21.	Luring Students to Read	194
22.	Helping Students Tell a Story	200
23.	Using Those Beloved, Obstreperous Machines	209
24.	Ready-Made Patterns	218
25.	When All Else Fails	226
26.	For Teachers Only	239

Index 249

Foreword

John F. Povey

Bilingualism and biculturalism are concepts that challenge the conventional interpretation of American history. This nation is based upon the principle of assimilation, "the melting pot." Those "huddled masses yearning to be free" were to become Americans, and America was defined by the English language and the codes of Anglo behavior. Surprisingly, the system worked reasonably well. Russians and Italians, Greeks and Swedes did become Americans. English was learned, and residual accent was intrusive for only a generation. Probably there was more hardship than is usually admitted, but the results seemed to justify the elimination of the inherited language and culture. Apparent success for many concealed those peoples for whom such simplistic and arrogant expectations of cultural adaptation were not acceptable. They did not begin with the immigrant's willingness to subjugate his identity to the mores of the promised land. These people, the Mexicans in the Southwest and, above all, the American Indians, saw this policy of assimilation not as the golden opportunity perceived by the immigrants but as an invitation to cultural suicide presented by powerful invading forces.

It is against this backdrop of history that we must understand the issue of bilingualism. In this country in recent years, most people assumed that new legislation would charitably provide a temporary educational control while the transition was made into the dominant culture. They have been appalled to discover that non-Anglos see bilingualism as a weapon to reinforce a different identity, a means of retaining a familiar and deeply cherished inheritance. None have expressed this attitude as strongly as the Indians, who have suffered more than a century of Anglo dominance.

The issue is clear. English is the essential tool for survival within the American system. How can it be presented so that it is perceived as providing an advantage rather than a threat? The experience of former colonial countries indicates a possible direction. In such countries the colonial language is employed for its necessary utility, but it is no longer seen as undermining the indigenous society because it is modified to new usage and made a vehicle for the expression of cultures and ideas unanticipated by those who first imposed it. That experience confirms that English can define even the most intimate concerns of those to whom it is not the mother tongue. When that is recognized, antagonism ends. The urgent need to seek techniques for individual communication becomes motivation for the vigorous exploration of the second language that has been resisted when it was seen as expressing only the oppressive majority culture that they were being forced to join.

The philosophy of the program outlined in this book can be subsumed in a dramatic declaration: English can be your language as much as ours. English can contain Navaho and Eskimo feeling, as it has already expressed cultures equally distant from British-American society. Only when that idea is taken to heart can the process of education in English begin.

In Indian schools where this approach was first attempted, the classroom problems were generally as clear as they were distressing. Indian students were failing lamentably where English was being taught by conventional principles. Yet all their future opportunities depend upon their achieving success in that language. Competence in English is the most essential and utilitarian obligation of their education. Unhappily, their inherited revulsion to Anglo educational priorities engendered specific resistance to their learning. Linguistic antagonism had to be removed, and this required a fresh incentive. Improvement would not be achieved by additional replications of those tedious formal exercises in grammar that they had already demonstratively rejected out of boredom. Implicit in all authorized texts was the unquestioned belief that several years of basic practice would develop an adequate functional usage. The books of rhetoric urged more intensive applications of established procedures, on the assumptions of dog training that repetition is the only means of imprinting knowledge in "simple" minds. Few educationalists allowed that there could be an approach diametrically opposed to the existing dull drill and workbook routine of established pedagogic methods. Those who pleaded for alternatives were usually dismissed as cranks rather than hailed as innovators. T. D. Allen was just such a person. She brought to the project her own skill as a writer, an understanding of the Indian way of life, and, above all, her inimitable sensitivity and warmth. The activities she encouraged in the classroom that are explained in this book created nothing less than a revolution. Terry Allen began her program, in contrast to the grammar texts, from the opposite end of the educational equation, placing function before practice, defining purpose before methods.

Without the desire for self-expression through the language, no improvement is possible in the language. That essential desire can only arise when the language is seen as providing the means for personal statement. The first step in the classroom was then to foster this desire—the students' admission of the utility of English.

Traditional teachers continue to argue the reverse. Until accuracy was achieved by their methods, how was it possible to imagine that the language could be used skillfully enough to serve any creative purpose? Allen saw advantages in reversing the stultifying results of that procedure. She reasoned that the only legitimate purpose of any language learning was the need to communicate. The desire to say something that someone would read with interest—that was the motivation that would produce improvement.

Better grades did not motivate Indian students. In fact, most Indians frown on such obvious marks of getting ahead of their fellows. In contrast, the essential human need to be heard, to be understood, had been sanctioned since the days of Tecumseh and Chief Joseph. If saying something and being listened to was what it was all about, then English was no longer merely an imposed academic subject. It ceased to be threatening and boring. No longer did it belong only to the enemy. It became an acceptable, even admired, vehicle for personal assertiveness. The difference in attitude and enthusiasm toward learning that this discovery occasioned in students was marked.

The first evidence in the school where Allen began teaching was the observable eagerness in students to manipulate the second language to the same effective purposes that their mother tongues were able to serve. This happier attitude would have effected a valuable improvement in classroom response, even if the product of such a technique had been dismal or trivial.

In fact, the work that students produced when following the principles outlined in this book proved not banal and commonplace but exciting and original — an outpouring of deeply felt emotion. It was a rich expression of students' essential and long-restrained Indianness made explicit and public in their ingenious and perceptive prose observations, but it was written in English.

Their early-draft English was not always the English of the school textbook. How could it be? Allen taught the professional author's way of getting the idea on paper and then revising as many times as necessary to make it readable and publishable — the method that truly motivates learning competence in grammar and syntax. Since students did their own revising, they saw and learned grammar in its functional capacity as a means to clarity.

Even so, some of the final-draft aberrant variations fretted orthodox teachers for their lack of formal accuracy. Yet the style was the more exciting and original for its first-language carry-over and flavorings. Freed from the expectations of the commonplace, these students instinctively devised their own English style, frequently modified by their mother tongues. They enriched rather than deformed the English language. Their writing provided new evidence that the English language has the flexibility to express many sensibilities far different from the tradition of Anglo usage.

The project, intended to stimulate general English usage, took on a life of its own. The creativity it induced provided examples for emulation that became the additional stimulus to new writing and wide reading at all learning levels in some 150 schools. It provided the material for anthologies published by commercial publishers and for an important annual sequence of publications presenting the best of the year's writing from each school. These anthologies were called appropriately enough *Arrow*—an Indian weapon that once battled the invaders. In this case their quiver encompassed words—experiments with poetry, intimate short stories, lucid descriptions, legends, beliefs—all in English.

In all these schools bulletin boards displayed fledgling efforts at verse. New school literary journals presented the work of the students to their peers. Publishing this material gave evidence of an exciting breakthrough toward communication. It supplied an added benefit, unanticipated in the original plan. The writing provided a body of readings by young Indians that other Indians and readers generally found fascinating. Those relegated to the remedial-language study rooms reserved to assist those with woefully limited basic skills eagerly examined the writings of their friends. Their reading incompetence proved to derive less from functional inadequacy than from a disenchantment with orthodox readers. A thrilled reveling in the Indian experience of this literature provided a hungry recognition of shared identity. This, in its turn, enhanced the desire to experiment, to try for themselves.

Amazing evidence of the creative potential of this system is contained in the work of Emerson ("Barney") Blackhorse Mitchell, a Navaho who had become a junior in high school with only minimal English-language skills. At the Institute of American Indian Arts in Santa Fe, New Mexico, where Allen began teaching, Barney elected to enroll in "Writing." His verbal acuity was all in Navaho, but, encouraged to explore English, he experimented with unyielding determination.

The result, in time, was *Miracle Hill: The Story of a Navaho Boy*.[1] "A true tale so entrancing that it recently went into a third printing," one reviewer said. Reviews in the *New York Times, Chicago Tribune, Los Angeles Times,* and many other review media were enthusiastic. The book is now available in paperback, and thousands of Indian students devour it in their reading periods. Normally they would be coping

---

[1] Norman: University of Oklahoma Press, 1967.

with contrived elementary tales foreign to their feelings and upbringing.

Barney merely exhibits to an extreme and remarkable degree the way that the teaching method works. By observing its techniques, Indian children and young people can be encouraged to explore English out of their own discovered need. It informs them that English allows an exciting potential for cultural expansion rather than a narrow bread-and-butter utility. To develop the possibilities of sustaining other successful young writers, students, even at the elementary levels, must be protected from having their imaginations stunted and inhibited by the pedantic restrictions of exact grammatical usage.

No one can doubt the virtue of good and correct English. The only argument is how to acquire it. Allen suggests an unexpected but tested policy that does not reject the achievement of exactness. She merely postpones this as a declared goal. In some happy way that necessary end is additionally supplied by the creative use of language. Allow the free exploration of words to begin with, and later much else, even accuracy, is added unto that usage.

Allen's educational experiment with Indian children is surely of enormous general significance. It has wide-range applicability. Although some of her success owes a great deal to her own ability and dedication, the technique is not so individualized that it cannot be transferred into the regular classroom and become available to other competent and intelligent teachers. Having tried out this approach for five years at the Institute of American Indian Arts, Allen took the method into 144 Indian and Eskimo schools from Alaska to Mississippi and from coast to coast. Other teachers, with her help, were able to work with success in the same way. Finally, she taught at the University of California at Santa Cruz. Her reversed approach to the teaching of English worked in all these situations.

The method is effective in wider contexts than those where students labor under the inhibitions of moving into reading and writing in English from a foreign mother tongue. Even with native speakers, teachers are encountering the dismaying discovery that English has become, in effect, "foreign" to them as well. Students increasingly resist traditional teaching materials and methods and are graduated from level to level unable to read or write. They too will achieve success when they are taught that vital truth: Here is your language, what do you want to say in it?

Allen's concept is so original that, once it is observed, it simply seems obvious: the excitement of creative and imaginative and honest writing should be regarded as the beginning rather than the end of language teaching. Such teaching eliminates the normal, dismal, classroom tasks and dismisses the belief that hours of tedious formality are the inescapable prerequisites of more innovative language use.

Probably, like all the very best ideas, this is not so new. The word "education," as we all know, is derived from the Latin and implies a "drawing out" of student skills. This is a happier and more productive technique than the common method of "pushing in" a block of resented and resisted information. It returns education to the students, asking them to determine their own needs. Allen's profound gift as a teacher and friend to many young students made this process of "drawing out" exciting in its potential and in its actual achievement.

In her modest way she would make no possessive claim for this method, though indeed it is surely her invention. In this book she is saying, "I have tried this method and found that it works. Can it help you too?" Those who do try it may also discover the ineffable pleasure of creating creativity. That is surely the most exciting sponsorship possible between teacher and protégé. Those who teach English, the language of one of the richest literary heritages, should delight in the possibility of acting as midwives to new writing. And if most of their young Miltons remain mute and inglorious, such teachers will still have the sensation of pointing out the most exciting road of all—the road that "should be taken."

Preface

This book evolved from my inability to be in 144 places at once. Those "places" were schools scattered from Unalakleet, Alaska, to Philadelphia, Mississippi, and from Riverside, California, to Cherokee, North Carolina. My being present when needed presented problems. I was working, finally, with more than 250 teachers and several thousand students.

We were in the business of helping students write well and read widely, in that order. We began through classroom demonstrations. When time and space intervened, a manual became necessary, and we soon supplemented that with a monthly newsletter in which my teachers and I exchanged experiences and suggestions.

Our method of work grew directly out of my twenty previous years of professional writing, editing, and publishing in many fields. George A. Boyce was responsible for selling me the completely foreign idea of teaching someone else to write. I was an author, not a teacher. Boyce was superintendent of the Institute of American Indian Arts in its first struggling year when I happened to visit it. I found a student body representing something over ninety tribes of Indians and Eskimos and an arts faculty of professionals. "We know these students can paint and sculpt and throw a beautiful pot," Boyce told me, "but we don't know whether they can express themselves in words. Many of them use English as a second language. Most have had poor language training in their grade schools. They need to be able to use the English language if they're to get along in any of the other arts. We want to add a written-arts studio. How about coming to help us?"

As we talked on for an hour and then two, Boyce kept

saying: "No one will rush you. We'll give you all the time you need. This will be the most difficult of all the arts for these students to master. We'll give you time."

That was 1963, and the time was right. The country was ready to hear what blacks and Indians and Eskimos had to say. Our students, never having been listened to, were all but bursting to speak.

My teaching was based on long years of sitting at a typewriter and on tips taken from my own teachers, especially Walter S. Campbell and Maren Elwood; from my first and best fiction editor, John Fischer, at Harper's; and from my reading. The core of my own method is not writing but rewriting. Most teachers assume that high school students will not rewrite. Since I had never taught, I did not know what high school students will not do. Before the end of our first semester my students were selling to national magazines.

After I had established the Written Arts Department in the Institute of American Indian Arts (IAIA) and taught there for five years, the Bureau of Indian Affairs asked me to go into some of their other high schools. "Train language-arts teachers to work on writing and reading as you have at Santa Fe," they said.

I started traveling to nine schools, working with as many of the teachers in all fields as wished to work with me but concentrating on the language-arts departments. Other schools soon wanted in, and by the end of four years we were reaching, directly or through summer workshops, 144 schools and were including elementary along with secondary grades. The University of California at Santa Cruz handled my contract the last five years of the project, and, during terms when travel money ran out, I also taught at the university level.

John F. Povey served as consultant on the project from the beginning. He went to many of the schools and learned to scale down his usual university-geared teaching to whatever grade needed him. Lawana Trout also traveled on occasion and did demonstration teaching. Anne Cathcart Hall spent one semester of her college career as a resident reading-writing teacher among the Sioux in North Dakota. Ronald Rogers, one of my early students at IAIA, finished college and accompanied me on school visits. Ron, I must add, taught exactly the way I had taught him, and he was highly successful. He is now teaching and writing among the Blackfoot in Montana.

In these pages you will meet many generous, born-again teachers: Ann Gulledge, from Albuquerque; Peggy Jo Hall, of Sequoyah High School, Tahlequah, Oklahoma; Mae Schense, of Turtle Mountain School, Belcourt, North Dakota; Cleta and Glen Morehead, of Mount Edgecumbe School, Sitka, Alaska; Alexa West, from Intermountain School, in Utah; Marianna Taylor, of Sherman High School, in California; Ruby Shannon, from Carson City, Nevada; that full-of-ideas teaching team, Julian Wharton and Carol Soatikee, of Concho School, in Oklahoma—the list is endless. I am indebted to all the teachers and administrators who took me, an outsider, in and lent me their students and poured out their own ideas and actually opened the way to bringing students of all ages into the exciting world of writing, of reading, and of being read.

Thanks to Mary Lois Mamer and the Kehoe-Mamer Foundation, we were able to publish beautifully bound annual contest books, *Arrow I* through *Arrow VI*. These now grace tables in hogans and wickiups and Native American homes throughout the country. The first four volumes were published as a paperback, *Arrows IV,* by a commercial publisher. It is still producing royalties and permission fees, which are passed on to student contributors. The publications and the financial rewards provide lifetime prideful symbols for student authors and for their families. The commercial paperback is included in thousands of school libraries and personal collections.

After our project expanded, our students were no longer exclusively Indian or Eskimo. We included many Caucasians, blacks, Spanish- and Mexican-Americans, and mixtures of all kinds. Our methods, arrived at on the job, worked well with all students who had previously been silenced and tongue-tied by traditional approaches to language usage. My teachers learned to write well themselves and wrote along with their students. School librarians worked with us and learned new ways to start students on lifelong adventures in reading. Student books stimulated school-wide reading and recruited new, enthusiastic writers who also had something to say.

We are convinced that you too, as an individual, can write

to be read. If you are fortunate enough to be a teacher, you can start an epidemic of writing and reading in your school.

T. D. ALLEN

Carmel-by-the-Sea, California

Writing to Create Ourselves

Introduction

    I wish we dident have to wright this because I hate to right. One resion I hate to right is because I cant right. in my hole life I have written only 5 letters—I hate to *"right"*—Wrighting is a dull thing writeing is the most dullest thing about school— I hate to right any thing and every thing—I hate to right. If you want some thing written Right it your self dont ast me—I hate to right boy do I hate to right. but If it werent for righting you woundent be reading this now would you so I hope I took up the hole tin minents because I hate to "RIGHT"!
    Oʜ Rɪɢʜᴛ—Time is up! ! ! !

The author of this essay was in the seventh grade. His sentiments and proficiency are fairly typical. He failed to sign his paper, so I cannot give him proper credit. I do give him credit for communicating two profound truths: (1) students hate to write because they "cant right," and (2) they long for someone to listen. Even this disgruntled boy hints at a wish: "but If it werent for righting you woundent be reading this now would you."

The aims of this book are:

    1. To take the mystery out of writing so that students can write with confidence and satisfaction.

    2. To lure students through writing into reading with ease and pleasure.

    3. To show methods and results of one experiment in teaching that may help you discover your methods and achieve your best teaching results.

    4. To find as a predictable by-product that your teaching will become stimulating, joyful, and highly successful in drawing from your students their own best efforts and self-discovery.

A brief description of how this experiment took place will help explain that we were not dealing with students more gifted than yours, that we were not working under ideal conditions, and that we did not have unlimited funds. In short, your students and your conditions are different, no doubt, but not necessarily inferior to ours. We are all in this together. Let us see how we can help each other.

This book, then, is the story of an experiment in teaching. I am telling it on my knees to those teachers who care deeply that our students are leaving school never having had the fun and satisfaction of writing well enough for someone else to read their words with interest, never knowing the excitement of reading for the sheer joy of letting words in their best order flow into them from the printed page.

It is my conviction, born of experience, that almost any teacher can lead students into reading and writing well. By reading and writing, students can grow toward their own highest possibilities. Without these skills they will settle for second best—in achievement and in sense of self—all their lives.

When Marva Collins and her students were featured on the television program "60 Minutes," viewers said: "She's a remarkable teacher." "It's her personality." She is remarkable. I'm very sure, however, that the teachers added to her no-longer-one-teacher school are also getting remarkable results. They are bound to have different personalities.

When my high school students had an anthology of poetry published by a commercial publisher and an autobiography published by the University of Oklahoma Press,[1] some people shrugged and called it a fluke. Later, however, another publisher brought out a commercial paperback anthology written by the students of the teachers we had taught to use our methods. Today poems and stories written by our students are in demand by publishers of textbooks and anthologies. Our former students are receiving permission fees for works written while they were attending grade schools and high schools throughout the United States. Many of these students use English as a second language.

---

[1] Emerson Blackhorse Mitchell and T. D. Allen, *Miracle Hill: The Story of a Navaho Boy* (Norman: University of Oklahoma Press, 1967).

It is in the sure knowledge that it can happen more than once that I would like to tell you the story of our experiments in teaching and in learning. Given what my students and I had learned and demonstrated, teachers in Bureau of Indian Affairs schools from Alaska to Mississippi and from the West to the East coasts were able to achieve results on a par with ours. I know for a fact that you too can use our experience to work out your own methods of teaching that will stir up equivalent student enthusiasm and achievement.

This book is for teachers of students who use English as a second language and for teachers of any students who will not or cannot read and write. It is not aimed at a particular age group or grade in school. I worked with students at all levels from kindergarten through university. I worked with teachers of first grade through high school.

The method we used is simple. It amounts to teaching upside down—writing first, then grammar. The method probably developed because I entered teaching not as a teacher but as a writer. I shared with students the techniques of writing that had been taught to me and that I had used through years of professional writing.

We approached the teaching of English usage not by the grammar door but by the writing door—letting students write what they wanted to say. We came to grammar—spelling, syntax, rhetoric—through revising material for reading. This is the way a professional writes, and many of our students became professional in the sense of being paid for their work. A few are now full-time authors and teachers.

Our method is based on two suppositions: First, each child, each young person, is an individual. No class is a mass. Second, each person's experience, no matter how brief (as for a kindergartner), is of value to him[2] and to the rest of us.

I often say to students that we are all interested in and write about just one subject. That subject is Life for Human Beings. When we write or read about nature and the animal world, we relate that information to life for human beings. What this means for students is that any part of life they have lived provides a good subject for their writing. Because

---

[2] For convenience, in this book "he" is used to refer to the individual student, to avoid the cumbersome "he or she."

each one of us is special—one of a kind—each one's view of what has happened to him is unique and thus adds to the sum of human experience, provided these experiences are written and shared.

I had become acquainted with George A. Boyce through some of his writings as an educator with the Bureau of Indian Affairs. In fact, my husband and I had included his *A Primer of Navajo Economic Problems* in the bibliography of our *Navahos Have Five Fingers*.[3] I met Boyce in person in Santa Fe, New Mexico, where he was superintendent of the new Institute of American Indian Arts (IAIA). The institute was a combined academic high school and art school—an innovative concept then being shaped by Boyce and his handpicked staff of educators and professional artists.

The school opened in the fall of 1962. I met Boyce in the spring of 1963. He had decided to add courses in creative writing to his Arts Department. After I had thanked him for what I had learned from his writings, Boyce started talking about the possibility of my setting up a writing section of his Arts Department.

He explained that many of his students—representing some ninety tribes of Indians, Eskimos, and Aleuts—used English as a second language, and that virtually all of them used English poorly. "We know that these students can paint a picture, weave a rug, throw a pot, dance, sing, sculpt, and such," he said. "We're not at all sure that they can express themselves in words, but we want to give them the chance. I do promise that if you apply for the job as our writing teacher, and if we hire you, we'll give you time. We know in advance that writing will probably come slowly, more slowly than any of the other arts. We'll give you as much time as you need."

His promise and my own curiosity made me apply, even though teaching school had never been a goal of mine. That fall I was assigned a large, light, dirty room with a long storage closet and, off one end, a tiny room with a window. My quarters had no furnishings except four paint-smeared worktables. I was granted scavenger rights to the storerooms

---

[3] Norman: University of Oklahoma Press, 1963.

on campus. After much hands-and-knees scrubbing, I started setting up the Writing Studio.

The discard piles in storerooms yielded scratched, cracked, wooden bookshelves. I took several of them. A low, round table suggested a place for books and magazines, so I took that. Books and magazines meant that there would be a need for comfortable places to sit while reading. I found a love-seat-size sofa and its matching larger mate. Two upholstered chairs would fill the space available around the low table. All these were so ragged and dirty that they had been given up as a lost cause by the dorms. I had to buy fabric and cover all the cushions. When I had done that much, the business administrator scrounged through a basement and found a metal desk that someone else had rejected because it had one badly bent leg.

Along one end of the room I made an island from the scoured tables and placed twenty chairs around it. My desk and my personal typewriter, together with bookshelves, a conference chair or two, and a metal file from salvage, became the teacher's end of the room. The reading center fitted into the middle. Bookshelves served as room dividers and filled the unpainted wall spaces between doors and windows. To fill the bookshelves, I went to the stacks of books that had been discarded from the library through the years and were destined to be burned. I wanted a feeling of books immediately, even though these dull, ragged specimens would be replaced as soon as possible. I bought a rod and hung a flowered curtain to cover a rusty sink and counter. House plants liked our room and grew to cover scratches and cracks in our tables and bookshelves.

We had plenty of light and space (some of you do not have those advantages, I know). I was allowed to order paper, pens, file folders, and such. Friends let me have used magazines. It took me more than a year to get a typewriter for students to use. In the meantime they used mine. When I needed a record player, the Music Department let me borrow one. Eventually I acquired a tape recorder.

One condition was perhaps more favorable than yours. I had classes all day, and students in the upper grades could, if they wished, enroll for two or even three consecutive periods of writing a day. Since partial classes overlapped, however, the teacher was always in danger of failing to instruct a few students or of boring some to death by repetition. You probably do not have that handicap. When I worked with teachers and students in more traditional schools, my conditions were very similar to yours.

Given your conditions and your students, you should be in for an exciting and delightful teaching turnabout.

Book 1

TEACHING ENGLISH UPSIDE DOWN

1. Why Try?

Schools endlessly revise their curricula, but the teaching of English goes on forever. English is one subject that is never left off the list of offerings or off the list of requirements. From grade one through graduate school students in this country are exposed to the study of the English language.

Still, when we pick up any newspaper or magazine, we are likely to be confronted with laments over the deficient state of reading and writing among students and graduates of our local elementary schools or of Yale and Stanford. Parents and educators are asking: "Why can't they read? Why don't our schools teach them to write? How can they get a job? How can they do the required work in any discipline when they can't read or write?"

Worried citizens vote down school bonds in local elections, saying: "No more money. With all the money they now have, our schools aren't teaching our children to read and write." University alumni funds dwindle before the argument that students are being graduated without having learned the simple, essential skills of English usage. Calculators may substitute for memorizing the times-nine table, but surely we can expect our schools to teach reading and writing.

School boards and teachers ask for more money. Government appropriations make possible learned surveys that generate costly new programs. Special teachers are hired and provided with funds for handbooks, new texts, classroom libraries, language labs, and supposedly literacy-stimulating activities—museum excursions, trips to Mexico or Europe, audio-visual equipment and materials.... The list is endless.

In this country, and around the world, skills in the use of the English language are essential to any kind of academic or living-making endeavor. These skills are threatened with extinction. Money that formerly went into teaching English grammar and literature is being siphoned off into teaching other languages—from the widely spoken and literature-rich Spanish to the dying dialects of thirty-member Indian tribes. Many university departments are devoted to the training of teachers who will work toward developing skills in the English language among students whose first language is other than English. All too often these efforts result in weakening the use of English.

A few years ago a battle raged between educators of the Bureau of Indian Affairs and the American Indian parents of children attending state and government schools. The educators, for sound, humane reasons, had decided that Indians should be taught in their own languages. Parents argued that they wanted their children to learn English so that they could function on an equal basis in their English-dominated world. Typically, the Indians succumbed to the louder argument and heavier placement of money, and the American Indian bilingual program went into full swing across the land. The same switch in viewpoint and money placement took place among Spanish speakers and the Chinese. It is taking place among Vietnamese, Filipinos, and others. We have been teaching other languages for so long that now we are being required to print election materials in two and three languages. Soon the number may be seven, twelve, or seventeen.

When bilingual education was still in the choose-up-sides phase, a Navaho student and I were asked to appear before an education conference to answer questions about our work together. The book *Miracle Hill: The Story of a Navaho Boy*, had been recently published. Two newly converted bilingualists, sitting rigidly apart from the group, listened to the questions and answers for a few minutes. Then one addressed my student in angry tones.

"Navaho is your language," she blurted. "Why didn't you write your book in Navaho?"

"Because," the young author answered quietly, "I wanted a lot of people to read it."

The claim of this book is that *they can say it in English* and that anyone who hopes to make his statement to a large audience had better learn to make it in English. That is true not only for those who have no other language but English but also for those in this country who have come to English from any other first language.

Certainly this is not to deny the validity of any and all languages. Spanish, French, Creek, Greek, German, Suquamish, Zulu, and all other languages (if they are spoken by two people only or even by one, talking to himself) are valid and should be studied, their nuances of meaning perfected and cherished. The most widely used American Indian language is Navaho (Athapaskan). Siouan runs it a close second. At least one hundred other American Indian languages still survive from among the three hundred or so once used in this country. We will all be the richer if we do what we can to preserve and nourish these various ways of observing and describing human experience.

The bare-bones fact remains that, for those who live in the United States at least, the ability to use the English language with effect is essential. Those who cannot handle English to their advantage are handicapped, and we are consistently graduating from our schools handicapped children and adults.

The solution to the problem lies not in money but in method. Reading and writing basics were taught in earlier days by ordinary, everyday teachers with no special equipment other than slates and tablets and a tongue-moist pencil. The method described here seems almost too simple, and yet it has been demonstrated and proved effective by teachers of wide-ranging abilities. Many of these teachers were skeptical. Most missed, at first, their security blanket of grammar rules. A few were never able to give themselves to the personal relationships and the required demands on their time. Most experienced a kind of conversion that resulted in happy teaching and happy, responsive learning. Their students are now literate.

The method prescribed and described here is built on three simple steps that almost any sincere teacher can take:

1. Believe it yourself and convince students that they have something of significance to say on the one subject in which every reader is interested—Life for Human Beings.

2. Discover each student's experience-based subjects, those on which he is the one and only authority and can, therefore, write well.

3. Keep students writing until they have said exactly what they want to say.

This method is grounded in the theory that language learning is a simple, natural experience—something that babies regularly accomplish. Skill in language usage happens as a direct result of self-motivated practice. It does not happen as a result of memorizing and applying rules of grammar.

This does not mean that grammar and syntax are four-letter words. I came across an explanation of their place in effective language usage in a most unlikely context. Hans Selye in his book, *Stress of Life*, says:

> What is the use, for example, of dissecting a sentence and explaining its structure? In actual speech you would never have the time to apply the rules of syntax and grammar by conscious intellectual processes. Still, people who know something about syntax and grammar use better language, thanks to this knowledge. You cannot teach a man how to express himself because it is the first rule of the game that his speech must reflect his personality, not yours. Moreover, few of the rules of syntax and grammar are absolute; the most unpolished slang is often more effective and picturesque than the King's English. All formal teaching can do is to explain the basic elements of language, so as to make them available for translation from conscious intellectual appraisal—which is impersonal, slow, and cold—into instinct—which is personal, quick, and warm.[1]

The method suggested in this book is based on the conviction that a student with something to say to a reader will learn to say it well. He will be motivated by the desire to be interesting, to be clear, and to be convincing. With that motivation, he will find the words and put them in the proper order to serve his purpose. No motivation of teacher or textbook can equal that.

---

[1] New York: McGraw-Hill, 1956.

2. Why Write?

Almost everyone believes that he learned to write in the first grade. Unfortunately, many students and adults later find themselves stuck on that first-grade, mechanical level. They cannot write a letter that conveys their desires or emotions clearly. They cannot write a successful application for work. They cannot write a lucid interoffice memo. They carry a thinking handicap through life because they cannot record and examine their thoughts on paper and use those thoughts as foundations on which to build more fully developed thoughts.

An even more far-reaching reason for students to write and to learn the art of writing (not merely its mechanics) is that, as someone has said, "any work of writing confers its first benefit upon its author."

A student, writing what he wants to express, is creating his personality. He is discovering who he is and what it is he has to say. He is learning to look at the conflicts within him and to sort them out in relation to the requirements of living with others. He is examining and setting goals for himself. He is learning to think in a straight line. He is developing a discipline. He is finding within himself legitimate sources of dignity and pride.

Once he has written and written well (well enough that someone else will read with understanding what he has written), he can never again be put down, nor can he put himself down as "just a kid" or as "just an Indian." He knows better. He has actually seen glimpses of greatness shine from within himself. He has read his own thoughts and found them bigger than he knew himself capable of producing. There they are—his uniquely personal experiences and ideas—in permanent form on the paper before him, and they could not have come from anyone else. They are his, and he is somebody.

In this, then, lies our first reason for teaching our students to write and also our first criterion for judging the worth of what they write. A piece of writing is valuable if it—or the effort a student has put into it—serves to improve its author as a human being. This does not mean that our standards for grammar and rhetoric need be low. Quite the contrary.

We expect and inevitably get improved facility in English usage as students write. If that were the only end product, it would be well worth our effort. To participate in a writing program such as that described here, students must spend long hours and years practicing to improve their use of English. We all need this kind of practice. For those who use English as a second language, such practice is essential. In addition, however, experience has led us to expect more.

The end product of this program can be publishable stories, poems, articles, and books. We have many such examples, published by educational and trade publishers, after only the briefest and spottiest training in our writing regimen as offered in Bureau of Indian Affairs schools. Our work has since supplied reprint material for practically all of this country's publishers of educational texts and anthologies. It has produced, in addition, many continuing writers and teachers.

Whatever the end, it is the time spent in writing and the human processes developed during that time that are more significant than any tangible printed page. This is true for Spanish-speaking students as well as for the English-speaking students who are choking off their own means of full expression and personal development with rote "you know's" and "far-out's."

We, as teachers, are concerned with unfolding, evolving persons, and writing can be one of our most effective tools. In addition, we can and should expect some highly desirable by-products—poems, stories, plays, essays, books. Along the way to these by-products, students will inevitably read more widely, practice standard English usage more consistently, and mature as persons.

3. What Is It Possible for Us to Teach?

Teachers of English work on a margin of time. More and more students in this country use English as a somewhat halting second language. Most of our students fall low on the scale of reading ability. As a rule grammar and rhetoric training have been persistent but ineffective in the grade schools, high schools, and colleges our students attend. Most of us have been trained as English teachers, not as professional writers or as writing coaches. If you as a teacher have some training or experience in writing for publication, this is a happy plus but certainly not a requisite for success in this program.

Given the conditions under which we teach, what exactly can we do to help students use the English language with imagination and power? Writing well is both an art and a craft. We certainly cannot expect all our students to become masters of the art of writing, any more than we can expect all students equipped with a chisel and a block of marble to become fine sculptors. A few individuals do seem to be born with a kind of writer's sixth sense. Some of them are to be found among Indians and Eskimos and among those who originally spoke Spanish or French or Tamil or any other mother-tongue language. Even they, however, need to learn the craft and the disciplines of writing. After that they will teach themselves and will become artists. For the most part, writers are trained technicians who, in addition, develop the art of writing by long-term trial-and-error practice. These writers were born with one big advantage—nobody could stop them from writing.

Most students are easy to stop, and the very methods and attitudes characteristic of our English classrooms could be prescribed as "stoppers." Red ink and grammar rules and, most of all, the hourly revelation to students that a teacher cares more about spelling and syntax than about what the student has to say—these are made-to-order stoppers. No teacher has a chance of turning a student on to writing who treats the student as if he were a defective, sputtering engine that is supposed to grind out compound sentences made up of words instantly spelled correctly and arranged in parsable order.

As teachers we can help students begin writing and keep writing until they teach themselves some skill in the art of expressing themselves in words. This book is aimed at helping teachers learn how not to stop students from writing. Many of your study materials and course plans—without intending to, of course—provide excellent methods for stopping students from writing. We can set up safeguards and replace the ineffective with productive experiments and exercises.

We can help make students aware of the world, of other human beings, and of relationships between things and people. Once a student has achieved this kind of awareness, he has material from which he can write. Usually he has material from which he is eager to write.

We can give students finger exercises that will help develop habits of observing closely and recording in detail through their sense perceptions.

We can provide exercises and games that will help students enlarge their vocabularies and, more important for writing, guide them in the choice of words for their denotation or connotation, their specific and intended imagery, and their excitement and fun.

We can stimulate students to read and make them aware of the techniques used by accomplished writers so that they are always exploring what they read as a textbook in writing, as a skill, and as an art.

We can help students develop appreciation for and readiness in the use of effective figures of speech.

We can acquaint them with interest-getting devices—with tricks of word selection, tense and voice forms, sequence, suspense, and the like—that give a piece of writing readability.

We can make them familiar with various poetic forms and guide them into the selection of the best form for whatever they have to communicate to others from their own experience.

We can give them in direct, outline form ways to develop a plotted story, a formal or familiar essay, a character sketch, and even certain kinds of poems.

We ourselves can learn how to recognize sparks among the ashes on a page and discover ways to fan those sparks into flame rather than smother them under a wet blanket of grammar rules.

Finally, we can provide students with a checklist of rules for readable writing and show them how to become their own critics. Every writer must learn how to do this because, ultimately, he is his own editor, his own judge, his own teacher.

4. The Five Doors

"What We're Learning About Learning" is the title of an article by Rita Kramer that appeared in the *New York Times* June 11, 1967. It reported that child-study experts had discovered that tiny babies understand only in terms of what they can see, hear, touch, taste, and smell. Even beginners in school cannot understand abstract explanations. They may repeat "one and one are two," but they cannot get the idea until they can touch a real orange and then are given another orange. Then something clicks.

Most good writers are well aware that all of us get our information about the world through our eyes, ears, taste buds, nose, and fingertips or skin. Writers also know what the baby experts learned, namely, "Lack of stimulation can actually change what a child sees or hears." Children born with all their senses who were reared by parents who could not hear lost their ability to hear well. In experiments monkeys were kept in darkness for long periods during their infancy. After that it was very difficult for them to learn to distinguish objects by sight, even though their eyes were not damaged. For writers beginning or established, this is a vital lesson.

The five senses are five doors through which enter all our information about the world, but these doors have a tendency to swing shut. The way to keep them open is to keep streams of information marching through, flooding through, so that the doors do not have a chance to close.

The sad truth is that we do not have to make an effort, such as putting infants or ourselves in dark places, to impair our sight. We can accomplish the same result simply by forgetting to look at whatever is before our eyes. We turn off our ears and actually damage our hearing simply by not listening to the wind, to the birds, to the traffic, to a scolding voice. Sometimes this is deliberate and protective. More often it is unconscious and careless.

What a pity that any of us loses his original awareness! Any healthy baby is "turned-on" every waking minute, keeping his eyes open and searching, his ears tuned to every sound, his fingers reaching, and his voice raised in protest when his skin is uncomfortably wet.

To write well, students must learn how a writer thinks. Then they must practice that way of thinking until it becomes habitual. My lesson on babies may sound babyish, but it produces results and does so with students of all ages and at all levels of development.

To much of the world, being able to write well seems mysterious—something that a few fortunate people with special talents can do. Those not born to be writers are doomed to look on in awe and admiration. This awe and admiration work to the advantage of teachers. Good writing is respected by practically everyone. A teacher who can guide students into good writing is considered a kind of magician. In fact, you too can be a magician.

I frequently go into a class for the first time and promise, with no qualms, that I have a trick I can use to make each one in the room an instant writer. "It's quite a lot like making instant coffee," I assure the group. I go on, then, to admit that making instant writers takes a little longer than making instant coffee, but not much. It also requires that each person who wants to enjoy the benefits of this magic must be a volunteer to help me with the trick. Next I ask, "Do you have a small baby in your home?"

For those who do not have a baby close at hand, I suggest that they think about the last very young baby they saw and possibly held. I have never found students too old or too young to listen intently while I remind them of a few facts about babies. "That baby you're thinking about can teach you more than I can about how to become a good writer," I tell them. "You don't actually need me, but I'll just remind you of some things you might forget to notice."

"That baby," I say, "has been born out of a dark, almost silent place, and is suddenly thrust into a world where everything is light and filled with colors and shapes and things going on around him, and he doesn't understand any of it. It must be like landing in the middle of an erupting volcano at first.

"That baby, however, is born with five doors through which he can get all the information he needs about his world. The great thing is that a baby starts, almost at once, to open up those doors and let information about his world walk right in. No self-respecting baby is going to be a dummy for very long—not as long as he has those five doors."

"I suppose," I go on, "that each baby learns things in a different order, but let's say that, first of all, he opens his taster door, and he learns that milk is warm and smooth in his mouth. It tastes good, and his tummy feels better when he has that warm white stuff inside him. Through his mouth he learns, almost immediately, quite a lot about this strange world.

"Maybe next he opens his eye door and starts looking around. He looks at walls and at the ceiling above him and at some strange lumpy shape beside him. Before long he wants to see it all at once, and he lifts his head and twists around. He just has to see everything, including what may be behind him. He must get it all into his eyes and start remembering shapes and sizes and colors.

"Soon, or possibly first of all," I continue, "he discovers that he can open his mouth and make an exciting sound, and he opens his ear door to listen. Then he finds that the shape beside him can make a different sound, and again he opens his ear door to listen. Before long he is beginning to know one sound from another, and he can tell which sound comes from the shape beside him and which comes from another shape that is getting closer and closer on his other side. He probably likes the sound he can make best of all, and so he keeps doing it over and over. Sometimes he makes his sound and learns that, when he does that, somebody else will make a different sound. He is learning about his world.

"Pretty soon he opens his smeller door, and something doesn't please him at all. Then he is likely to make his sound as loud as he can in protest. In time someone takes that bad odor away, and something soft and smooth is being rubbed on his skin, and suddenly the air around him smells like talcum powder. He stops yelling and learns that he can make little humming sounds and then cooing sounds and splutters and burps and oooohs.

"Now," I say, "we have five doors too." I let students rehearse along with me—eyes, ears, a smeller, a taster, and feelers or skin. Together we point to our eyes, ears, noses, mouths, and we wiggle our fingers. Then I ask a startling question: "Did you know that everything you have learned since you were a tiny baby has come to you through your five doors? You've seen it, tasted it, heard it, smelled it, or felt it. There is no other way for anybody to get information and learn to live in the world."

I push up my sleeves in true magician style. "I'm getting close," I warn, "to turning all of you into instant writers, so watch and listen."

I usually pick up a tablet or a clipboard and poise a pen or pencil above it. "This 'baby lesson' is one that all good writers know, and now you know it, too, so you're partway along the road to being a good writer. If you are ready, we'll go the rest of the way. Here it is.

"If, when you write, you will put on paper exactly how something looks to you (size, shape, color), how it tastes to you (sweet, sour, bitter), how it sounds (melody, clatter, beat), how it smells (stinky or fragrant), and how it feels (warm, smooth, rough), you can make something wonderful happen.

"If you write here, on the tablet, exactly how it looks, tastes, sounds, smells, and feels to you and . . ." I turn the tablet around so that they can all become my readers. "Turn it around so somebody can read what you have written, and right here on the page is where the magic happens. If you have written it exactly that way, when someone else reads it, he will not read just words. He will see with his eyes what you saw, he will be able to taste what you had for breakfast, he will hear the notes of music you heard, he will smell the flower you sniffed, and he will feel the broken rock wall you skinned your knee on when you climbed over it. You can hand your reader, not words, but the experience exactly as it was to you. There! That is the magic trick, and now it is yours. It's the trick good writers know that you didn't know till now, the trick you could have learned from your baby brother or sister. Now that you have it, you can start practicing, and you can be a good writer with your very first sentence, provided you remember to write in just that way."

"Of course," I have to admit, "writers practice a lot. The reason they must practice so much is that they keep forgetting the trick. They have to go back once in a while and study that tiny baby again so that they will keep remembering to write the way a baby learns, the way everybody learns. Now, I suggest, let's practice a little."

My ways of helping students practice are almost as many and varied as the classes. The way I select usually depends on what is available for sensory examination. Teachers at Intermountain School will remember that I brought to our first meeting red and yellow leaves I had found beneath the trees on campus. I gave those teachers the "Five Doors," or "baby," lesson, and they wrote far better than any of them knew they could. In a few minutes they learned a great deal about fall leaves and even more about how to express themselves in words.

In Alaska in January, leaves and grasses were almost impossible to obtain without stripping the houseplants in the schoolrooms. So we used the most readily obtainable stimulus —paper, lined tablet paper. Plain lined writing paper, one sheet to a student, became our "thing." It was at hand, it was expendable, and it was so common that students were always astonished at what they learned from something so common.

My first use of paper was at Mount Edgecumbe School, in Alaska. Cleta Moorhead, the teacher I was helping, suggested paper when we failed to find anything else to use with the incoming class. Quickly we laid a sheet of lined tablet paper on each desk.

I had never used anything so bland with my classes at IAIA. I had given each student a plastic cup filled with tea, or we had used cookies and candy that looked like pebbles. As I shall describe later, with my first class at IAIA, I had used seed pods. Here in January with snow to our knees, we had paper.

The class of sophomores arrived, and I gave them a quick lesson in the Five Doors. Then I turned to the paper. I asked them to leave it flat on their desks and look at it.

What shape is it? What color? Is it the same color all over?

Individuals react individually. Sheets of paper from the same tablet varied in color from white to cream to gray. The lines on the paper were blue or purple or baby blue or green and reddish. When I asked them to hold the paper to the light, students saw clouds, blotches, dirt, popcorn, and waves. It felt to their fingertips like sandpaper, like silk, and like dough, or it tickled.

They smelled the paper, and it smelled like wood, like paste, like alcohol, like dust, like gasoline. Most were surprised that paper had an odor.

I suggested that they listen and asked, "Does paper have a voice?" They thought not at first and looked baffled until I started waving my sheet of paper in the air. Soon they were full of ideas. They flapped their sheets in the air and it sounded like music. It could be made to have a beat. They wadded it and listened. It sounded like rain and like fire and like a dozen other noises. They tossed it on the floor, and it whished. When I mentioned tearing it rapidly, it sounded like a gun, like pants splitting, like bacon frying, and like a zipper. Torn slowly, the paper sounded like shuffling feet, like whispers.

Finally, I said, "Now eat it." While they were still in shock, I added, "Tear off a little corner and taste it. Does it taste like anything you've ever tasted before? How does it feel on your tongue?"

When that class was over, school was out for the day. Cleta and I made ourselves a cup of tea. Across the room one student, Grace Antoghame, lingered at the typewriter. She seemed to be doodling with the keys. She barely shook her head when we offered her a cup of tea. So we sat down to plan our writing follow-up for that class for the next day. Before we finished, Grace got up and ambled out. When we were ready to leave, we straightened the room. Cleta pulled from the typewriter the sheet Grace had carelessly left. Just before wadding it up, she looked at it. Grace had written:

> She came today and taught us to see, feel, and taste a plain, white fourth-a-sheet of paper that sounded like thunder, chuckled like a small child, crunched like snow and crackled like potato chips.

A small piece of paper that felt as smooth and as rough as my bitten-up fingernails. A tiny piece of paper that tasted like yesterday's snow that's been aired out too long.

She gave to us the products of writing, the products we have and yet kept blank and unused. The servants we pushed and shoved aside to the drain of laziness. Letting them sleep a dreamless, meaningless, useless sleep."

This is not a finished piece of writing. Sentences are not complete. Some words are not the right words. Grace would, no doubt, be the first to say that she did not intend for anyone to read it in its first-draft form. It clearly indicates, however, that she had fully investigated a piece of paper from the point of view of a child experiencing paper for the first time. That is the whole idea—the first step in writing well is to establish the habit of observing and making comparisons, using the five senses for collecting data and reporting the details of experience.

You may wish to remind your students to use their five senses by giving each one a cracker or a pebble or a quilt square. You may wish to try this experiment with different objects as a warm-up writing exercise for the first five minutes of each class period for a month. Or you may prefer to use it at the end of the class period, sending students out with this reminder of the fun and necessity of turning on all five senses to write.

My first class at IAIA was crowded around the long table in the Written Arts Studio. I gave the students a brief oral introduction to the Five Doors of sense awareness. Each student had a sheet of paper and a pencil. I tossed onto the table a handful of milkweed seedpods. I asked students to examine the pods, do whatever they wished with them, and then write impressions, using their five senses.

They tore the pods open. Some blew on the fluffy seeds at first to keep them in the air. Some swatted at them. Some examined them closely with their eyes only. Some started pulling off bits of fluff. A few became adventurous enough to nibble on the seeds. Soon most were writing tentative notes. One or two were writing rapidly in more or less complete sentences.

"I would enjoy seeing your paper," I told them, "when you are ready for a reader."

The results were not great literature, but the results within some of the students were profound. In the five or ten minutes required for telling them about the Five Doors, and in the ten minutes of fun and laughter while each personally examined the seeds and pods, the students learned basic and vital lessons in writing. Several of those students went on to become professional writers. The story of that one class session was recorded months later by one member of the group, Blackhorse ("Barney") Mitchell in his book *Miracle Hill.*

A sophomore student in Ann Gulledge's class in Albuquerque, New Mexico, was so impressed by the Five Door idea that she wrote me a letter:

Dear Mrs. Allen,

   I was so glad when you first came to our classroom because you taught me something new, and that is the five doors. I am so proud that you taught me something new because no teacher ever told me about it before and again I want to Thank you very much.

Sincerely yours,

Eunice Jane Coriz

P.S. I used the 5 doors when I wrote my mom.

Ann Gulledge used fall leaves with her sophomore students at Albuquerque Indian School. At the time, in October, Carl Vicenti wrote: "An oval shape, rough edge, yellow thing. Smooth and thin, sour taste and dirty. Comes from a tree. Blowing in the grass."

In January he looked again at what he had written and revised it, writing more nearly complete sentences and adding a personal relationship—"has to be raked up." Now it read:

   An oval shape rough edge leaf, smooth and thin. Has a sour taste, and has a funny smell too, with yellow color. Comes in autumn when it gets ready to snow. Dirties the grass and has to be raked up.

In February, Carl decided to shape his experience with the leaf into a poem. To do this, he addressed the leaf as if it were a person. Personification is a professional writer's way of waking a reader's interest in an inanimate object. Now the reader can identify with Carl's leaf. In his last line of this version the young poet added the hint of universality that is characteristic of good poetry. Here is the recurring cycle of seasons and the oneness of things and people in the march of time.

>   You rough edge, yellow thing
>   Very smooth and very thin.
>   Blowing in the grass
>   Wet and moist
>   Dropping off a tree,
>   Lying there real still
>   Waiting for the snow to fall.

Finally, Carl eliminated unnecessary words (two "very's" and "dropping off a tree"—where else?). Then, instead of telling, he showed his reader by translating "real still" into "eyes shut," and made his reader feel "holding your breath":

> FALLEN LEAF
>
>   You, rough edged, yellow thing
>   With a sour taste.
>   Smooth and thin
>   Blowing in the grass
>   Wet and moist
>   Lying there, eyes shut,
>   Holding your breath,
>   Waiting for the snow to fall.

It is still not a finished poem, and Carl may be still working on it, for all we know. Have we read meaning into the words? Certainly. All authors know that occasionally they write better and bigger than they know how to write. That is the witchery of words.

The author selects words that best convey his experience, and those same words convey to the reader whatever richness his own experience has built into them. Carl's revisions and rewrites moved from rough-draft notes based on sense awareness (truth), toward meeting standards of English grammar, toward making writing an art by adding the interest-getting device of personification. Revision normally follows a similar path, and herein lies the obvious value of creative writing as an aid in teaching English as a second language, in teaching grammar and syntax, and in teaching most of the arts of communication to almost anyone.

The student with something to say is self-motivated toward learning to say it well. On the way to this end he is criticizing and correcting his own English usage and revising himself toward excellence. To begin this process, he needs only a way to get off the starting line.

The Five Door lesson—or the "baby lesson," if you prefer—quickly gives a student of any age the place to start and the way to start writing well with his first sentence. Sense impression feeds out those first hard words. The validity of each person's sensory reactions is unarguable. The endless variety within the five-sense responses holds a writer's interest and reaches out directly through the senses to readers.

What more can you expect of one brief teaching session than that it spawn the kind of self-awareness doodled out on the typewriter by Grace or keep Carl writing over a period of months or prompt Eunice to use the Five Doors to write a letter home? During that one first session at IAIA, Barney wrote the makings of a poem that eventually turned into a published book.

5. Here and Now

Following is a method of exercising fingers and senses to get students into the habit of writing the sensory detail that makes it possible for the writer to communicate with his reader. It is not a method for producing finished pieces of writing. It is what preliminary sketching is to an artist—a sketch may be incorporated in a finished painting, but it is not the painting nor even a finished drawing.

Even though you may be impatient to see finished stories and poems, you cannot afford to skip this step in the process, any more than a concert pianist can afford to neglect practicing scales. Most musicians practice scales to the end of their careers. Most writers would produce more good writing if they warmed up with an exercise in Here and Now whenever they sat down to work.

The words "scales" and "finger exercises" may carry the wrong connotation. If they make writing sound like drudgery, they are misleading. Here and Now experiments are fun. They lose their value when they are approached in any other way. They call for free, spontaneous reactions. No structured writing form need be remembered and followed.

Here and Nows are snatches of writing that impose no requirements from rules of grammar. They can and should be sketchy—quickly caught impressions pinned or tacked to paper in the easiest way possible. Students who dread the chore of writing should find in this kind of exercise "just fun," as Indian students say. Teachers too will find them fun and should do some or all of these experiments along with their students.

"Here and Now" is a term frequently used by psychologists and teachers, and you may come across it in various contexts.

What does it mean for our purposes? It means simply that we and our students capture a moment in time and the immediate environment of a given place to turn on the five senses and record everything.

Introducing Here and Now to Students

As an exercise in writing, try introducing Here and Now to a class:

"For a few minutes, we are going to open all five of our sense doors and make notes about what we hear, feel, smell, see, and taste. The trick is in getting it down on paper exactly as it is to you. We are all sitting here in one room, but each one of us is an individual, with our own special senses, and all the things around us are a little bit different to each one of us. In that little bit of difference lies the secret of your special writing style and of my special style.

"When we write, we are saying to a reader, 'This is the way it looks to me. This is the way I hear it. This is how it feels when it touches me.'

"If each of us writes honestly, exactly as it is to us, no two of us will write exactly the same things about how this room looks, how it smells, or what we hear. Always try to find the exact word that reveals how it is to you. For now, however, don't worry about spelling or sentence structure or anything else. Simply catch it on paper as it is to you right now.

"You may turn on your eyes first and then your skin and then your ears, or your way may be to do it more nearly as it comes to you—all at once. This is the way we finally write a good story, as if we are taking the reader along and letting the story take place around him—its sights and sounds and feelings going on all at once. You may, if you wish, write Here and Now in that way, but don't forget to turn on all five senses. Don't be content to look and forget to listen, for example. Do both.

"Write in the present tense and in first person. Keep jotting down sense experiences as they are coming to you at the moment of writing. For now, try not to remember other sights and odors that you are reminded of from the past. Keep it Here and Now. When you can no longer do that, when you get distracted by something outside the room and have trouble coming back to the here and now, then the experiment is over, and you should stop."

Suggest to your students: "I want you to write one Here and Now in this classroom as soon as I tell you to start. Also, I want you to have a notebook beside your bed in your room and to write one Here and Now when you first wake up in the morning, before you get out of bed. Then I want you to continue writing Here and Now experiments in many different situations, at different times of day or night.

"For someone else to read and understand what you write in this way, it should not be necessary for you to tell where you are or what time it is. A well written Here and Now will make time and place clear. At the beginning, however, I would like to have these dated and the time of day given in the upper right-hand corner of the page. Your name goes in the upper left-hand corner.

"I want to read some examples so that everyone knows exactly how this writing experiment works. These examples were written by students at the Institute of American Indian Arts."

Read one or two examples when the exercise is introduced. Later, you can read from your own students' work—with their permission, of course.

Examples Written by High School Students

HERE AND NOW

As I pour the icy amber-brown liquid, it foams down and around the translucent forms stacked haphazardly in the glass. The foam threatens the rim but, with a profusion of cracklings, sinks to the level of the vaguely cubed ice forms.

My eyes, traveling the length of the glass, notice a strange family of bubbles anchored to the bottom. They seem to peer fixedly—pleadingly—through the glass. Suddenly the bubbles split, then form a vertical chain which missils up through the amber until it is shelved on the underside of the marble-like ice.

The ice filters light to eerie shades of yellow and reflects the dark red amber of the liquid, as it holds the bubbles. The bold, molded patterns of a cube weigh down the helpless bubbles. Finally, the chain inches in ascent once more, threads between the marble-ice, up, up until it merges with warm air.

I pick up the cold glass and slowly lift it. The icy marbles caress yet pain my lips. The cool amber liquid slides welcomely down my throat. The fountain of miniature droplets explodes to tickle my nose.

NOTE: This I found interesting to write about. An ice cube in a glass of Pepsi! Never have I seen anything so beautiful and eerie.... I liked the subject so much I decided to write about it again from a wider point of view.

Two large bubbles stare through the side of the glass like bulging eyes. Silently, smaller bubbles push at them until they slide around the ice, upward to the thin, black line where they disappear. Above the line, a grey strip sits diagonally on the other side of the glass. My eyes follow the grey strip until it meets a blank grey wall—a gentle curve, mostly hidden by a Pepsi bottle and a glass.

As I rise, my eyes search this drab grey cylinder to find what it holds. Dwarfed, misshapen cubes float, neglected, in a dark grey pool. Each little shape nestles in my hand as I fish out a few of the smallest. One by one, I plop the glassy forms into the liquid. Ice clacks like Gypsy castinets against ice, and I hear an occasional gurgle as each drops. Then quiet, and I take a drink of my pop.

—Patricia Irving

HERE AND NOW I am aware of the New Mexico State Fair atmosphere. My friends and I are standing in front of the building facing west. This is an exciting place and moment for me and for everybody. People are strolling, laughing, riding, wondering, carrying, and eating. The clouds are getting dark so all the red, yellow, blue, pink, and orange colored lights are going on. Like a dream, the rides are spinning their lights in the dark. Under the colorful decorations are people enjoying carnival music. Many stands give out the odor of snacks. I hear many sounds made by the people and the music. I am kind of tired and my feet are aching like cramps, I feel like sitting, but it's crowded and wet. My mouth tastes like hot dogs and pickle from what I just ate.

—Grey Cohoe

As I sit here, on this beautiful day, I feel the cool refreshing breeze blowing my hair with a slow drowsy stroke. My black sweater is absorbing the heat from the warm sun. The gum in my mouth is a nuisance with its rough-smooth texture, but

I can't keep from occupying my jaw. As I wiggle my toes, I feel the sweatiness between them. In the distance I see the monstrous incinerator, the home for litters. I faintly hear gay whistling of someone, and someone walking down the sidewalk with hard steps and another walking with light, dainty steps. I barely hear the zum-zum sound of the cars and the busy townspeople's chattering sounds, like bees buzzing. I must have fallen to sleep 'cause I hear nothing, I see nothing.

—*Madelyn Samuels*

HERE AND NOW I'm aware of modern art before me. I can still taste the spinach I ate for lunch . . . and the peaches. At this moment, I feel quite hungry. Before me is a painting which I can't understand. My first impression is that it's not art at all. Colors and different shapes seem to have been thrown together. By chance it came out right.

God created the world—the highest artistic creation known to man. He didn't just slap materials together. He created a miracle of color and composition. In my opinion, chance shouldn't have anything to do with art.

With my second glance, I am beginning to see the abstract figures forming specific shapes, like in a dream. At one corner I see a big orange circle shape with a touch of white, brown, and green. Since I'm hungry, it suggests a fresh, juicy orange. Gosh! I wish oranges grew that large! At the top right corner, I see a green oval shape. This suggests an ice-cold, luscious watermelon. Right above the center there's a cylinder-like shape, fading into a background of black. In the middle is a touch of black, white, and a fleshy redness which suggests a roast ham. I'm beginning to torture myself. It's best that I continue my journey on campus.

—*Curtis Link*

The two paragraphs above are not good examples of Here and Now writing. They are included here because they clearly show how very difficult it is to stay in the Here and Now.

HERE AND NOW a thump, thump moves across the library, fades, and quickly dies with the slam of a door. Dull murmurs drift about on the thick air, then seem to fill the spaces between the colorful books, sitting sedately in the shelves.

Tables scattered regularly beside the laden shelves mirror the multicolors of the books. The colors are only shapes, floating unreally on each tabletop.

Too many books—a tall, proud red one; a short, stubby black one; a just-right yellow one; and a fat, blue one. Between them settle the whispers.

A high drone interrupts the air as a fly cruises about my head. With a tired little buzz, it lands on my hand and begins his bath.

First, the wings—brush well with hind legs. Now, to scrub the sides a little and rub the other legs. Carefully, he returns to the dainty task of massaging his wings. Only the oversides are done today. First one—very carefully, then the other. Now, he scrubs his hind legs together and, refreshed, buzzes off on his merry way.

— *Patricia Irving*

HERE AND NOW I am aware of an unusual adventure at night and far out from our school. Our picnic is going all right at this moment. I am full and tired from walking around in this soft soil. I am sitting on our water canteen, tasting the strong, black coffee. The coffee burns my mouth, but it is good tasting because it is boiled on an outdoor fire. As I hold the cup to sip, the steam waves against my face, smelling like coffee grains. . . . Our fire is huge, flaming into the black space around us. Smoke is visible only against the yellow, orange, and red flames. As the smoke disappears into the dark atmosphere, only the sparks it's carrying shine, but it also disappears into the night sky among the twinkling stars. The fire reflects all our near environment. Once the firelight hits an object, it breaks into the darkness. I can see our bus and a car and students, standing around the fire. The mountains are dark monster objects, surrounding us as if we're in a bowl. I can feel the heat, striking one side of me and it colors us all orange. My eyes are irritated by the dry-wood smoke. This night makes me feel that I'm in a world of my own. In the dark it is quiet and cool, but I hear singing by the students. The soft folk songs make me feel like going through the clouds. Best of all are the crackling and sparking sounds from the burning fire.

— *Grey Cohoe*

Open All Five Doors and Write

Now, you and your students are ready to write.

You will find that some students take to this exercise and enjoy it very much. Others may make a feeble attempt to write one or two paragraphs and then want to give up. Usually the student who does not enjoy writing Here and Now exercises is the one who has not fully caught the idea of reporting exactly and fully all the impressions he gets through his five senses.

This exercise cannot be helpful or fun if a student persists in writing in general terms or refuses to examine his own sense perceptions. Sometimes a reminder from the teacher that he is not putting it down in sufficient detail will help a student turn around and start over. Looking, listening, tasting, smelling, and feeling—while perfectly natural for a baby—are for many of us lost arts. To regain them takes an act of will at first, and then something similar to a religious conversion may take place.

Coming alive to sights, sounds, tastes, odors, and textures can happen in a flash. Then, given persistent practice, this new awareness (lost since babyhood) can become second nature again. In this second-nature stage is where good writers live. From their accurate observations, through their five senses, come their ideas. In seeking to record exactly and honestly, they build rich, connotative vocabularies. In the practice of writing and rewriting, they learn to say clearly and honestly whatever they wish to say.

"Tell it like it is," is the current (ungrammatical) way of asking for honest speaking and honest writing. This kind of writing is interesting because it carries the personality of the writer, his individual sensory responses to his world's stimuli. Honest writing has a person caught and revealed in it, and we are all interested in alive, aware, and responding people.

Once you and your students have learned to write Here and Now, you are ready to write There and Then. This is an exercise in total recall. Again, it is a kind of trick, but one that has paid off for every successful writer who ever lived. Those students who have caught the feel of writing Here and Now can now choose whether they will write of their immediate situation or will put themselves into some other time and place and write There and Then.

For beginners this exercise should also be written in the present tense and in the first person. The mere mechanics of catching an experience on paper in the present tense and first person helps the student remember to let the setting or action he is recalling unroll around him as if he were again in the middle of it. If the place or the scene recalled is to become a portion of a story or article, the writer can readily transpose to past tense and third person, if he wishes. The writing will still retain its "live" quality. This is the easiest way for beginners to achieve in their writing a sense of immediacy and reality.

Followup for the Teacher

We do not ask of this experiment that it be anything more than a warm-up for writing. It is not expected to be or to produce a concerto played before an audience. The alert teacher will, however, watch for seeds that can be watered, fed, and cultivated into full-blown poems, stories, articles, plays, or possibly letters. We can never afford to pass up an opportunity to encourage a student to go on with a finished piece of writing when we come across a sentence, paragraph, or even a word that reveals special excitement, knowledge, or awareness.

Exercises often simply set students to writing, and their finished pieces may have nothing at all to do with the immediate or remembered experience caught on paper. In Here and Now writing, however, a certain mood will sometimes be captured later in a poem, or an observed action may form the basis for a play or story scene or for an anecdote used in an article. When you, the teacher, find anything at all on these or any other papers presented by students—bits that strike fire with you—suggest to the student that he may have at his fingertips the stuff of a polished piece of writing.

These exercises should never be given half-attention reading. You are not looking for grades; you are mining for a person. Sometimes the simplest-sounding statement may, on a second, searchful reading, glint and sparkle off the page.

"You read meaning into your students' papers," one education specialist accused, and this is true; however, the student who writes one sentence beyond his immediate comprehension can be encouraged to keep reaching beyond himself until he consistently writes profound truth and honest emotion. Please do not make the mistake of settling for too little. You are cheating your students when you expect from them anything less than their best.

Elementary-school boys and girls, maturing high school and university young people, even grandparents in continuing-education classes respond positively to my reminding them of something they all know but do not think about very often. I put the reminder in the simplest possible terms. I ask: "Do you have a brother or a sister?" (some do, and some do not). "If you have a brother or sister, do you look exactly like that other member of your family?" (if I ever came across identical twins, I could still go right on with my questions). "Do you and your brothers and sisters always agree on everything?

"I wonder why you don't see everything in just the same way. You have the same mother and father (at least one or the other is the same). You were probably born in the same hospital or in the same house. You've been fed from the same recipes. Why is it that you don't look exactly alike? Especially, why don't you think alike so there would never be any disagreements around your house?

"Well, the reason is that each one of us, even before we're born, is given a design and our cells grow and multiply according to that pattern. Where does the pattern come from? We all know the answer to that. Your mother gave some of her genes, and your father gave some of his genes, and they combined into a special set of genes, and that set belongs to you (of course, you know what kinds of genes I mean; you may be wearing your dad's or your mother's blue jeans, too; I'm talking about the genes in your DNA pattern).

"That special pattern has in it genes from your mother's father and mother, from your father's parents, and from the father and mother of your grandfather and of your grandmother on both sides of the family. It gets to be really fantastic when we start thinking back to how many genes have gone into making each one of us. That does explain, however, something important about us here today. When we think about it, it stands to reason that each one of us has a pattern that is all our own. No wonder we don't see things exactly the same. No wonder we argue. We are one of a kind even before we're born.

"But that's not all. From the minute we're born, each one of us starts living in this big, bright world, and different things happen to us. Some of us are allergic to milk, and so we may start life on a chemical formula. Some of us get sick and have good or bad hospital experiences because of that. Some of us, as we grow up, move from town to town or from country to country. Some of us stay in the same place all our lives. Some feel happy most of the time. Some are always singing the blues or the blahs.

"The things that happen to us make up our own pattern of experience. We respond to our set of happenings in the ways that our genes suggest. When you put all that together, it's no wonder that I'm an oddball. There's the oddball that looks like me and thinks the way I think and does the things I do. Then, there's the oddball that is you and you and you. Each of us is one of a kind.

"The reason we need to remember this here and now is this: Everything that happens to us and everything we do about it has to do with Life for Human Beings. If you are sixteen, you've spent sixteen whole long years discovering what life is like to you. If you are seven—seven years is a long time, two thousand five hundred and fifty-five days—you've been up against hard problems and found a way to solve them. So, in my opinion, you—at whatever stage you are now—have a great deal to share with the rest of us about what life is like to you. Since you are one of a kind, if you don't tell us what life is like to the special, one-of-a-kind human being that is you, then, forever and always, one piece of experience will be lost.

"Your way of seeing, your way of hearing, your ideas that you are forming because of what happens to you are ideas that we all need. We'll all be missing something helpful, if you fail to tell us what it is like to be you.

"One of a kind we get born into this world. We arrive here wanting a good life. It doesn't turn out that way all the time, but we keep trying to make things better. We soon discover that if we are to have good lives other people must have good lives too. Everything we discover about how to make life better for ourselves is something we need to let other people in on. Frequently we get good ideas from something that someone else has discovered and told us. Mothers and fathers spend much of their time telling us, 'This works best,' or 'Do it this way and you'll be happier.' Another way of telling is in books and magazines.

"Someone writes what he has discovered about Life for Human Beings. We can read it, and then we know it too and can use it. Through reading, we can learn how to make our lives good from people who were making discoveries about it a thousand years ago and through all the years between then and now. Through writing, we can report our discoveries to people who will live a thousand years from now.

"It's for all these reasons that I'd like to help you tell your one-of-a-kind story of what Life for Human Beings is like and to help you say it in such an interesting way that other people will want to read it and learn from you."

6. "What Shall I Write?"

Students have brainwashed teachers into expecting a minimum of effort on written work. The first question following almost any writing assignment is, "How long's it hafta be?" The "hafta" implies minimal interest in the assignment and minimal standards for the finished piece. The teacher is trapped into setting minimal limits, and even those usually bring forth groans from the class. This pattern of attitudes and interaction must be broken if we are to lead students into the fun of writing that normally precedes learning to write well.

The only good tool for breaking up the pattern is personal interest—set the student to writing something that catches and holds his interest because it is what he, and he alone, knows all about. That subject is the story of his life.

"Old stuff," you say?

It is, of course. Educators frequently tell jokes about the eight-year-old who has written her autobiography three or four times.

"My students are too reticent. They won't write about themselves," you may object, and with good reason. When the purpose for the assignment is explained, however, and the fears of students are taken into consideration in advance, the Life Story comes close to being a surefire starter.

Students who do not yet know the teacher will usually assume that the reason for the assignment is that the teacher is nosy or is trying to get information that might be used against them. A full explanation of how the assignment is to serve the class purposes of the students themselves will make all the difference between success and failure. In fairness I must add one other provision. That is, this pump-priming assignment does not work for every teacher.

Peggy Jo Hall, at Sequoyah High School, Tahlequah, Oklahoma, noted one fall: "Started my creative writing class with a great deal of uncertainty. You start with the Life Story, which frightens me. The idea that students will spill their guts out on cue like turning tap water on and off—well, some do, and it's embarrassing for them and me. No, I won't let them, I think."

Anne Cathcart wrote from Fort Yates, North Dakota: "Life Story. They hated this assignment, and I can't truthfully say that I was terribly enthusiastic about it either." (This surely tells us something. I doubt that any teacher has a chance with any assignment that he or she is not enthusiastic about. I agree with both Peggy and Anne that they should give this assignment a wide berth, at least until they have a change of heart. Enthusiasm is catching, but another attitude is even more catching—lack of enthusiasm.) Anne went on, "Very few of them [the students] turned in a Life Story or even worked on it. Even fewer did it in the detail that is necessary. Definitely a failure."

Elbert Hubbard said, "The world is moving so fast these days that the man who says it can't be done is generally interrupted by someone doing it." A recent newspaper item that appeared in the *Los Angeles Times* (long after my work with Anne and Peggy Jo) explains, more scientifically than I ever tried to, why the Life Story assignment did work for me and for others of our teachers.

The article describes a room filled with people who sit scribbling intently in thick notebooks. "Once in a while someone shuffles, coughs or sighs, but the intensity holds. There are few dawdlers because everyone knows the subject he is writing about intimately; better, in fact, than anyone else in the world, for it is his own life. . . . He does not have to think about style or arrangement because he has already been instructed that he is to write freely, without censure or judgment. . . . This is not a class for writers. It is, instead, an Intensive Journal Workshop. . . . Its creator, New York psychotherapist and author Dr. Ira Progoff, calls it 'a unique, modern therapeutic tool which enables all persons, regardless of age, social or educational background, to begin where they are and progressively draw their lives into focus.'"

Drawing life into focus—that is what all writing is about,

and, for me and for others of our project teachers who tried it with success, the Life Story does point out to students their own areas for focus. It says to them: "This is what I know. This is what I am. These are my subjects for writing." For the psychotherapist the intensive journal (more structured than we attempt) is pulling heads together. Our Life Story, too, does very much the same.

So the teacher's reason for the Life Story assignment is to help the student reach his own readiness to write and to discover experiences from which he can make his own future writing assignments. These must honestly be the teacher's reasons. All information gained must be considered strictly confidential. At the same time, a Life Story, written as suggested, will surely become the basis for a new and deepening understanding between student and teacher.

This understanding plays an essential role in the development of the student's writings. When this assignment is finished, the teacher will know just what it is that Linda Brown or Johnny Nez or José Sanchez is attempting to say in subsequent writings. Nothing more surely discourages writing than to have a teacher who has misunderstood a first-draft piece of a poem or story try to make suggestions from a point of view entirely different from that of the student's.

To the question regarding the Life Story assignment, "How long's it hafta be?" you can safely answer: "As long as you want to make it. This is for you, not for me. Just be sure that you don't leave out anything because that might be the very experience that could be the basis for your best poem or story or play."

You, the teacher, should know whether or not you need to assign a due date. I prefer not to. I do, however, watch for signs of lagging along the way, of boredom, and of readiness to get on with other writing. Frequently the reminder to use the five senses proves an instant cure for lagging and boredom. Some students will never finish this assignment, and it becomes worth almost nothing to insist. Occasionally a student will falter and stop on this, write on something else for weeks or months, and then decide to finish his Life Story. If your schedule is such that you must assign a due date, then do so. If some students wish to keep writing, you can always extend the time. I suggest allowing an extension if the student is still interested and eager to write more.

A spiral-bound notebook in an 8-by-10- or 9-by-12-inch size is the best format for this assignment—something not too bulky to carry and with few enough pages to lure a student into filling them all. Actually, students who start will astonish themselves, provided they write in detail, using all five of their senses. A kind of chemical reaction sets in, once we start recalling in detail on paper—one sense stimulates another, and the precise sense impressions stimulate the memory. Most Life Story writers set down far more than they thought they would remember.

In addition to the notebook, you, the teacher, must make provision for privacy. When you make the assignment, stress the importance of not sharing Life Stories among students. The story becomes violated in this way, and the writer soon loses interest. The student must consider this a "dear-diary" kind of commitment, never to be passed from student to student during the writing.

In the same spirit the teacher with a locked cabinet or file can secure the story's privacy by locking it up between writing sessions, if a student wishes. Few homes and especially dormitories provide lock-and-key privacy. If your schedule permits students to work on their Life Stories during class sessions, it is a simple matter for you to lock them up until the students' next writing time. If your schedule does not permit in-school writing time, you can still offer safekeeping for notebooks the morning after a night writing session or over the weekend. The mere act of offering locked protection gives the assignment the proper air of integrity. It is under these conditions that the exercise performs its ultimate function, for the student and for the teacher.

Make the assignment in your own words instead of reading it. The ideal way is to make it to each student privately, looking him straight in the eye. It can still be a personal experience even when the assignment is made to a class, provided you become familiar with all its facets in advance and provided you honestly believe that your students can reach whatever goals they set for themselves. Students will detect faking at this point.

The Life Story Assignment

"Please write the story of your life, from the time you can remember anything until you are thirty years old."

This is a bit of a shocker. Now that you have your student's or students' attention, the explanation can be given in detail:

"This must be written in the same way that you have been writing Here and Now. It must be written in first person, and present tense is a big help in keeping you into the details. Start by remembering eyes, ears, nose, mouth, and fingers or skin. Include from the past—home, family, play, school, toys, friends, teachers, summers, sicknesses, sadnesses, hurts, lonely times, decisions, happy times, achievements. Include about the future exactly the same, plus training, profession, travel, marriage, children, dreams—everything as if it had already happened.

"The way to work is this: For everything that happened to you before today, *imagine* yourself back into the setting, into the time, and among the people. Then write as if it were Here and Now. When you are writing into the future, ahead of today, again *imagine* yourself into the exact setting, among the exact people, in the exact time, and write everything as you want it to be when that time in your life actually arrives.

"Your great-grandparents, your grandparents, your immeidate family—these cannot be changed now, but they are an important part of the person who is you today. As for the future, imagine and firmly believe (because it is true) that nothing stands in your way of being and doing whatever you want to do—nothing, that is, except possibly you—your failure to make a plan and your failure to aim high enough.

"I have several good reasons for this assignment. They all have to do with your success in writing and, in the end, they have to do with your success in life. My reasons are these:

"1. Not until you have examined your whole life—past, present, and future—do you know yourself what it is that you have to say on paper. Of course, we can't expect readers to want to read what you say until you have something important to say. That 'something' will reveal itself all right, never fear, once you take a good look and really know *who you are.*

"2. In order for me to help you say exactly what you want

to say, I need to know who you are and what it is that you have to say to a reader. This assignment will help you, my student, and me, your teacher, get acquainted. This is necessary, not because I am nosy but because I am the one who wants to help you say clearly and in an interesting way anything and everything you have to say.

"3. In writing your Life Story, you, not I, will select your subjects, your style, and the form in which you will write. Not that you will think about these things as you write rapidly, getting it all down in rough form. When I read your story, however, I will find parts of it that you have written in such a way that they make me sit up and take notice. Some parts you may not really be interested in as you write. You will write them just to get them out of the way, and I will be able to tell this from the way you write. Other parts, even when you may not be aware of it, will interest you greatly. These parts will come off the paper filled with excitement. They will show me the style in which you can write best, and they will give you ideas and subjects enough to write and rewrite into finished poems, stories, articles, or plays for the rest of the year—and possibly, enough for the rest of your life.

'*Warning.* Write alone. Don't show this to anyone but me. Especially don't show it around among your classmates. It is nobody's business but ours, and it is my business for no reason except that it will show me how to help you write. Tell all and tell it exactly the way it was and will be. Your sins and silliness will be safe. I am not going to criticize—not now or at any time you are in my class—what you choose to write about. My job is to help you to write well whatever you want to say on paper for someone else to read.

"So, turn on your five senses and let yourself go. Write rapidly. Pay no attention to anything except getting it on paper in sensory terms. Grammar and spelling we can work out later. Do write it so I can read it. If you can't, I'll ask you to type it from your notebook, but I really don't want it typed at first. The *you* will come out better through your fingers from the tip of a pen than it will through a typewriter. Write it by hand, and I promise to do my best to read it.

"You will need to work hard and fast, in class and outside. I am [or am not] giving you a due date, but I want you to get all the way to being an old person of thirty before you give me your story. Getting all the way through is a part of the experience that will be of real benefit to you. Your own interest in writing the story thins out if you let someone else read it before it is finished. I don't know exactly why, but it does. This is your personal story. Don't let anyone else have a chance to stick pins in it."

Once this assignment is made, you will have all kinds of surprises in store. Even though you assign a due date, you cannot expect to get finished life stories on that date. This assignment must be—and you must be—flexible.

I suggest that if a student loses interest or bogs down before the end of his story it is well to ask him whether he is ready for you to read as far as he has gone. If he gives permission, I urge you to read slowly, searching all the way for this student's self-revealed future writing assignments. Make marginal notes, especially those that ask questions. The following chapter explains in detail the kinds of markings I make on students' written material. You will doubtless develop additional marks of your own.

At this stage in your relationship with your student, encourage, lead on, assume that the experience described is of value to others, ask questions that help the student to become more aware of his five senses, and make suggestions that show your personal interest in what he has to say.

Relax. Enjoy. Encourage. Look for ideas and for the soul hidden beneath the words.

When George Boyce was nearing retirement and had begun work on his first book, he asked me to read his manuscript and make suggestions. He knew a thousand times more than I did about his subject. He had received a great many honors and recognitions. Even so, I marked his manuscript in exactly the way I mark student papers—suggesting that he add sensory detail at one point, asking him to clarify his meaning at another, questioning, prodding, encouraging.

Later his wife told me, "George was so pleased with the help you gave him. He said, 'She must think what I have to say is important, or she wouldn't have spent so much time on it.'"

If my marginal markings could give him that much assurance, think what that kind of attention, coming from you, can do for a beginning student writer.

7. Now That You Have Something on Paper

If you have some Here and Now experiments or a Life Story manuscript on hand, remember that these are raw-materials packages. They are not finished pieces of writing and probably never will be. You could receive an exception. If you do, you will recognize it by the effect it has on you as you read. Even then, the chances are good that it will need a lot of polishing before it is finished.

If, instead of reading words, you see pictures, hear sounds, smell odors, feel your skin crawl, or taste food or dust or juniper berries, you will know that you have a writer or potential writer in your care. In fact, any word on a student manuscript that makes you see something from a fresh point of view is exactly what you should be looking for as you read.

Good writing comes from within the student. Its source is the real or imagined experience of that student. It is, in that sense, uniquely his own, and he is seeking his own personal way of expressing something real. Almost always, with this kind of material, the writing is free, more like talking than like writing.

Whatever you do with Life Stories or any other student writing, do not make the mistake of letting broken rules of grammar blind you to honesty and freshness of expression. This is not to say that you should forget about grammar. Nobody can expect to say anything on paper and be taken seriously unless he is willing to learn and use to his advantage the accepted forms of standard English (a few excellent exceptions now in print serve to confirm this rule, of course). One delightful feature of writing, however, is that it can and does develop in stages.

Writing Is Rewriting

Revision is a basic technique of writing. It can be made less onerous if it is presented to students as a means of avoiding embarrassment. Students who are unsure of themselves can be reminded that if they *say* something and their words do not come out quite right, they are embarrassed. They may agree that often they hesitate or refuse to speak for fear of embarrassment. Writing, on the other hand, can be corrected before anyone else reads it (with the possible exception of a trusted teacher, who does not quite count, since he or she is there to help students avoid embarrassing mistakes and wrong impressions). Often, this suggestion alone is sufficient to gain student acceptance of revision.

Assume, then, that if your attitude is open, accepting, and sympathetic, you and the student will be able to work together toward a finished, grammatical form of whatever manuscript he produces. Your attitude toward the student's first drafts will set the pattern for your work together.

First of all, you must have a relationship in which the urge toward creativity can grow. Red, uncompromising markings ("Sp.," "Tense," "Never end a sentence with a preposition," "Wrong word," and all the other scolding marks that deface honest first efforts) often serve the same reputed purpose as waving a red flag in the face of a bull. A student's explorations into creativity can grow and flower only under careful cultivation and weeding, appropriate feeding, the right amount of water, and an ample supply of sunshine.

Your expectation can justifiably be well above the known ability of each of your students. When I began working with American Indian and Eskimo students, I was warned that it would take them a long, long time to produce good writing. This seemed a reasonable expectation. My students, however, soon dispelled this assumption. Given basic instruction in reporting sense impressions, many students turn in first-draft manuscripts that contain vivid, perceptive writing. Sometimes it is a word only. At another time a phrase rings out with complete honesty and keen insight. Occasionally an entire piece of writing is unified, direct, and true, though almost never are all the words correctly spelled and the rhetoric flawless.

How to Recognize and Nurture Creativity

1. Expect more of a student than you can at first prove.

2. Praise everything in a manuscript that is more vivid, more aware, more perceptive than you have found in that particular student's last piece of writing. This can mean praising one good figure of speech, or a particularly lively verb. It can mean praising a word spelled properly if the student has not spelled it correctly before.

3. Make notes immediately for yourself (and later for the student) of his grammar needs. Never lose sight of high writing standards, but you may delay stressing them to the student until he himself sees the need in terms of his desire to say something that is important to him that he hopes others will read.

4. Never settle for mediocre effort. You may have to settle for a mediocre piece of writing, but a student who is to make anything at all of writing must be urged toward his top performance whenever he writes. Top-performance standards must be set for each student individually.

Our Way of Marking Manuscripts

Our way may not necessarily be better than other ways. If we agree now on a method of marking, however, we can understand each other throughout this book. Since my way of marking has kept many students writing until they were ready for a trade publisher, I feel safe in recommending it to you. Many other teachers have had the same kind of success with this marking method.

Writing detailed comments through student manuscripts is basic to the strategy of this program. True, marking in this way requires a great deal of time. True, you have too many students. Still, suppose you try it on the Alcoholics Anonymous principle—one day at a time.

Get students writing by the methods suggested in the first part of this book. Somehow manage the time necessary for marking manuscripts in detail for one day, for one week, possibly for three weeks. By then you will be so interested and will be seeing such growth in your students' abilities that your twenty-four-hour day will stretch enough to allow you to continue.

To save time, we use a kind of shorthand that fits into margins and between the lines of a manuscript. Students can easily learn to translate our markings.

Please read through each piece of raw-material writing once without a pencil in your hand. Read for general impression. Read for enjoyment. Read as a reader, not as a teacher. Be sensitive to your own reaction, particularly to your emotions. Are you amused? Horrified? Touched? Frightened? Depressed? Left with no feeling, one way or the other?

Now you are ready to read again with a blue or black pen in your hand.

MEANING TO THE AUTHOR

Is this something you'd like to develop as a poem?
I usually ask this question in a margin beside a passage that made me feel any strong emotion. Not all such passages turn into poems, of course, and some of them should not. Still, as a student considers whether or not he feels strongly and would like to write a poem, he is discovering a great deal about writing:

1. That it is his personal reaction to objects, events, or people that is the stuff of writing.
2. That good poetry usually grows out of deep emotion.
3. That he can find release from his strong (often self-injuring) feelings by diluting them in ink and spreading them on paper.

If a student feels deeply enough about anything that the feeling comes across to you as you read his casual writing, he probably has the makings of a poem in that particular experience. You may want to discuss it with him or suggest on the margin of his paper (1) a possible beginning line or ending line (your off-the-top-of-your-head suggestion may inspire the student to try his hand at one of his own); (2) a possible form —ballad, free verse, limerick, haiku, ode, lyric; (3) the possible tone—humorous, loving, patriotic, satirical.

Know your student, and you will know whether it is enough merely to suggest that he has the seed that can be cultivated into a poem. Some students need, particularly at first, to see you waiting, almost holding your breath, expecting them to come forth with something good. An extra note or two on the margin can make these students itch to get started.

Is this something you would like to develop as a story?

I ask this question in the margin beside passages that contain a great deal of action, describe new experiences, reveal tense personal relationships, have to do with hard decisions, and so forth.

Real people discovering what life is all about—what makes life good, how to triumph over personal or social problems, what to believe, how to get along with family members, friends, or enemies—this is the raw material of stories. When you find any hint of this in a student paper, that material can be presented in scenes and the scenes arranged into a story.

Is this a person you would enjoy writing about more fully?

Family members are frequently mentioned in students' first writings. If we were to judge by American Indian and Eskimo student writing, we could hardly fail to conclude that grandmothers and grandfathers are the most deeply loved people in the world. The grandparents of Indian, Eskimo, Spanish-speaking, Vietnamese, and many other students provide unusually interesting material for character sketches because many of them are standing astride two cultures, and their points of view are pertinent to understanding these peoples.

Occasionally a student will write out his hatred for someone who has mistreated him. This too is valid material for a character sketch.

You've expressed an opinion here that might make a good article.

Magazine editors are often eager for material written from almost any ethnic point of view. Remember, though, that your students (whether they have lived on a reservation or in a ghetto or in a war-torn country) are young people. They have strong opinions and fresh insights on various growing-up problems, and these can be developed into articles.

You may have a how-to-do- or how-to-make-something article here. You sound like an authority on the subject.

Many of our students are experts in special kinds of fishing, hunting, trapping, rodeo riding, dancing, singing, drumming, beadwork, basket weaving, ethnic costumes, cooking of special foods, regional fauna—in a thousand things that others would like to know and would, therefore, read about. Watch for indications of these special bits of knowledge on papers and in conversations with students. Articles on how to do or make something are always in demand, and your students may well be authorities with firsthand knowledge necessary for teaching others in step-by-step articles.

✓ *Good!*

A small check mark will fit above a word, in a margin, or in any small space. In my code it means, "I like this." I use this mark generously and am usually rewarded with extra effort by the student.

You can do better. Try to improve this.

I mean by an × that the expression is not clear or that the student has not given his writing enough thought at this point.

×

Incorrect spelling.

All teachers know this one. I usually correct spelling errors on a first draft, however, rather than marking them. I even correct spelling on several successive drafts if I feel that the student is struggling with more fundamental values—meaning, clarity, accurate detail, for example. My reason is that I do not want to stop the student from revising. A sea of *Sp*'s on a returned manuscript can be most discouraging. The student is likely to think: "The teacher doesn't care about what I'm trying to say. All teachers care about are their silly rules." I do not see any harm in avoiding that stopper for a while.

sp.

Often a student who is sincerely trying to write a poem or an essay and who repeatedly comes across the proper spelling of a word he needs will learn the correct spelling in passing. If he persists in spelling the same word incorrectly in his later drafts, then I insist, as a last step in finishing a piece of writing, that he look up words and spell them correctly. At that stage in his writing he is willing to learn how to spell because proper spelling then serves his own purpose. It makes his work look professional and thus wins him a literate reader.

You may discover better motivation. I had a college professor who read student papers with a pair of scissors in his hand. When he came across a misspelled word, he clipped the upper-right-hand corner off the paper and read no more. We spelled correctly to get our papers read. I am not sure that elementary and high school students are ready for this method, but you may want to try it.

Keep together words that belong together.

This series of letters in a margin usually amuses a student at first, and amused is not a bad state of mind in which to

ktwtbt

53
Now That You Have Something on Paper

revise. Accidental word or phrase order happens to the best of us in first drafts and frequently in later drafts, for example, in the classified ad "Cow for sale by lady with red-and-white spots," or in the really confused classic that has been attributed to various famous people, "What did you bring that book that I didn't want to be read to out of up for?"

A teacher or any reader, coming fresh to a manuscript, will stumble over these oddball arrangements, but an author is often too close to what he intended to say for him to see the difficulty until it is pointed out to him. Occasionally, a strange sentence structure results in translating into English from an originally learned language. In that case the teacher may need to go into a long explanation (which is the student's chance to learn something about sentence structure). The native English speaker can readily revise, once you point out the trick his words have played on him.

Transpose.
I usually mark the body of the manuscript (using the professional editor's curved line over and under) to straighten out letters, words, phrases, sentences, or paragraphs that appear in reverse order to assure greatest clarity and effectiveness.

Start a new paragraph.
Train students to look at a page of prose writing after it is typed. Solid blocks of print frighten a reader. Sometimes the formal rules of paragraphing may need bending a little to provide print-shy readers with enough space on a page to keep them reading. My rule is: Paragraph partly by eye. It is usually possible to discover some slight subject change, if you must justify shorter paragraphs to make a page look readable.

Too many sentences begin with ing *participial phrases.*
Beginning participial phrases are habit-forming, it seems. A writing style that begins every paragraph with an *ing* word or that runs three sentences together with participial opening phrases becomes monotonous. Such sentences are to be used sparingly. A more direct statement is usually stronger and clearer.

In addition, all initial participial phrases need checking for one pitfall: the opening phrase that does not refer to the grammatical subject. Strunk and White give a typical example: "Being in a dilapidated condition, I was able to buy the house very cheap."[1]

clar.   *Clarify. I don't understand exactly what you mean.*

Again, if the confusion can be blamed on second-language problems (vocabulary, syntax, or whatever), the teacher will need to explain and help the student make his meaning clear in English. I usually say, "Tell it to me. . . . Now write it that way, and we'll revise from there."

Most students who use English as a second language can make their meaning clear when they speak. They may tighten up and stumble over grammar rules when they write. A personal feedback in which the teacher can say: "I don't understand. Can you say it in a different way?" can quickly show the student his problem and help him to correct it in his own words.

A student who has no second-language hurdles can usually manage his own revision (once the lack of clarity is pointed out to him). He may argue, however, "It says just what I mean," or "There's no clearer way to say it."

In such cases I usually find that a sentence or paragraph has arrived on paper containing only part of what a student was thinking when he wrote. In the effort to say something briefly or in striking terms he has left out an essential word or phrase that is clearly a part of his thinking. The student honestly believes that he has said it all and will be astonished when he cannot find the complete thought in his copy.

Sometimes the writing is not clear because the writer forgot the reader's Five Doors. He may be trying to *tell* his reader something instead of *showing* it. He has probably selected words high on the ladder of abstraction instead of presenting images of sight, sound, taste, smell, and feeling. To clarify such a passage is a mere matter of translating into sensory terms so that the reader can experience for himself whatever the writer wants him to know.

Often passages are unclear because they are not specific. Caution students to watch for sentences that cause the reader to ask When? Where? Why? How long? Who? Answer such questions, and the passage will become clear.

Develop into a scene.

This is the marking I often use opposite passages of sweeping, ground-covering narration. If the story development depends on the action being described, then usually it should not be skipped over hurriedly.

A writer's judgment is not something that can be handed over from me to you or from you to your student. Judgment

---

[1] William Strunk, Jr., and E. B. White, *The Elements of Style*, 3rd ed. rev. (New York: Macmillan Co., 1979).

develops, normally during and after a great deal of writing and rewriting. You, the teacher, if you have read widely, have been conditioned to expect the progressive steps in a story or article to be presented fully. If something is presented fully, you know from your reading to expect that passage to be used to bring the story or article to a satisfactory conclusion.

Most of our students have not read that much. We can hope that they will read widely, and we can provide them with reading material (something many of them have not had at home). As they read, they will begin to sense which parts of their writing need the blow-by-blow treatment. Until this sense develops, you can lend students a little of your intuition.

Nar.

Turn this into narrative. Eliminate most of the detail.

This means that a scene is developed unnecessarily. It is a marking I seldom need. Still, an occasional student whose writer's sense for selectivity is not yet developed will tell everything in the same wealth of detail. This leaves his writing with no emphasis because it has too much emphasis.

The action described may slow the story action, or a developed scene at this point may give the wrong impression of its significance. Most students' natural antipathy for writing more than is necessary helps them avoid this hazard, but we cannot depend on that. Selection must become a positive skill.

If you, an experienced reader, feel impatient with the time required for reading a passage, the chance is good that it could have been told quickly in narration. Most students can learn the art of selection.

Cliché

Say it in your own words.

Most clichés were good the first time. With much use they get worn out. Say to your student writer: "Tell it as it is to you. Relive it in your memory and write as it passes before you. Remember your five senses. Put on paper the sensory qualities. Your own personality will shine through your five senses and make yours a fresh statement." The word "cliché" in the margin will remind your student of all this after you have explained fully a time or two.

Active voice

Transpose from passive voice to active.

Beginning writers are normally self-conscious. They can talk all day, beginning every sentence with the word "I." When they take pen in hand, they fall into the passive voice in an effort to avoid "I did this" and "I did that" and "I" and "I" and "I."

Instead of writing, "I'll always remember walking through the cemetery," beginning writers are much more likely to write, "Walking through the cemetery will always be remembered by me." Somehow that "I" at the beginning of a sentence feels too bold.

Occasions arise when the passive voice is useful and right. In general, however, the active voice is more direct and less wordy and makes a stronger impression on the reader.

The habit of trying to hide the "I" can be broken with practice and some reminders in the margins of early drafts. Soon the student will begin to feel uncomfortable with the few passives that creep into his first drafts. That should not, of course, keep the writer from using the passive voice when it better serves his purpose.

Too many words ending in "ly" are monotonous.

Monotony is not the only sin here. If the student gets into the habit of selecting the exact nouns and verbs and, when necessary, adjectives for what he has to say, he will need very few adverbs. Usually the idea in the adverb can be included in the noun and verb if these are chosen for their connoted meanings. Excellence in writing depends partly on making one word do the work of two or of ten. When in doubt about which word to choose, always prefer nouns, then verbs, then adjectives but in limited numbers.

Point of View.

Poems and stories are usually written from a single point of view, that is, through one person's eyes. Changes in viewpoint must be for a good reason and require a conscious transition (even though it may be nothing more than an extra-line space that serves as a signal to the reader).

Beginning writers will do well to practice staying behind one pair of eyes, one nose, one set of ears, tastebuds, and fingertips. Switching point of view is a skill to be learned after the single-narrative viewpoint is mastered. For any student who is having trouble with this, I recommend writing first drafts in the first person. It is a simple matter to transpose to the third person in the finishing stage of a manuscript.

Put this away overnight or for a week while you work on something else.

A piece of writing may sound deathless at the moment of creation, but after it and the author have cooled off, it can turn out to be contrived, too studied, or confusing. Many of the problems will be apparent to the author after a cooling-off period. Passages that need this treatment may be spotted by the teacher when he finds the student deaf to suggestions for improvement.

Such passages often evolve as a result of long searching through the thesaurus for an unusual word, piling up adjectives instead of selecting the exact one, or getting carried up into the rarefied air of abstraction during the heat of creation. No fault of this kind is fatal. A period of bed rest can usually bring about a cure. Neil Snortum suggests that his students read such writings later, coming at them coldly "like something slid under your door while you slept."

Cc ?

Critics' circle?

This margin marking means, Shall we have this duplicated and get criticisms from the class? This can be done anonymously but need not be. Sometimes the author prefers to have his name on the copies and to take suggestions and criticism openly. Sometimes a student will choose to wait until he has made one or more revisions before letting anyone else read his work. Sometimes he will choose not to show his work to the class. I respect a student's choice.

In time most students who are serious about learning to write well will discover the values of class criticism. I have had students criticize me for not using this technique often enough, and I think they are right. Open critiques provide opportunities to educate all members of the class in almost every phase of writing, provided the teacher remains in charge. From a roomful of beginning writers can come many good opinions and reactions. From the teacher must come the reasons why and most of the suggestions for solutions to problems.

Open sessions for criticism harden the soul a little—something most writers need. Skins need thickening a little, too, but the teacher must watch for the appropriate moment. Too soon can be fatal.

Research

You need more information, don't you?

I use this marking when a student reveals an interest but does not have enough information to flesh out his subject. Students often write a sketchy sentence or two about a family custom or a tribal ceremony and then finish lamely, "My uncle knows all about this."

This is the point at which I suggest that he talk with his uncle. Interviews, particularly when they span a generation or culture gap, are of great benefit to both participants. In addition, the student who is eager for writing material almost invariably learns more than he thought he wanted to know. He often acquires material for several pieces of writing. Any broadening of knowledge is of use to a potential writer. He may never write an article or story about what he learns in an interview, but whatever he does write will be enriched by his deeper understanding.

Words repeated by accident are circled.

I circle words that show up too many times and too close together. Three or four blue circles around the same word on a page point up these first-draft accidents. The author then searches for synonyms.

For generalizations and broad sweeping statements.

This is the marking I use most often. I've saved it until last because, while you may forget all the others, you must remember this one. This is the one marginal note that can turn your students into authors.

This is your gentle reminder to the student that he has forgotten to use his five senses. You and he will have the fun of watching dull first-draft sentences come to life and dance off the page as the student responds to these notes.

This is a variable marking. "Show me" is probably the one I use most. A student introduces a character or a setting without action or visual details. I cannot picture the scene in my mind as I read. The student can, of course, because he has been there or has seen the person. He has all the information, but he forgot that his reader needs it, too. A reminder will call it to the page.

"I can't see it," I write in the margin. A student has written, "After a good breakfast, I went to town." I, his reader, cannot see (or taste) his breakfast, and I cannot visualize his going to town. He has not told me what he was wearing or whether he was afoot, on horseback, or in an army tank. The writer knows, of course, what he had in mind. He forgot to let his reader know. Until the reader knows, he cannot enter into the experience.

When marking student papers, ask, in the nearest margin, the questions that come into your mind as you read. You *will* have questions, if you read as an interested human being, not merely as a teacher. Your questions will show a student where he has left out detail that will make his story or poem clearer, more sensory, more effective.

In addition, the student will appreciate the attention being given to his experience, and his writing will improve for that very reason. We all like and need a good listener. You must be that to your students. So few people have ever listened to them. Teachers, for the most part, are too busy talking. Let us listen for a change and put our questions in writing on the page. Our students will strive to write well enough to fill us in on everything we need to know to understand what they have to say. Thorough, thoughtful marking in the margins says to a student, "Here's one teacher who is paying attention and believes that I have something important to say."

If you can, go the second mile: type your comments on the students' work. This procedure is not for all teachers. If you have ninety-five students, you will not have the time or energy (except possibly for a few who show exceptional promise). If you do not type or do not have a typewriter, this procedure will be too time-consuming. If you do type, however, you will be able to write a paragraph or two almost as fast as you can think your reactions to a piece of writing. The results in student effort and enthusiasm are exciting.

The sample comments below would be more helpful to you if you could see the first or second drafts that prompted them. Most of the manuscripts that inspired them, however, were handed back and polished into finished stories or poems. My students did benefit from finding sheets of paper clipped to their work with comments such as these:

> Gerald, you have the makings of a story here. I assume that the boy is to be your main character. If so, you must make your reader like him. If he merely steals the paints, your reader will turn against him, but you can change all that. Most people will forgive a child for taking something, but only if he has strong motivation. You need to make us believe that the boy is a real artist. Paints are as essential to him as bread is to most people.
>
> How about putting him in a situation where he sees colors that most people don't see? Others in his class answer the teacher's question about some object in the usual way. Your boy sees it differently. When he says what he sees, the class, the teacher—everybody—thinks he's crackers. He simply has to show them.
>
> Now, you see, he is motivated, and your reader is in there

rooting for him to get some paints—by hook or by crook, if necessary—and show the world.

This may not be the way you want to do it. Any number of ways will work. The point is, by some means you need to motivate the boy and make the reader pull for him. Once you have done this, you'll have the form of your story. Shall we give it a try?

Louise, your short pieces make me think you might enjoy trying your hand at haiku. Remember, that's a traditional Japanese form that we studied briefly—a kind of word game with rules to make it more fun. Shall we review the form? Content: Usually starts with something from nature—flowers, birds, trees, seasons suggested, if possible. Then the poem makes some comment on life—something suggested by your observation of nature.

Form: Three lines only:
Line 1 has 5 syllables.
Line 2 has 7 syllables.
Line 3 has 5 syllables.

Haiku suggests meaning rather than spelling it out. The best ones require more than one reading, and then the reader does a kind of double take and says, "Oh, I see!"

Maria, think of a poem as something designed and planned like a picture. [Note: Maria was a painter and printmaker.] It must have unity, and this begins with your first line because your last line depends on the first. Very often it is as if you had an enclosing circle that defines the shape of your idea. This can take the form of repetition of words (especially repetition that builds, that is, takes on added meaning; a word can be like a stone that takes on polish as it rolls).

However you do it, all your ideas should be neatly tucked in together like a dozing cat with paws and tail confined in one simple, complete design.

In this poem you might suggest the completion of the idea with a change to an upbeat color at the end. That, however, is up to you. Find a way to fulfill the promise of your beginning and complete your design.

Larry, use images to describe purely mental or emotional states. Sensory images are more individual and more expressive than names of things. Sense impressions can carry not only what the poet means but all that he feels. It's as if you roll thought and feeling into a ball and throw it, all in a wad, at your reader. I know you can do it because you have before. I'm reminding you of your Five Doors the way I keep reminding myself when I write.

David, the skillful writer makes his reader feel what he himself has felt. Good writing has very little to do with printed words on a page of paper. It must be a shared experience. If you look long and honestly at your experience and give it in sensory terms to your reader, it can be for the reader as if you wrote it in tears or blood or in ripples of laughter. He will no longer read your words; he will suffer or enjoy as you did. You will be speaking not to his brain but to his eyes, ears, nose, tastebuds, and skin. I know you can do it. You have proved it to me.

Jerry, a story shows (and I do mean shows) a moment of change in a character's life. If you intended to show that, I've missed it, so perhaps it isn't clear enough (I'm the average reader you are testing your story on, remember). The change should be definite and clear, and it should manifest itself in some symbolic action—something the character does that will convince the reader that he has really changed.

I think you are being hobbled by things as they are. I want you to write from reality, but it should be *from*. To write things just as they are is not art; that is candid-camera shots. You have a good character in Kenny and some good situations. You've handled your dream sequences very well, it seems to me, but your story as a whole needs some rethinking. Shall we talk about it?

8. The Raw Material of the Writing Game

Words are a writer's raw material. He needs many and varied words at his disposal. He needs to be able to make them jump through hoops at his command. All too often these days, so-called writers are not writers but celebrities. Most of the words they use are of the four-letter genus.

James Lipton, in *An Exaltation of Larks,* says:

> Our language, one of our most precious natural resources, . . . is also a dwindling one that deserves at least as much protection as our woodlands, streams and whooping cranes. We don't write letters, we make long-distance calls; we don't read, we are talked to, in the resolutely twelve-year-old vocabulary of radio and television. Under the banner of Timesaving we are offered only the abbreviated, the abridged, the aborted. . . . Before it is too late I would like to propose a language sanctuary, a wild-word refuge, removed and safe from the hostile environment of our TV-tabloid world."[1]

Lipton's book suggests a fascinating word game that you and your students may enjoy playing: the game of richly connotated categories for things and people. Students can be asked to bring in one category a day for a week or for a month, or this may be a game that only one or two will enjoy from time to time with the teacher.

"Neologism" is another game that may appeal to the class. Those who especially enjoy it should be encouraged to coin new words and phrases or to make new uses of words that add to or change their meanings. Such changes often come about by listening to the sounds of words or by deriving original

---

[1]James Lipton, *An Exaltation of Larks: The Venereal Game* (New York: Viking Press, 1968).

words from onomatopoeic values. This requires a good ear and a pinch of imagination. Examples are the names of Edward Lear's animals: Yonghy-Bonghy-Bo, Bisky Bat, the Pobble who had no toes, and so forth. The writings of A. A. Milne give us sneezles and wheezles. Wallace Stevens's "thunder's rattapallax" suggests wordplay that may inspire your students.

New words sometimes come from language blending, and those students who know two or more languages should be eager to give this a try. English has been enriched by almost every language that has touched it. Natives from Mexico who inhabited what are Texas, Arizona, and New Mexico before the Pilgrims landed on the East Coast and who first owned California provided the English language not only with place-names but with much of the cowboy tradition—its sombreros, remudas, rancheros, and all the rest. The official language of the United States should hang its head in shame at having picked up so little flavor and sauce from its first inhabitants. Some Indian place-names were taken over, but there the enrichment largely stopped.

Another way to create new words is to telescope sounds and ideas. The line "Worlds of wanwood leafmeal lie" from Gerard Manly Hopkins contains two telescoped words. "Wanwood" has in it the ideas of colorless and dark and suggests the sound and notion of wormwood. "Leafmeal" telescopes seasons into one image—from leaf to crumbled fertilizer.

These are highly sophisticated word games that are played by good writers. Your students will enjoy attempting them, at least, and they may excel at the language-combining method of creating new words.

You and your students can learn new words and correct spellings and enjoy word handling through the use of commercial word games. Game racks seem to sport new word games every Christmas. Scrabble you know, of course. Also try Royalty, a game that usually sends students to the dictionary, to sit looking up words while the game languishes on the table before them.

Other word games abound on the shelves of your all-purpose drugstore or stationery shop. Undoubtedly new ones will keep appearing. Watch for them and try them out with your students. Do not be deluded into thinking that students learn as a result of being told or that, to do any good, the "medicine" must taste bad. Learning can be fun and certainly takes place faster if fun is the only purpose the students suspect.

A simplified form of classroom Password can be adapted from the television game. You need no more equipment than a blackboard or a good memory for keeping score. Divide the class into two teams. Select one student from each team to leave the room while a word is being decided on. Then practice one-word definitions from first one team and then the other until one representative wins for his team. A word guessed on the first clue counts ten points, on the second clue nine, and so on. If the count runs downhill to 0, there is no score for either side, and a new word is chosen.

Password helps students increase their vocabularies. It helps with specific word meanings and also with the connotations of words, since a clue can be not a synonym but any word that suggests the target word. This game helps students develop a fun-with-words attitude.

Another classroom game can be useful in getting students to recognize the difference between denoted and connoted (fact and feeling) word associations. The rules should fit your classroom situation and can be as simple as this: Write a list of words on the board. Ask the students to divide a sheet of paper down the middle. Have them head the left column "Fact" and the right column "Feeling." In the columns have the students write both kinds of definitions.

This game can be more complex and more helpful if you have students give dictionary definitions orally and discuss whether a word makes them feel elated, hungry, sad, proud, disgusted, or whatever. Then, let them try to find a word with a similar dictionary definition and opposite connotations. This works best when the words are used in simple sentences. For example: "She barged into the room." The connotation is: "like an elephant in a pansy bed."

When we change the verb that means "entered," we can immediately bring to a reader any number of different and even opposite images: "She tripped into the room," "She pranced into the room," "She ambled into the room," "She slithered into the room," and "She slunk into the room." All the examples are to be preferred over "She entered the

65
Raw Material of the Writing Game

room," which is completely neutral and nonconnotative and, therefore, carries no image to the reader. He cannot possibly see her enter, and yet, with the same number of words (one in this case) the writer can and should draw a picture. What kind of picture is up to him, and he should be very sure that he draws the picture he intends.

If the author wants his reader to like "her," he probably will not have her barge into a room. Barging is for battle-axes or domineering women, and we do not pick them for our heroines at first sight (if her heart of gold is to be lying there undiscovered until the author unveils it later, he may very well intend to point up the contrast in the girl by having her barge into the room). If she happens to be shy through and through, the author should introduce her to the reader by showing her as she slips or edges into the room. The reader will supply the connotation "shy," and the author will not be put in the amateur's role of telling his reader that the girl is shy. Readers believe nothing that an author tells them. They believe everything that an author shows them (or makes them hear, smell, taste, or feel). "Seeing is believing, but feeling hath no fellow."

Another essential word study for a writer has to do with generalizations and specifics. Someone has said, "A generalization is a plateau where a tired mind rests." While an occasional generalization is good and necessary, the mark of an amateur writer is vagueness. Vagueness is usually found in the gray upper atmosphere of generalization. Up there the reader sees no outlines of sizes and shapes, he sees no color, he hears no quarter notes or trills, he tastes no pepper, he never feels the sting of sleet on his cheeks.

Students enjoy climbing or descending ladders of abstraction or generalization. The wordplay can move in either direction, up or down. Start with a specific object at the bottom of the ladder and add words slightly broader and more general on each rung of the ladder until you bump your head on the flat, spread-out abstraction of each word's ceiling.

Read Magazine for March 1, 1969, contained excellent help with the generalization problem of writers. In an article entitled "Let's Get Specific," the authors show on color bands a detailed picture of a particular Corvette (a picture a writer can show in words). Then they move up toward gray with "orange Corvette," "car," "motor vehicle," "land transportation," and finally "transportation." As an example of what happens to meaning when general words creep in, they finish with the sentence, "I got into my transportation and drove it away toward town." From that sentence it is impossible to see any image because the reader does not know what to picture — a car, a pickup, a tank, or a horse and buggy. Everyone who wants to write well must learn that generalizations are bound to sneak into most first drafts. He must train himself to recognize them and mark them for revision. Revising then is as simple as placing one foot after the other down the rungs of the ladder until he himself sees, hears, tastes, feels, smells the specific object and gives the exact sense reaction, instead of the abstraction, to his reader.

Increasing the ability to write exact impressions requires building vocabulary. Aids are found everywhere. The *Reader's Digest* carries two features regularly that students should see: "It Pays to Increase Your Word Power" and "Toward More Picturesque Speech." Some students may want to clip back issues and make themselves a reference book. If you use the school edition of the *Reader's Digest,* many additional helps are offered.

I found the writings of Indian and Eskimo students somewhat "thin" in that few of them had read widely in the English classics. They could not enrich their own words through the use of literary allusions. (They have classic oral literature and frequently alluded to enrichment materials from their own cultures. Unfortunately, most of their English-speaking readers had no background for understanding these allusions unless they also gave full explanations. Explanations defeat the charm and economy of an allusion, of course.)

Stock your classroom with aids to word usage. These should include an up-to-date unabridged dictionary (*The Random House Dictionary* is a good one, the *Oxford Universal Dictionary* is another, and new ones keep appearing), a thesaurus (or several inexpensive paperback copies), small dictionaries from various editors, possibly a rhyming dictionary, and dictionaries of whatever languages other than English that any of your students know or hear at home.

Word origins, often fascinating, serve also as aids to remembering words and meanings. Search for these, keep your own notebook, and let students in on the fun whenever you have occasion to use a word with an interesting family tree. Add to your classroom library, if you can, books by Bergen Evans and Edwin Newman and others that have to do with words. Your classroom should be a well-stocked word factory, its equipment always in use, its products (writing and reading) continuously moving along the assembly line.

We all know that we can lead a student to a book but we can't make him read. Sometimes we can lure him to read, and often we can see to it that he receives either the training or the glasses, or both, that make reading more comfortable for him. Writers simply must read—to get information, to study how others write, to motivate and heighten their own writing drive. Any good writing program is also a reading program.

Writing and reading—one activity stimulates the other, and we can help both along. We can place books and magazines in a student's way so that he can barely pass without stumbling over them. Many of our students have never had this kind of environment in their homes. A reading center or corner in a classroom is invaluable, provided it is kept up to date and attractive. Time for reading must be provided. This should be time for reading anything and everything— reading for pleasure and to form the habit.

A teacher who loves to read can spread the virus through his classes simply by talking with enthusiasm about what he is reading. School librarians plead for suggestions about what to buy. Help them. Lend your own books to students. Books collect less dust when they are being read. You will lose a book occasionally, but you can write it off your income tax as a professional expense.

I know one surefire way to turn an entire school population into determined readers. For a little while, at least, you may see only the tops of heads in hallways, gym, and classrooms. The hat from which you pull this magic can be a small, inexpensive mimeographed book of your students' writings. When a collection of student writings is distributed school wide (preferably at an assembly called for the purpose or with some appropriate fanfare), no student in the school can resist reading what a few of his classmates have to say.

Poems, stories, articles, gripes—whatever—they are all interest-grabbers for their authors' fellow students (naturally authors should be asked to autograph their works).

Books of student writings mean extra work for teachers and for students, but the results are worth the effort. Students want their work to appear in book form only after it has been finished and polished to a stage as near word-perfect as they can achieve. Each publication date serves as a spur. It is good to publish at least each semester. Quarterly publication, if you can manage the time and costs, is even better. If you must settle for publication once a year, be sure that your book is finished and distributed well before the end of school. You do not want to miss seeing all those heads buried in your students' writings. The students certainly should not miss that show of interest in what they have to say.

Keep your publications as inexpensive as possible. Duplicate the pages by whatever means available in your school office. If you have nothing more than a hectograph, use that. A mimeograph can turn out a very attractive book. Some schools are now able to duplicate by an offset process that can produce books of professional appearance.

Are any of your students enrolled in typing classes? If so, they can practice by cutting stencils or making letter-perfect copies for offset. Find a student who will make a drawing for your cover. Colored paper is usually no more expensive than white. Use whatever materials and time are necessary to turn out attractive books. Students need a dose of pride now and then.

Students will gladly spend time before or after school helping collate and staple the books. A strip of tape around the spine keeps staples from pricking readers' hands and gives the sheets the look of a book. The mere act of typing and putting together attractive presentations of their words adds to students' will to write well and boosts their self-image.

I have worked in schools where one of these simple little books has brought would-be writers out of the woodwork. Once fugitives from anything connected with reading or writing, they discover that classmates (no more literary than they) can write lucidly and hold the interest of readers. They discover that they too have something to say and are eager to learn to say it in such a way that others will read it.

9. Is It a Poem?

Books on poetry and how to give it birth are abundant. Many approaches are available in texts and school magazines and in the autobiographies of poets. All I shall attempt here is to show you how my teachers and I helped our students get started.

Indian and Eskimo students dispelled one of my illusions on my first day of teaching. I more or less grew up assuming that modern-day boys were football players, not poets. To my delight, male Indians and Eskimos brought to class no prejudice against poetry or against any other form of writing. Many tribal warriors were orator-poets, highly skilled handlers of words. Our students assumed from the first that we were dealing with the stuff of bravery and influence.

Most of them did not know the saying "The pen is mightier than the sword," but they believed it, and none considered writing a sissy game. "Poetry" was not a dirty word to them. Later I learned that my communication classes at the university enrolled as many male as female would-be poets. The current trend toward erasing gender roles may not greatly affect football teams, but it should wipe out all traces of male reticence in signing up for the poetry team.

I usually introduce poetry as a game. Like any other game, it has rules. Rules make any game possible, and they certainly make playing more fun, as well as harder. A baseball game in which the umpire allows as many strikes as the batter wishes is no fun at all. A game of Scrabble in which words are spelled as the player chooses soon becomes a squabble. So, I tell students (with my tongue halfway in my cheek because no poetry rule applies invariably), poetry is played by rules. The rules make the game harder to make it more fun.

Our students, once we got them started, had fun with words. They had fun with various simple writing patterns. Once started, potential poets study and play with words until they teach themselves to bring forth good poems. We have no doubt that students with no special bent toward writing poetry continue to read poetry at times, after they have finished school. We are sure that those students now enjoy life a great deal more than they could have without our push in the direction of keen observation, word selection, and the experience of stepping off into the space world of poetry.

>   . . . it is difficult
>   to get the news from poems
>   yet men die miserably every day for lack
>   of what is found there.[1]

Our first assumption is that your students are not already poets. Some will have written a few verses. Most, when you first face them in a classroom, will not be readers of poetry. Few have had poetry read to them. Reading poetry in class may serve as the wedge to crack open the door of indifference. Seek out the anthologies compiled for children and young people. Dozens are available in both hardcover and paperback editions. Select from them poems to read aloud that have a strong musical beat or whose subject matter is close to your students' own experience.

I have never read William Stafford's "Fifteen" to a high school class without hearing a hush of recognition and kinship in the room.

Read poems by A. A. Milne to first- and second-grade classes and be rewarded with a roomful of giggles and a quick willingness to try writing poems themselves.

John Keats said of poetry, ". . . it should strike the reader as a wording of his own thoughts, and appear almost a remembrance."

John Ciardi says, "What one must always comprehend of poetry is that it is an experience the reader must re-live."[2]

---

[1] From "Asphodel, That Greeny Flower," by William Carlos Williams, from *Pictures from Brueghel: Collected Poems* (New York: New Directions, 1954).

[2] John Ciardi. Introduction, *How Does A Poem Mean?* (Boston: Houghton Mifflin Co., 1959).

When you read aloud in class about some experience foreign to your students' age-group or life-style, they have no way of reliving the poem. Along with the recognition and reaching out that our students found in the poetry we read to them, we approached the now-let's-do-it-ourselves stage somewhat as a coach approaches basketball—as a game with enough rules to make it fun while the players develop some skill at dribbling, racing down the court, and shooting at the hoop, occasionally making a basket. This was all in the manner W. H. Auden suggested to a would-be poet. We were "hanging around words and listening to them talk to one another."[3]

The form a piece of writing takes should be the choice of its author. To have a choice, he must know something about the forms available to him. At the beginning of his writing experience, he should have chances to dip his toes around the edges of the deep pool we call Poetry with a capital *P*, and that stands for pool.

A few students may insist on climbing onto the high board and diving into the middle of that pool. The poems of some beginners are astonishingly skillful and expressive, even profound.

In an interview Isaac Stern spoke of music as a continuing process of self-education. The same must be said of writing— and yet he also told of hearing a nine-year-old play a piece by Niccoló Paganini with seemingly little effort and great brilliance. He commented, "Thank God, she hasn't learned how dangerous it is."

Something similar happens with our students. Later, if they are to be poets or accomplished handlers of words in any form, they will learn how dangerous it is, and they must learn to overcome the dangers. Meantime, if they have written a brief poem, they have made music—at least to their own ears and egos. Novices have little need for bravery among words. Grown-up writers must move daily through the danger, gaining courage one step at a time and never ceasing to move with caution and respect for the danger.

Our theory with students (to mix the metaphor) was to get them into the zoo. Let them enjoy the fun there. Without

---

[3] Quoted in ibid.

that, they would never know whether they wanted to become wild-word tamers. Those who do will develop their own timing for confronting the uncaged lions.

The contribution we can make is to speed up students' willingness to begin playing the game and to lead them by the hand as they feel their way deeper and deeper into the world of words—the world all of us must live in from day to year to lifetime.

Among elementary and high school students I found at first a great deal of bafflement about what to write about and how to write it. At the university level, about half of my students knew what they wanted to write and in what form. One girl said, "I don't know how to write a term paper. That's what I want out of this class." So, in our communications class, that is what she learned to communicate.

A young man wanted to communicate by playing the koto. He did that, but he also communicated in words the history of the instrument, and he described on paper the traditional achievement levels a musician can attain and the manner in which proficiency is recognized—similar to the different-colored belts awarded in Karate. In addition to his research and writing, he gave class performances that helped train all of us in the art of listening—hearing music in the unfamiliar intervals of the five-note scale, in the sharp, bell-like clarity of the struck strings.

My high school students and I usually found their subjects and forms within their Life Stories. I asked questions on margins: "Poem?" "Character Sketch?" "Think you have a story here?" Or I made suggestions: "Show me. I can't see it." "I'd like to know more about this." "This line strikes me as being poetry. Do you want to develop it?"

Life stories do not always work, however. Some are written in such sweeping narrative that characters and events are nothing more than a blur. Some students cannot or will not write them. The teacher must then find some other base to stand on while nudging each student into writing.

One girl from the Pacific Northwest refused to write a Life Story. She did write a few feeble first lines, but I soon saw that I must find some other way to get her started. I tried every approach I knew, but nothing worked. Finally I placed a record player in the closetlike room off my classroom. I gave her two or three recordings of an actor reading the poems of Edna St. Vincent Millay.

That first day with the recordings, Aggie sat in her cubbyhole through the class period, through all but ten minutes of her lunch period, and through the study time that followed. The next day she listened again. The following day she brought me her first poem. It was not finished, and unfortunately I do not have a copy of her first draft. I made a suggestion or two on the margin. We talked about it. Her finished poem, her solo flight was:

THE SEA IS MELANCHOLY

As sad and salt as tears,
The sea is melancholy.

It sings a song its mystic own,
The minor, melancholy sea.

Listen! Hear its Orphean melody,
Lamentations of the sea.

Coaxing, luring, nudging me
To run barefoot toward joy.

—*Agnes T. Pratt*

From then on, Aggie wrote poetry and read other authors' poetry morning, noon, and night. Emily Dickinson soon usurped Millay's first place in her list of favorite poets. Aggie's own poetic insights and skills grew, and in short time she became a poet published by highly respected publishers.

She wrote memories of home and wrote out her frustrations at boarding school. Dormitory life crowded her. One day she stormed into Written Arts Studio early and slapped a sheet of paper on my desk. From the doorway, as she rushed off to another class, she called back, "I'm going to call it 'I'm Only Going to Tell You Once'":

Shut up, and leave me be.
I'm lonely,
Can't you see?
Take your serpent slit-eyed grin
And squirm beneath a rock.
If you can recall what door

>   You slithered under to come in,
>   Use it when you slither out again.[4]

Once she began writing in terms of memories and then of emotions, Aggie had no more difficulty discovering the arenas in which her poems would perform.

Some students are willing to write, but they cannot think of a proper subject for anything as awesome as a written piece to be shown to the teacher. Calvin O'John wandered into my class at IAIA, never having considered the possibility of writing anything. He entered into the spirit of our "baby" lesson and the exploration of our Five Doors. Soon he came to class and sat down immediately to write. He never wrote a Life Story as such, but neither did he ever find himself with nothing to say. Once his pen started moving, the fascinating inner world of Calvin appeared as if by shadowgraph on the page. One day, after bending over pen and paper for about twenty minutes, Calvin handed me the following:

WHAT SHALL I WRITE ABOUT TODAY?

> What shall I write today? Well, there are a number of things to write about. At times I sit here and think of what I'll write. I start, but end up writing any kinds of words on my paper. I started to write about a tree, but the tree didn't want me to write about it. The other day I wrote a short story about a dog and was going to give it to my teacher next day. But the dog, somehow, got hold of it and chewed it to pieces. One time I wrote about a horse. The horse liked it so much that he gave me a ride. That was the horse I told you about before that wouldn't let anybody on. I am quite proud of myself. I was going to write another ghost story, but the ghost at my house said, "No." I don't know why. However, some of the ghosts around our town are writing about us. They have already written a story about me. I was quite pleased. I once started to write about a face, but I didn't feel like going on with it. There are a lot of things to write about, I always tell myself. Let's see now, what shall I write about today?

I myself have days like Calvin's. The problem: What shall I write about today? Or, how shall I go about writing? Poetic forms can offer ideal answers to these quandaries. Short lines,

---

[4]These two poems by Agnes T. Pratt were first published in *The Whispering Wind*, ed. T. D. Allen (Garden City, N.Y.: Doubleday, 1972).

lots of legitimate space on the page—these offer easy outs. They suggest that almost anybody can finish a piece of writing quickly. They provide bait for reluctant and uncertain students caught shivering on the brink of "writing."

The distinguished poet Robert Graves painted for us a picture of a poem that shows the reasons why most students like reading and writing poetry once they are introduced to its possibilities.

POEM:
A REMINDER

Capital letters prompting every line,
Lines printed down the center of each page,
Clear spaces between groups of these, combine
In a convention of respectable age
To mean: "Read carefully. Each word we chose
Has rhythm and sound and sense. This is not prose.[5]

Rhythm, rhyme, format, significance, space to breathe—from these comes poetry. A poem can be complete (and therefore satisfying to its author) in as few as two short lines or even in two words. The sustained effort necessary to complete a short story or an article is beyond most beginning writers.

The rules of different poetry games appeal to students' sporting instincts. They like knowing the rules and being challenged. Some of the rules themselves almost start the pen moving. The basic rule, that of using and writing through the Five Doors, is a self-starter. Almost any sense impression hands us the stuff of poems, and sense impressions are piling up on us continuously. Using the Five Doors is like a game rule in that it offers enough chance of success and threat of failure (forgetting) to challenge students to give it a try.

Catalog, cinquain, haiku, limerick, clerihew, and dozens of other forms are appropriate for getting started. Ballads, odes, sonnets, epic poems—these may come along later. Little poems can serve as field trials for everybody.

As I was exploring my way into teaching, almost everyone

---

[5] From Robert Graves, *Poems, 1968-70* (New York: Doubleday, 1970). Reprinted by permission of Collins-Knowlton-Wing. The poem can also be found in *Zero Makes Me Hungry: A Collection of Poems for Today* (Glenview, Ill.: Scott, Foresman, 1976).

I read on the subject started by having students write in the haiku form. I tried it but soon tired of watching students count on their fingers. That and the ineptness of their seventeen syllables, as compared with skillful haiku, convinced me that this form requires more insight into words and into life than most beginners possess. Later I was not so sure. All through my own experience and that of the teachers who worked with me, we found an occasional student who played Paganini like a pro with haiku. Usually, however, we did not begin with that form.

Frequently we started, and got classes started, by doing two things at once. After introducing the Five Door way a writer thinks, we reminded students that writers, in addition to thinking by way of their senses, must practice a lot so that the conscious awareness of eyes, ears, nose, taster, and feelers becomes a habit as natural as breathing. If they do not practice, we warned, they are in danger of forgetting what makes the magic between writer and reader. We often began by practicing as a group.

My beginning practice period with a class may take one of a dozen tacks, depending on the students' grade level and their readiness to become involved. We may begin with the examination of a piece of paper with the five senses described in chapter 4. As we explore the paper's secrets, we write a class description on the board. To that practice activity I usually add another small lesson in writing: the suggestion that the reason we write is to share our experience with other people and, if we can, to relate what we have learned about life to what our readers know from their experience. "After all," I say, "we're all in this world together, and we'd like to make conditions as happy for each other as we can by sharing exactly how things are to us and thinking how our experience might help us all. For that reason we might ask ourselves another question: "'What is writing paper good for?'" I write on the board: "It's good for. . . ."

Class suggestions usually run the gamut from spitballs to airplanes. Then I ask, just before the last bit of space is gone from the board, whether the class will permit me to add one line to that final list. I add, "And for writing a poem."

Then I read aloud from the board (with as much rhythm as possible) what the class has written. Students are pleased and surprised. After all, they wrote it, and it is, in very fact, a poem about a sheet of paper. The students regularly ask, "Can we copy it?"

This is a catalog poem. It is a good poem in that it is not merely a list but a list in terms of sensory qualities. Many good poets write poetry in catalog form—Walt Whitman, for example, and Elizabeth Barrett Browning's "How do I love thee? Let me count the ways," for another. The work of these poets may be better, but their form is the same as ours. Quality can be upgraded.

If class time permits, students should copy the poem. Remember, writing confers its first benefit on the one who writes. Even copying provides exercise in writing, rehearses the process of five-sense awareness, and confirms the proud feeling of having written a poem. If class time does not permit, then the teacher or an aide should copy the poem from the board and duplicate it for each class member.

We are almost always doing two or more things at once when we teach. Cinquain is a five-line form with a grammar lesson hidden in its depths. It also demonstrates several techniques of poetry. I find it particularly helpful to introduce this form as another class exercise that students can, immediately afterward, succeed at individually.

I explain the form of cinquain:

"Cinquain starts with: Line 1—a noun subject."

I explain: "A poem is about one subject. It can be about almost any subject, and any one-word subject will get us started so that you can each learn how to play this game with words. In addition to being about one subject, a poem normally has a beat or a rhythm. So, for that reason, we'll have a poem with more rhythm or beat if we select a noun subject that has at least two syllables. A one-syllable word, all by itself, doesn't have much beat. It drops with a thud off the end of the tongue. So let's try to find a noun subject that has two or more syllables so that our voices will rise and fall (or fall and rise) when we say it.

"Line 2—two adjectives describing the noun subject.

"Remember your five senses when you pick these adjectives. What does an adjective do in a sentence? Right! It modifies the noun subject." (Sh-h-h! Grammar lesson in disguise.)

I frequently reject general adjectives on the grounds that I cannot see "pretty" and I cannot hear or touch "peaceful." This and every other piece of writing the students do will improve a thousand percent when general, abstract words are replaced by sharp, clear impressions that our five senses are ready at any time to hand us.

"Line 3 — three verbs.

"To be sure that we have something happening in our poem — action is interesting — let's use verbs in their 'ing' form. 'Run' is a good verb, but 'running' suggests a picture of action and it also keeps the rhythm going.

"Line 4 — a sentence or part of a sentence.

"This line makes some comment on what we have written. It is a summary of what it's all about, or what it has to do with life in general. This line relates our subject, as we have described it and seen it in action, to something bigger. It tells the reader why we are calling his attention to this subject, describing it for him, showing how it acts. This line should suggest: Think about this. Do you feel in your bones what I mean, even though I haven't told you everything I know about it?

"Line 5 — a one-word, if possible, synonym for the noun subject.

"Some writers merely repeat the one word from the first line and make that their line five. We aren't, however, allowed many words for this kind of poem. Each word we use should carry as much meaning and feeling and suggestion as possible. If we can think of one word that adds a little something more to the noun subject of this poem, that something-more word is the one to use for line five.

"Notice: In poetry, in a story, in a term paper, one thing we write insists that we write the next thing. Unless our writing moves in this way from the beginning to the end, it cannot take a reader along, clinging to its shirttail."

With no more introduction than this, Glen Morehead's high school class at Mount Edgecumbe dictated, as we explained each line, something like this:

Line 1 — noun subject	Teachers
Line 2 — two adjectives	Dressed up, solemn
Line 3 — three verbs	Explaining, scolding, correcting
Line 4 — statement	They are getting us educated
Line 5 — synonym	Slave drivers!

This poem was so successful that members of that class wrote cinquain poems for weeks, in class and out. They typed them and taped them to the walls of the classroom and in the hall outside their room. Everyone in school read them, and many students decided, "I can do that, too." Cinquain became epidemic, as it did in many other schools.

Intermountain School, at Brigham City, Utah, was an incurable carrier of this strain of the poetry bug. The teachers at Intermountain also introduced and worked more than any of the other schools with the diamanté, or diamond-shaped poem (◊), and turnaround poem variations from which students learned lessons in grammar while producing short poems that gave them satisfaction. In addition, they gained a certain prestige among their classmates when these and other writings were beautifully published in the school's own printshop.

We did use the Japanese haiku form at times, usually after exploring less demanding patterns. Traditionally, haiku has no punctuation, no rhyme, no title. As mentioned earlier, it has three lines:

Line 1—five syllables.
The line contains a specific, freshly observed sensory image.
Line 2—seven syllables.
This line follows on and is required by the first line. It elaborates on line one or adds another sensory image that helps build a total picture or a complete experience for the reader.
Line 3—Five syllables.
In expert haiku a kind of chasm opens up between lines two and three. The skilled poet asks us to leap off into space and trust him to help us land safely on the other side.

When we filled our classroom walls with students' haiku, we often added others from books by haiku creators.

One student haiku may serve to illustrate:

> Tightly gripped paintbrush
> Paper and adoration
> Child's view of mother.

This haiku, written by Libby Alexander when she was a

student at IAIA, does not adhere exactly to the Japanese traditional rules. It does not start with nature. It does not suggest the passing of the seasons. Still the seventeen-syllable count and the leap of faith drew forth a successful poem from a student who was having trouble getting started.

The syllable count does not always come out right in translation, but this can be explained to students if we decide to show, along with their haiku, some truly excellent examples from masters of the form:

> Stupid hot melons . . .
>   rolling like fat idiots
> out from leafy shade!
>
> —*Kyora* [translated by Beilenson]

> Ah! I intended
>   never never to grow old . . .
> Listen: New Year's bell!
>
> —*Jokun* [translated by Beilenson]

> For a lovely bowl
>   Let us arrange these flowers . . .
> since there is no rice.
>
> —*Basho* [translated by Beilenson][6]

> Snow melts
> and the village is overflowing
> with children.
>
> —*Issa* [translated by Henderson][7]

> The sky is the blue
> of the world's beginning—from my wife
> I accept an apple.
>
> —*Kusatao* [translated by Keene][8]

At IAIA we worked on rhythm with a Cochiti drum: ta-*dum*, ta-*dum*, ta-*dum;* or ta-ta-*dum*, ta-ta-*dum;* or *dum*-ta-ta, *dum*-

---

[6] Peter Beilenson, trans., *Japanese Haiku* (New York: Peter Pauper Press, 1955).
[7] Harold G. Henderson, ed. and trans., *An Introduction to Haiku* (New York: Doubleday, 1968).
[8] Donald Keene, ed., *Modern Japanese Literature* (New York: Grove Press,

ta-ta, *dum*. A bass drum, a guitar, or a pan and spoon can be used to demonstrate the same rhythms and emphases.

Those who wish may rhyme their poems. I always warn that what they have to say is more important than that two words sound alike. "Don't let your reach for rhyming words pull you off your horse. If you do, you'll never arrive at your destination, which is a poem that conveys to a reader something you believe or feel."

We explain the fundamentals of rhyme for those who want their poems to rhyme. We say: "Rhyming is done entirely by ear, not by spelling. A near miss by ear test is not good enough. In its simplest form (which is all we need at first), if the end syllable sounds like the end syllable of the intended rhyme word, you have a rhyme. If the two words do not sound alike, look for another word."

Young children very much like rhymes in their poems, both those they read and those they write. For older readers and writers rhymes are not much in style these days. Poets from more leisurely eras gave themselves sufficient time to discover rhymed words that often added to the effect and essence of their poems. "If you have a month or a year for writing your poem, you probably can find telling rhymes," I tell students. "Or, you might get lucky." Actually, some have runs of luck I can scarcely believe.

Whether a student is writing poetry or prose, I warn against rhyming by accident. Rhyme should have a purpose, and it should establish a repeated pattern. A reader, coming on a rhyme in a poem, is trained to expect other rhymes to follow. He is disappointed if the poet happens on one rhyme and then abandons the idea. I emphasize that we, as beginning writers, cannot afford to disappoint our readers. Readers should be kept happy, angry, excited, or stirred to love or battle. They should never be let down.

Young children can become so interested in what they have to say that they forget about rhymes. Usually their beginning writings are better for that oversight.

1956). For other examples see James W. Hackett, *The Way of Haiku: An Anthology of Haiku Poems* (Elmsford, N.Y.: Japan Publications, n.d.); James W. Hackett, *Haiku Poetry* (Elmsford, N.Y.: Japan Publications, n.d.); and Kenneth Rexroth, trans., *One Hundred Poems from the Japanese* (New York: New Directions, 1955).

At a village as remote as Unalakleet, Alaska, all midwinter visiting helpers are utilized to the utmost. For that reason, I was asked to work with every group from kindergarten through the senior class in the town's independent college. The second-graders had me scared. I had no idea whether I could get them started writing. Fortunately they had a fine, flexible, responsive teacher, Susan Hanson, and they were ready.

I began by explaining briefly how a newborn baby learns about his world. Then I told the class that I had never been to their part of the world before and that I was almost like a newborn baby here. I said, "You can teach me about Unalakleet and about what you do in the summer when school is out. All you have to do is show it all to me, just the way it looks to you. You can make me hear how it sounds, give me the odors that are around you, let me feel things through my skin, make me taste your food and your weather."

They did not instantly write deathless prose and poetry; they were still having some mechanical problems with writing and spelling. Yet they began at once to think the way a writer thinks. After a few reminders by their teacher and me in the margins of their first drafts, most of their writings began to come to life.

At first, for example, Mike Haugen wrote three lines about his dog:

>I like my dog
>I like to feel my dog's hair
>He feels soft.

His teacher and I asked: "What color is he? Can you show us what he does?" We reminded him to remember all Five Doors. We still did not get a finished piece of writing, but Mike immediately improved his observation and his writing skill. Most of all, he wanted to write, and he became prouder and prouder of his poem as it took on life through the sensory detail he wrote into it:

>MY DOG
>
>I like to feel my dog's hair
>And see him sit in the sun
>And go to sleep.
>I like to hear him bark and howl

And I like to watch him stretch.
I like to see him lie in the sun
I like to smell his fur
And touch his nose.
He feels soft.

— *Mike Haugen*

Gordon Katongan wrote only half of "Egavik" on his first try. He wrote as far as "And we went home to the blockhouse. There was a camp across the river. We stayed there about three months."

I wrote in the margin: "I don't know what a blockhouse is" and "Can you show me that camp?" His finished poem is one that never fails to tickle my fancy. Perhaps it is not as grammatical as you would like, but where will you find as much visual impression and psychology condensed into telegram length as in "Mom gave us some gum / To not eat berries"?

EGAVIK

I like going to Egavik.
Once I saw a moose there
When I was picking berries.
Mom heard a motor
It was Dad.
Mom gave us some gum
To not eat berries.
Dad came and
They had coffee.
They waited for Grandma
And we went home to the blockhouse.
It was a big house with many rooms.
There were three old houses
And a camp across the river.
There were many fish in the river.
We could see a cold storage
And a reindeer slaughter house
With many rusty nails in the boards.
There was a big corral
With a fence around it.
It reached all the way up
To Strawberry Hill.
There was a pond by Big Point.
We stayed there about three months.
I like going to Egavik.

— *Gordon Katongan*

A similar lesson in the five senses to be learned from a baby calls forth different levels of expression from different personalities and from varied levels of experience. For example, from a junior at Hallsboro High School, Hallsboro, North Carolina:

IT COMES

It comes.
You wish it wouldn't,
You can't stop it.
It rides slowly and people take notice.
It comes.
Everything old, dirty, soiled,
Everything man has brought down to his level
Is fresh, clean, pure, and ready for
Man once more.
It comes.
The life which once belonged, belongs again.
It comes.
And his tears run over the earth.
The hills, mountains, and valleys
Quiver with the thought of new life.
It comes.
It goes.
I wonder . . .
Will God cry tomorrow?

—*Jodi Bradley*

From a Navaho senior at IAIA:

THIRST

What's that, over a distance?
White puffs of gray-shadowed clouds!
Thirst dried my smile—
Not as of sandstorm
Or grit of snow, but—
As if it placed a bucket
And waited for a drink.

At the male voice of thunder
My heart stormed with beats of joy.
Slowly . . . blue shadows spread
Over the nearest butte.
Rain approaches,
Wetting its path down the slope
Of our droughty land.

Are my sheep in?
No, don't bother to prepare!
Stand still,
Spread your arms as to worship.
    Rain!
        Rain!
            Rain!

—Grey Cohoe

From a nine-year-old at Concho, Oklahoma:

HOW TO EAT A BEAN

How to eat a bean—
You can taste the bean first
If you do not like it
Do not smell
Hold your nose
And eat it.

And then drink something!

—Leland Biemens

To Karen Nanouk, a second-grader in Alaska, beans had a different connotation which she was able to convey in her poem.

CAMPING

In the summer
I like camping.
We fish
We catch fish
We hear the rod
Go "hoooo"
When it is time
To pull the string up
And on the hook
Is a fish
That smells as good as
Melted snow
And yellow sunshine
And when we cook it
It tastes as good
As beans
Maybe better.

—Karen Nanouk

Writing through the five senses is for all ages and for all writing, of course, even term papers. For that reason, it is worth as much practice and as many reminders as are needed to help students establish the habit. Letters home or to friends should improve almost instantly. The "baby," or Five Door, lesson has in it, in literal fact, a bit of magic. The trick will work, and it proves itself most readily in poetry. Almost any student can be lured into trying something that is as much fun and involves as little risk as writing a short poem. Since he can, by remembering to use his five senses, achieve some level of success that is recognized by his teachers and peers, he is willing to try again and again.

If that student stays at the small-poem level, at the very least he is learning to use his language. At best he has a chance of being read in his school magazine or in a published book. Given time and enough reader encouragement, the student may well choose to move on and try his hand at a sonnet or song lyrics or an epic poem. Possibly he will wish to move into that great big world of prose.

10. Building Blocks for Prose Writing

Just as hogans, tipis, mansions, and penthouses are one- or many-roomed structures, so are the forms of prose writing. A complete piece of prose can be a scene or a number of scenes. So too a room, whatever its purpose, may stand alone. Five rooms or hundreds of rooms may be required to complete a structure. If multiple rooms are needed, the individual rooms are connected by doors, hallways, arches, stairways, or elevators. It is the same with scenes. If this sounds at first like some vague generalization or too juvenile a lesson, it is not.

The Scene (with a capital *S*) is a literary building block made up of five ingredients.[1] Composing a good scene requires a method that can be learned. Once a learning writer has mastered the method, he can use it in writing short stories, plays, novels, legends, opinion pieces or essays, how-to articles, personal letters, book reviews, term papers—in short, any kind of prose writing that depends for effect on enlisting the interest of the reader. I shall use the word "story" interchangeably with "prose writing." In today's literary market almost all prose writing is developed in terms of characters, problem solving, and cause-and-effect action.

If you were planning to make a beautiful, perfectly tailored jacket from a piece of material you would buy a paper pattern. For a fine-tailored story you have the material from

---

[1] "Scene" as I use it here is not my personal discovery. I learned it from Walter S. Campbell at the University of Oklahoma. Campbell was the founder of the writing program at the university, a truly great teacher, and successful author (sometimes under the name Stanley Vestal). According to him, he was never able to sell a short story until he discovered and began to use this Scene pattern.

your experience (or you have acquired it from relived research). Fortunately, you can tailor any number of stories from the same pattern—a set of one-size-fits-all directions for cutting the pieces and sewing or lacing them together. As with the making of little poems, any student who wishes to can follow the pattern guide. Given the pattern, Scene making immediately loses its mystery.

The five steps of the Scene, outlined below, should be explained and illustrated in class. Students should find Scenes in magazine stories and articles and number each of the five steps. Read the Scenes in class. Act them out. These exercises should be repeated and repeated until no student can ever again sit down to read without immediately recognizing the steps in the Scenes he comes across. He should be aware of Scenes he witnesses between students in the dormitory, between brothers and sisters in the home, between teachers and students in the classroom, between players on the gridiron.

Scenes and their connecting links make up our lives. The rules of writing are valid not because the ancient Greek writers said so but because, early in the history of civilized man, someone observed that human beings act and interact in certain predictable ways. The writer must be a student of human nature. Our paper pattern helps us take notice of what happens in life all around us. Using the pattern, we can cut and sew our observations into works of art.

In outline, these are the five steps in a Scene:

1. MEETING—A meeting takes place between two or more persons, a person and an animal, or a person and a force of nature or variations of these.
    a. Time
    b. Place or setting

2. PURPOSE—One or more characters in the meeting must have a purpose which is made clear to the reader. The purpose is best when it is a Cross-purpose.

3. ENCOUNTER—The character with the purpose attempts to accomplish it on one or all of the following levels:
    a. Intellectual
        (1) Characters may give information
        (2) Characters may get information
        (3) Characters may argue

   b. Emotional
    (1) Characters may seek to impress
    (2) Characters may seek to persuade
   c. Physical—the character with the purpose takes what he wants by force.
  4. FINAL ACT—Here the character with the purpose can
   a. Win
   b. Lose
   c. Draw
  5. SEQUEL
   a. New state of mind
   b. New state of affairs
   c. Connecting link to upcoming Scene

Now let us consider each of these steps and ways you the teacher can use to present them to your students.

The Scene Meeting

Until two characters meet, reader interest is likely to be low. One person can sit alone and think, or, as the old joke goes, sometimes he just sits. In either case, an observer (the reader) cannot see much happening or anybody trying to accomplish anything. The reader has nothing to root for, so his energies are not in any way engaged. Once he is introduced to a character, however, he can usually be depended on to read long enough to find out whether anything is about to happen. During the time he is reading for this purpose, the writer must keep him comfortable, and, to be comfortable, the reader needs to know:

1. Where he is.
2. What time it is.

  All good writers put the reader at ease by placing him in a specific setting and by indicating whether he is expected to imagine himself back in time to 1776, forward to the year 2000, or merely to last night or to tomorrow morning.
  As readers, we are so accustomed to this that we may not be aware of its mechanics, but writers know the necessity of putting a reader immediately at ease. They know that a reader will feel bewildered and lost unless he can locate himself in time and space.

A story as simple as "Pat and Mike met on the street one bright morning, and Pat said . . ." contains the necessary orientation—street and morning. Given only that much, the reader or listener imagines a street for himself and sees the morning sun slanting down on the two characters walking toward each other, perhaps coming together in front of a store, and stopping to talk. The reader-listener does not have to worry about where and when Pat and Mike met. He can give his attention to finding out what they have to say.

If the time and place are important to the outcome of the story, the writer must show the reader a particular street and, perhaps, a wet, gray morning with trees bent low before a gale wind. If nothing much depends on the time or setting, the writer may give the reader a bare hint and allow him to imagine his own street and morning. He should never leave the reader completely up in the air at some vague time in some indefinite place. If he does, the reader is very likely to feel so uncomfortable that he will throw the story down in disgust.

Whenever possible, during the Meeting and during each step of a Scene the writer is expected to keep the story moving while giving the reader whatever information he needs to understand what is happening. This is not always easy, but the author who is aware of the need can soon learn to set up habits of writing in an active, ongoing way.

The Scene Purpose

At least one character in the story must have a problem, and he must urgently need to solve that problem when the story starts. (The urgency would be minimal, of course, in an article on "How to Catch Fish in a Dry Lake"—unless the angler was starving. For our purposes, however, we can still claim that all prose pieces of writing present a problem.) The Scene Purpose is to solve the main character's problem.

The problem can call for either a mental or a physical solution. If the problem requires a mental solution—that is, if the character can solve the problem by making up his mind—we are dealing with a story of decision. If the problem requires a physical solution—that is, a change in conditions—then we are dealing with a story of action and achievement.

It is essential that the reader know exactly and very soon after he begins to read what the character or characters are setting out to do—the precise, narrowed-down Purpose. The reader needs to know whether a character's Purpose is to make up his mind to take the job in Istanbul or turn it down or whether the character must make changes in his way of living to clear his good name and marry the girl he loves. In the first case, this is a story of decision. In the second, the character must change conditions to marry the girl, which is his Purpose.

In either story the reader must know the character's Purpose. If he can be told the Purpose without stopping the story, the reader will continue to enjoy all this. If the author is not skillful enough to give the Purpose without stopping the story (and poor writers do get by with this sometimes), the Purpose must, nevertheless, be made clear to the reader.

Example of stopping to tell the reader:

> Harry knew that Evelyn would never marry him as long as he lived way out there in the country in that house that had running water only when it rained. The fact remained, Evelyn was the only girl in the world for him.

Example of getting on with the story while showing the reader the character's Purpose:

> "I'm sorry, Harry," Evelyn said and her voice sounded as if she really meant it, "but I'm a city girl. It's all I know."
> Harry let her hand go and drew back. They'd been through all that a dozen times. "You know there's no market for the farm right now. If we lived there and fixed up the house a little—I could repair the roof so it wouldn't leak, and, if I painted the barn . . ."
> "It just won't work out, Harry. We'd be a year fixing up that place and then five years and ten. I do love you, I admit, but when I get married, I want to live, right off, not wait ten years to start living."

Dialogue is, perhaps, the easiest way of giving Purpose while getting on with the story. Nobody is concerned, however, about an author having an easy time. Too much dialogue in a story or article is the mark of a lazy or amateur author. So, let us try it another way that requires far less space than dialogue:

> Gray dust plumed out behind and billowed into his face as Harry gunned his rusty old cycle down the country road toward town and Evelyn. By gee, they could have a good life together, even while they fixed up his old farmhouse, and somehow he had to make her see it.

Cross-purposes are implied in the above example, and Cross-purpose is always more interesting than mere Purpose. You have Cross-purpose in a Scene when two or more characters each has a purpose and one cannot accomplish or achieve his goal without the other necessarily failing to accomplish his purpose.

This is not as complicated as it sounds. For instance, if Harry accomplishes his purpose of marrying Evelyn and taking her to the farm, she must give up her purpose of remaining a city girl.

If one character purposes to kill another character, the second one undoubtedly purposes to stay alive. If one wins, the other loses.

When Cross-purpose is made clear in your Scene or story, the reader will take sides. He will be rooting for one character or the other, pulling for his favorite to win. This is a surefire way to keep a reader interested—enlist his backing for a character who can possibly win (accomplish his purpose) but who seems to be failing by letting someone else win for a time. This reader enlistment is always worth far more than it costs in extra planning of Scenes.

The Scene Encounter

When two or more characters meet and one or more has a specific purpose to accomplish, something is bound to happen. What happens is an Encounter, and it takes place on one or on all three of these levels: intellectual, emotional, or physical.

In an intellectual encounter one or all of three things can happen. The character (or characters) with the Purpose can:

give information to another character, get information from another character, or two or more characters can argue.

This does not necessarily require dialogue, although it often does. If you use dialogue, other ways of imparting information will also be useful to the author.

For instance, suppose two people are approaching each other on a sidewalk. When they get near, both step aside and lower their eyes. What information is given in this brief encounter? The observer knows that either they do not know each other or that they are deliberately avoiding each other. If this Encounter occurred in an ongoing story, the reader would know whether these two are acquainted; so he would know, without question, that they are deliberately avoiding each other. The author has shown the reader rather than telling him—always the more effective way. Showing provides the reader with a sensory image. Telling may make so little impression that a reader will ignore it, forget it, or disbelieve it.

Gestures or hand language and body attitudes, clothing, and unconscious reactions such as blushing or perspiring—all are ways of conveying information without actually using dialogue. These, plus the exact words of characters (dialogue), all have a place in the Scene Encounter. For example:

> Suppose Tom Begay and Kee Yazzie meet on the bridge in Gallup. Mr. Begay asks Mr. Yazzie for information, inquiring, "Where did my son go?"
>
> Mr. Yazzie may answer in many ways—depending on his Purpose. He may say, "Up toward the post office." This is a worded answer in which the words denote their dictionary meaning.
>
> If that is all he answers, both the reader and Mr. Begay would probably start looking up the street for the boy. Suppose, however, that after Mr. Yazzie gives that answer, he pokes out his lower lip and tips his head back over his shoulder in the opposite direction from the post office.
>
> In that case, the reader and Tom Begay would know that Kee Yazzie was afraid of his words being overheard. He still wants to give the correct information to the boy's father, but he does not want to be caught tattling on the boy.
>
> In which direction do you think Mr. Begay would move to find his son? Obviously the nonword gesture would give more information than did the words. It would also make a stronger impression on the reader than the words made.

Now suppose that when Tom Begay asks Kee Yazzie about the boy, Mr. Yazzie answers, "Over behind the *hoskitti.*"

The reader might or might not understand Mr. Yazzie's meaning immediately, but Mr. Begay would know that Mr. Yazzie was really saying, "It's none of your business." These are words that have a connoted meaning different from their denoted or dictionary meaning. To understand, the reader must be given additional information, and this too can be given in words or in action.

If Mr. Begay's face turns red and he grabs Mr. Yazzie around the throat to choke the information from him, the reader will instantly know that Mr. Yazzie's words were an evasive answer and that he was protecting the boy, probably in something the father would not want him doing.

Choking, of course, is out of the realm of the intellectual and into the third way an Encounter can develop—namely, the physical. It would be possible for our two Navahos, however, to keep this on the intellectual level and to argue. For example:

> "I don't know where he went."
> "I'm sure you know. You're just trying to keep it from me."
> "I tell you, I don't know."
> "But you were with him. He must have said something."
> "He didn't say anything."
> "But you know where he was headed when you left him."
> "I don't remember."
> "You couldn't forget in five minutes."
> "I wasn't looking."

This argument could very well lead our two characters onto the emotional level of the Scene Encounter.

Remember that the character with the Purpose is seeking to accomplish his purpose. In this case, Mr. Begay's Purpose is to find his son. He has given the information to Mr. Yazzie that this is his Purpose. He has asked information from Mr. Yazzie, and they have argued. Now, he still has not found his son, so he needs to do something more. He can do one of two things:

1. He can try to impress Mr. Yazzie by making himself very important.
2. He can play on Mr. Yazzie's emotions and try to persuade him to help him find his son.

Mr. Begay can do one or both of these in this way:

1. The character with the Purpose may seek to accomplish his Purpose by impressing one or more other characters with the importance of his Purpose or with his own personal importance. He may be implying, "If you don't help me, I'm in a position to make you sorry."

How could Mr. Begay pursue the achievement of his Purpose on this level?

> He might say, "Yazzie, I'm representing our district on the Tribal Council. If you don't tell me what you know about my son, you'll be sorry."
>
> Or he might say, "Kee Yazzie, you said you'd be responsible for my son if I let him come to Gallup with you. I'll never trust you again."
>
> Or he might simply pull himself up to his full height, turn on his heel, and stride away. In this way he would imply, "I'm too dignified to lower myself by begging for information from you."

Still, there is another way for Mr. Begay to seek to accomplish his Purpose. That is on the emotional level:

2. The character with the Purpose may seek to accomplish his Purpose by appealing to the other character's emotions — make him feel sorry, make him feel obligated, make him feel that his own happiness is at stake, make him feel ashamed, and so forth.

How could Mr. Begay pursue his Purpose on this level?

> He might lower his voice or even wipe a tear from his eye and say, "Look, old friend, I need your help. That boy is as precious to me as your own little Betty Chee is to you. I'm worried about him. There are too many drunks in town tonight. Something bad could happen to my boy. You know how it is, my dear friend."
>
> Or he might say, "Cousin, my wife will kill me when I get home, if that boy isn't with me. You know what kind of spot I'm in. Your wife is just like my wife — crazy with worry about the kids."
>
> Or he might play on the idea of fatherhood, which has almost as much emotional wallop as motherhood. "Kee, I'm

the boy's father. I love him more than anyone in the world. If anything happens to that boy when I'm responsible for him, I'll kill myself."

Finally, the character with the Purpose may try to achieve his Purpose by physical force. Using our same example, Tom Begay might, in desperation, grab Kee Yazzie by the arm and force him to go along and look all over town for the boy. Or, he can knock Kee down and hold a knife to his throat until he tells all he knows about the boy's whereabouts.

The Scene's Final Act

At this point in the Scene, the character with the Purpose can:

1. Win—accomplish his purpose.
2. Lose—fail to accomplish his purpose.
3. Draw—give up (at least for the present) or change his purpose.

By some decisive act the reader must know that the action of this scene is finished. This often happens when the character with the purpose leaves the Scene as the winner, as the loser, or with the matter in a tie.

If Tom Begay walks off the bridge, the Scene is almost over. He may very well have another Scene with his boy, when he finds him, but that Scene will start with a new encounter. When that Scene is written, that will be another building block or another room in the edifice.

The Final Act is usually physical, but it can very well have other elements in it. Tom Begay could get tired of all this and decide, "That boy is a senior in high school and big enough to be responsible for his own actions. I'm not going to worry about him another minute."

This would be an intellectual and emotional decision (which he probably could not keep), but it would be symbolized by a Final Act, such as walking off the bridge toward home. When the Scene breaks up, this is the Final Act. It is not the end of the Scene, however, and many amateur writers think it is.

The Scene Sequel

This answers the question, "What are the results for the story of the Scene we have just been through?" Unless we are talking about the last Scene in a story, the Sequel provides the reader with the logical consequences of what has happened in the Scene (occasionally, the author can assume that the reader will understand the consequences without having them spelled out for him, but usually he needs an indication in some form).

All Sequels except that of the last Scene make clear:

1. The new state of mind of the character with the Purpose.
2. The new state of affairs resulting from the Encounter.
3. A connecting link between the Scene just completed with a Final Act and another Scene about to open with a new Meeting in a new time and place, a new Purpose, and a new Encounter.

The kind of Sequel, obviously, depends on what happened in the Scene. Suppose we say that, for a bit of violent fun, Tom Begay actually chokes Kee Yazzie until he is unconscious.

The new state of affairs is:

1. Kee Yazzie is lying on the bridge, instead of standing on the bridge.
2. Tom Begay has fixed it so he cannot possibly learn from Mr. Yazzie anything about his son.
3. Tom Begay, whose son may be in danger, has now put himself in danger. The police will be after him, and that will make it even harder than before for him to find his son.

The new state of mind is:

1. Tom knows he has done wrong, and he looks down at his friend and is ashamed or even horrified.
2. Tom is worried now about where he will get information concerning his son. He knew that Kee Yazzie knew where the boy was, but who else knows?

The connecting links between this Scene and the next are:

1. Tom must find somebody else who knows about his son.
2. He must search the town and find the boy with no help from anyone.
3. He must find a place to hide until all of this blows over.
4. He may follow whatever other course he is able to devise.

The Scene that follows can involve a meeting between Tom and the police, a meeting between Tom and his son, a meeting between Tom and his wife, a meeting between Tom and a violent rainstorm (rain in the face might waken Kee Yazzie), a new meeting between the unconscious Kee and Tom Begay, in which Tom tries to get rid of the evidence of what he has done (and this may delay him too long for him to save his son from harm) . . .

Here we have the basic paper pattern for cutting out a story and lacing it together in such a way as to hold a reader's interest. The secret of the pattern's style lies in this: EACH STEP OF A SCENE CAUSES THE NEXT STEP AND EACH SCENE MAKES THE NEXT SCENE NECESSARY.

The late playright George Kaufman used to say of a play with a bad third act, "The trouble is in the first act."

In terms of our building blocks with which we started, the Sequel of a Scene is the door of a room or the hallway between rooms. The reader is well trained (by his other reading) to move from Scene to Scene the minute the time and place of a new Scene-Meeting are indicated.

We are all accustomed to very brief transitions:

> Meanwhile, back at the ranch . . .
> The next day, when he arrived at school . . .
> In the early part of the sixteenth century, when Henry VIII became King of England . . .
> Later that afternoon he stormed into the house . . .
> She wept until he came home from work and she heard his key in the lock . . .

Sometimes all we need is an extra line space on the page. We know that as a signal that the author expects us to move to another setting or to a different time. Movies are forcing us, with their frequent jump cuts, to become Olympic-grade hurdlers as we follow the scenes of their stories.

The reasons for brief Transitions between Scenes are:

1. The Scene (with its Encounter and, therefore, conflict) holds a reader's interest far better than any other unit of writing. Transitions are fairly dull. If movies can train our brains to leap through time and space, the stories we read need not slow down much for our necessary adjustments.

2. A reader gets comfortable with a time and place (setting) and feels at home there while a Scene takes place. He does not enjoy getting himself oriented in a new time and place, so the good writer (always considerate of his reader's feelings) moves him as quickly and painlessly as possible, letting him in on what he needs to know to understand and not be confused by the Scene to follow.

3. Transitions make variety possible. With them, we can include in one story Scenes in places as different as the Blue Room of the White House and the fire pit outside a wickiup. We can range in one story from next year to the day the Spaniards arrived in New Mexico and found the land occupied. Without time and place transitions, we would be stuck in one setting, and we would have to fill in everything, day and night (dull as they may be), during the times between Scenes that really tell the story.

Sometimes it is important to a story to know that the main character rushed to the store and bought a dozen eggs. If she had enough money to pay for them, she probably did not have a Scene with the storekeeper. If she went and returned without hitting a dog or Grandpa Ebenezer on the way, she probably made the trip without entering into a Scene. She may have spoken to Grandpa or patted the dog on the head. Unless these acts are to be important later for the story development or unless we need to know that she is the kind of person who loves dogs and old men, the writer probably would not tell us about it.

If, however, it is important to know that she has no food in the house and the hero of the story is coming for lunch, it does indicate to the reader a good deal about her ingenuity (and something about her guest) if the reader knows that she can make a spectacular omelet and that she digs money for the eggs from the bottom of her handkerchief box. Going to the store to get the eggs has now become an important cause-and-effect link in the story, even though it is not developed around a Scene Encounter involving intellectual, emotional, or physical conflict.

It has required a great deal of space to explain the Scene. It can be explained more quickly in the classroom. Whatever the time required, however, is time well spent. In addition to a detailed explanation, students should be put to the task of finding fully developed Scenes in magazine stories. The stories in age-graded educational magazines and any of the popular national magazines will serve class purposes in finding and analyzing Scenes. Even articles are built of connected Scenes (usually called anecdotes). If possible, ask friends to save old magazines for you so that students may cut out, paste into notebooks for themselves, and mark the steps of Scenes for study.

Cause and Effect

These are the words to remember when planning stories. A character with an urgent purpose sets out to accomplish that purpose and meets another character (or force) with a purpose. The result of the Meeting is a Scene. That Scene sets up conditions (a new state of mind and a new state of affairs) that cause another Scene. Whenever one Scene does not cause ensuing Scenes, the story line is weakened, and readers are likely to drop by the wayside.

Beginning writers should wake up each morning, repeating to themselves, "Cause and effect, cause and effect, cause and effect." They should go to sleep at night, reviewing the day and connecting all that has happened into series of cause-and-effect Scenes. This is the way an author thinks.

All this may seem too technical for your beginning writers —juniors in high school or eight-year-olds or those entering college with limited reading and writing skills. Actually, beginning or seasoned storytellers all have the same needs if their stories are to be of interest to readers. The pattern for a scene relieves the uncertainty and fear. Once the pattern is tried, scenes almost write themselves. My teachers and I repeatedly proved that, if a teacher knows the appropriate questions to ask, all the feeling and information necessary to a good story can be brought from inside almost any student and put into words on the page.

Ask any ten-year-old would-be storyteller, "Why did Linda throw her math book and hit Roger's ear?" The author will know the answer. Suggest that the reason (scene purpose) be added to the first draft of the story. Ask: "Did anything happen before she threw the book? Did she try to tell Roger why she was mad?" Finally, "How did Linda feel after she saw the blood? Did she do anything about it? What did Roger do?"

These are simple, natural questions. The reader needs to know the answers to such questions if he is to enjoy the story to the end. A teacher, asking skillful questions based on the techniques known to every professional writer, can call forth from authors of any age fascinating, human stories of real worth to us all. Why should writing techniques be withheld from our students, condemning them to exercises in grammar and syntax that lead nowhere, as far as they can see, except to more exercises? Even beginning authors can someday play Paganini. The music is within them. Let us help them with their fingering and bowing.

11. A Story Is a Structure

The word "story" for our purposes means any and all prose writing, plus ballads and epic poems that also tell of characters in action. That is a broader definition than can be found in most dictionaries, but the present-day style of prose writing makes the old definition out-of-date. So for us a Story may be in the form of a play, a novel, an epic poem, an incident reported for a newspaper, a character sketch, a legend, a joke, an essay, a television script, a how-to article, a fantasy, or what have you. Story, for us, means strands of characters in action woven together into a strong cord to which a reader can safely cling until it leads him to its end.

What Is a Story Not?

It is not a lot of interesting happenings typed out and clipped together.

It is not the first idea that pops into a writer's head and onto paper to be dressed up a little and palmed off as a story.

It is not an exact reporting of something that really happened. "But I know it happened just that way because I was there," is not a valid defense for a piece of writing, unless it is the report of a fire for the newspaper. Even then, it would be better reporting if it were shaped by a knowing hand. Photography can be art, but only when an artist composes the picture, clicks the shutter without shaking, and develops the print. "Art is not the truth," Picasso said. "It is a lie that makes us realize the truth."

What kind of architect would say, "I have a great idea for a choir loft, so I'm going to build a cathedral"?

Suppose he immediately gathered up carpenters and stonemasons and announced, "All right, men, I don't know how the rest of it looks, but I know exactly how I want the choir loft. We'll build that first and trust to luck that the rest of the cathedral will come out beautiful and awe-inspiring."

About then, somebody should be after that architect with a butterfly net. Beginning authors, however, are always trying to build stories in this way. Or else they say, "It looks too hard," and do not attempt it. In truth, their years of grammar lessons do not prepare them for anything as awe-inspiring as building a story. Even though we have brought them along far enough that they can gather the material and mold a building-block Scene, they must learn how to fit building blocks together into a sound and beautiful structure.

Remember, when we dealt with poetry, we settled for getting students started to write, using forms that gave them satisfaction enough to keep them writing. So in dealing with Story we aim to get beginning writers started. We will make no attempt to deal with abstractions and symbols that rightly occupy the dreams and typewriters of many full-fledged authors. Our aim is to provide step-by-step guidance that will lift the veil of mystery and enable beginners to write stories that are satisfying to them and of interest to readers.

We plan to give students opportunities to write and to make their first efforts simple enough for them to write with some personal satisfaction. Given this much, we know that they will not sit frustrated in grammar classes through the rest of their school years. They will have a chance at the benefits that writing confers on writers—benefits that are job connected, that enrich their lives, that might possibly, if they so decide, lead to a career.

The Blueprint for a Story

Good stories are planned in advance. Some writers put their plan on paper in outline form. Some (with sharp memories) keep their story plans in their heads. Almost all good writers change the plan somewhat as they write. Characters become real people, and they have a way of speaking up when the author expected them to duck their heads and gaze at their feet. Or, in advance, it may have seemed to the author that when the bronco bucked off the hero, he would get right up and walk away. Still, when he came to writing that part of his story, the author might very well decide that this was all too easy. The hero should be really hurt and not be able to walk away. The author then decides to change the next two scenes, even though the end of the story will remain largely as he planned it originally.

Unless a story line changes somewhat during the writing, the chances are good that we are dealing with a dull story and an unimaginative author. This does not wipe out the necessity of a blueprint for beginning writers.

Before the author starts to write, he should know the following about his story:

1. The Beginning
   a. The characters
   b. The problem facing the characters
   c. Time, setting, and tone
2. The Body
   a. The attempt (or attempts) of the characters to solve the main story problem
   b. The complication with the hidden solution
3. The End
   a. The hidden solution that solves the problem
   b. The loose ends that must be tied so that the reader is satisfied

The Builder's Specifications

The bare outline given above is easy to remember, but it needs to be filled in and rounded out if students are to know how to plan their stories.

In the Beginning, know the Characters.
Before deciding even to attempt an outline, a student should consider: Do I know the characters well enough to write about them convincingly? Most writers do not invent their characters from whole cloth. They usually piece them together from snips and snatches of real people—the eyes of one, the laugh of another, the miserliness of another, the limp of another, the sweaty palms of another. In a sense an

imagined character may also be real because he acts and thinks as a real person does.

It is a good idea for a beginning writer to have an actual picture of his main character before him. If he can draw, fine; or, he may want to use the appearance of a person in a magazine picture. Perhaps he will paste it on a page on which he lists other characteristics that he has fitted together to round out a real character.

Start characterizing the actors in a story immediately. People (readers) are interested in people. A very fine teacher, Maren Elwood, titled one of her excellent books on writing techniques *Characters Make Your Story*.[1] Life for human beings is our one universal subject, I tell students. We are all interested in people, and readers (you and I) are especially interested if we see people in actions that reveal their characters. The good author will continue to characterize his actors all the way through a story. In the beginning, however, he should catch a reader's full attention by showing a main character in action that reveals the kind of person he is. If possible, he also shows that the character is up against a hard problem.

A word about what we mean by "showing in action":

An author can legitimately write, "Mary went to town." "Went" is an action verb. "Town" is a destination that gives Mary a Purpose for the scene. We also know that our character's name is Mary.

If Mary's trip is not important to the Story and you do not care to emphasize it, then this simple presentation may serve your purpose. If, however, Mary is an important character and her going to town is something you want your reader to remember, then it will require different treatment, such as:

> Mary raked a comb through her short, auburn hair and flung her green sweater around her shoulders without bothering to change from her denim work shirt and jeans. She ran down the front walk and cut across the street toward town, barely escaping before old Mr. Hamilton, his nose almost touching the windshield, his eyes narrowed against the sun, brought his rusty jalopy to a clattering stop beside her mailbox.

[1] Boston: Writer, 1973.

The differences between the two versions are obvious. The first gave no sensory details. The second uses sight and hearing—simply showing what the author saw and heard when he imagined it. Imagining fully—letting it happen before your eyes as if it were a play or a movie or real life—this is the secret of bringing words to life. It is the secret for making people (our best subject) real and events believable.

In the Beginning present the Problem.
The story problem dictates the main character's story purpose, of course. This must be made clear to the reader almost immediately, and it must be a problem that the reader can care about. That is, the reader will stop reading unless he cares about the main character and really wants him to be able to solve his problem (achieve his purpose).

A good story problem (good because it makes the reader care) is one that places something of real value at stake. The best story problem is a life-and-death matter, since life is our most valued possession. This is the reason why war stories are perennial favorites. It is also the secret of the classic western (the wolves or the Indians will get you, if you don't watch out). It is possible, however, to make values of far less importance seem crucial to a reader. The ways are: first, make the reader care about the character with the problem; second, make the thing-at-stake of supreme importance to that character. Once this is done, the reader will take the side of the main character and will be pulling for him. When the reader cares to this extent, the solution of the problem (accomplishment of the purpose) is as urgent to the reader as it is to the characters in the story.

In the Beginning establish the Time, Setting, and Tone of the Story.
Time and Tone can and should be quickly indicated in passing (that is, without stopping the characterization or the laying out of the problem) so that, for instance, the reader will know immediately that this is happening in 1861 and is to be a Civil War story with the main action taking place in a slave's cabin on an old plantation. It is just as important for the reader to know at once if he is being asked to transport himself to a longhouse in upper Washington state for

a naming ceremony in 1980. This kind of information can usually be given like a baseball pitcher's windup—on the way to introducing characters and story problem.

The settings a writer can make come to life for his reader are those the writer himself knows intimately—the swimming hole back home, the dorm room, the council lodge. These he can recall through his five senses. Then the trick is to give only enough detail to form a total image in the reader's eyes, nose, ears, and so forth.

In the Beginning, then, the writer is running a kind of three-ring circus, and still he must not appear to be out of breath. He gives necessary information in passing, without stopping his introductions of characters and problems.

In the Middle (or the Body) show attempts by characters to solve the Story Problem.

See the previous chapter on Scene and present these attempts in scenes, always remembering the principle of linking scenes from cause to effect.

In the End of the Body reveal the Complication that contains the Hidden Solution.

This is not easy and is not always necessary, but in most good stories a Complication (a further difficulty that develops) provides the Solution to the Story Problem. Writers who look as if they are sleeping are sometimes working hard at figuring out Complications with Hidden Solutions. A Hidden Solution means that the character, in attempting to solve the story problem, performs an action that backfires. For a time it looks as if he has made things so much worse that he will never be able to solve his problem. In accord with the law of Cause and Effect, however, the worsened situation actually provides a way out.

Walter Campbell used to say, "If you can't get a character out of his predicament, it is probably because you haven't made it hot enough for him."

The added complication, growing out of the character's effort to solve his problem, makes it hot enough for him that a way out will present itself. Such complications can sometimes be fatal for the main character. Usually, however, another character has been in training during all or part of the story to take over the purpose and carry on.

Look for and give students opportunities to look for Complications with Hidden Solutions in magazine stories. Mark them. Cut them out. Keep a file.

To test whether I was giving you an impossible assignment, I picked up a current magazine from my coffee table. It contained a one-page story by Will Stanton, a thoroughly professional author. This story is made up of character sketches of a cat, Sadie; a sheep dog, Walter; and the family. In this story, the family and the dog have a combined and single purpose: just once they must come out on top in an Encounter with that cat. Sadie, the cat, has her own Cross-purpose: she intends to remain top dog around that household.

Scenes take place, one Encounter leading to another. Walter, the dog, and the family come out of each Encounter a little the worse for wear. So Walter and the family fail in Scene after Scene. One day, though, it happens: Sadie falls into a full tub in the bathroom and goes dripping down the hall looking more sheepish than any sheep dog. Ah ha! Sadie has, at last, lost one trick. But the story cannot end here.

Father, gloating, tries to recreate the steps that led to Sadie's downfall, and he, in turn, is caught by Walter. At the end of the story Father feels and looks utterly foolish. He and Walter agree that Sadie has won again.

Sadie, failing, has complicated her purpose. In so doing, she wins again over the characters at Cross-purposes with her.

In the End the Problem is solved and the reader is satisfied.

In many stories the end of the body and the end of the story overlap. It is hard to draw a line, but that is not important. The essential requirement of the End is that the reader is satisfied. He should finish reading (or leave the theater or turn off the television) and say, "Yes, that is the way it had to be."

The way an author makes an ending satisfying to the reader is that he prepares for the End from the beginning. Everything that happens in the story is working toward the End. Nothing included in the story can be left dangling. The story is not finished until all loose ends have been tucked in or snipped off. Is there a better argument for planning a story before you start to write?

12. Capsule Lessons in Writing

Learning to write is a lifetime endeavor, as any author will tell you. We make no pretensions toward teaching our students everything. In the one year or even in three or four years during which we may be able to work with one student, he will occasionally produce some excellent writing. If writing turns out to be his forte, he will continue to learn through practice and further study. Meantime, our students read because they want to. Grammar becomes no longer a bugaboo but a tool they use with comfortable skill. Finally, our students (even of one year) no longer regard writing as some mysterious, unattainable art form reserved to the special few. They have written and written well on occasion. For the rest of their lives, they know that they can communicate with others on paper.

Teacher and student should seek out and read a few of the many books available on creative writing. We would urge you to buy for your classroom at least one copy of *The Elements of Style* by William Strunk, Jr. and E. B. White.[1] This work contains most of what you can learn from a book about pragmatic English usage. The rest comes from practice and from living. A personal literary style derives from the writer's personality as reported through his own individually tuned five senses.

To keep growing in the art of writing, it may be helpful for students and teachers to have various reminders at their fingertips in brief, rememberable form. We suggest that you mimeograph sheets with suggestions such as those that follow. The use of different-colored paper for each unit seems to help

[1] New York: Macmillan Co., 1979.

in remembering where to look for the reminders needed at a given moment of drafting or revising and polishing.

As you and your students read and discover techniques by writing, you may wish to add other sheets to your collection. Perhaps you will duplicate lists and capsule suggestions you find in the second part of this book. My teachers were full of ideas for stimulating and improving student writings.[2] In the meantime, here are those we have found students actually needing and referring to as they write.

Forms of Discourse

Some teachers find it useful to ask students to underscore, using a different color for each, the different forms of discourse in magazine stories and articles. A piece of writing, so underscored, shows at a glance how its author worked. In any case, the following reminder sheets are useful for students to have at hand as they write:

> NARRATIVE: Tells quickly, usually in past tense, what has happened
>
> Use: To connect scenes
> To make time and place transitions
> To give information necessary to the understanding of the story, especially information not so important that it needs emphasis
>
> Remember: Narrative saves space. Select carefully where you use it, and it will help you cut stories that run too long. An unimportant Scene can usually be transposed into a sentence or two of narrative. Ask: "Is this Scene essential to the development of the story?" If the answer is no, use narrative.

---

[2] The information in some of these guides for prose writing came to me originally and are adapted from my best teacher, Walter S. Campbell. These "devices," as he taught them, are contained in his *Advice and Devices* (New York: Doubleday, 1950). Although no longer in print, this book is available in libraries.

Weakness: The reader creates for himself no precise image and, therefore, is inclined not to believe what you tell him in narrative form.
Color me BLUE

DIALOGUE: Conversation between characters in a story

Use: To reveal character and motives of the speaker and of other actors in the story
To carry the story forward
To show emotion—tone of voice, inflection, and so forth
To keep individual characters immediately recognizable—using characteristic or habitual words or phrases ("tags" of speech)
To top off the action—the crest of the wave, not the whole wave
To emphasize

Remember: A character thinks, then acts, and speaks last.

Weakness: Dialogue is slow. It requires too much space, and it may tempt the author into overuse and into getting sidetracked from his story. Characters have a way of talking on and on, in spite of all the author can do to stop them.
Color me BLACK

DRAMATIC ACTION
AND PANTOMIME: The Scene, a blow-by-blow account

Use: To present all story developments on which much depends
To attract reader at beginning of story or article
For reality—reader will believe anything the author shows him through his eyes, ears, nose, skin, and tongue

Remember: Scenes are the building blocks from which stories are constructed.

Weakness: You cannot show all that happens in a Scene—Time, Place, Meeting, Purpose, Encounter, Final Act, and Sequel—as quickly as it can really happen. A scene, fully developed, slows the action. The reader may become impatient.
  Color me RED

DESCRIPTION: Presents through the five senses

Use: To call attention to the qualities of things, not their names and labels
To make the story believable to your reader
To characterize—a person's appearance, the way he does things (the facts about a person that we get through our five senses affect our judgment of him and also openly demonstrate his character).
For crossing thin spots in the story—calls attention to sensory impressions to divert your reader from thinking and wondering whether you are putting something over on him
To create glamour, atmosphere, glitter—makes things brighter and larger than in real life
To transport the reader into the world of imagination (see *Through the Looking Glass* by Lewis Carroll).
To indicate time and place transitions

Remember: A reader will not believe anything you tell him. He will believe anything you show him. Seeing is believing. So are smelling, tasting, feeling, and hearing. Dynamic description is more interesting than static. Describe in this order: size, then shape, then move in close and show details—long shot, medium close, then close-up.

Weakness: Description tempts writer into using too many adjectives and, in turn, too many adverbs.
  Color me GREEN

EXPOSITION: A statement of fact or an explanation

Use: To compress
To summarize
In the fifth step of a Scene

Remember: Readers will not believe anything you tell them, and exposition is telling. Either show a reader or be sure that you entertain him while you tell him something. If he enjoys learning what you tell him, he just might remember it. The liveliest form of Exposition is *epigram*, but epigrams are hard to come by. They must be witty or clever and must seem spontaneous.

Weakness: Exposition says to the reader, "Stop and think!" This is dangerous. Stopping is the antithesis of movement, and movement—getting on with the story—is the basic principle of prose writing.

Color me YELLOW

SCENE OUTLINE

I. MEETING
  A. Time
  B. Place
II. PURPOSE—preferably Cross-purpose
III. ENCOUNTER
  A. The appeal to reason
    1. Give information
    2. Get information
    3. Argue
  B. The appeal to emotion
    1. Push—impress, pull rank
    2. Pull—persuade (God, mother, flag)
  C. The appeal to force—fists, guns, bombs
IV. FINAL ACT: The person with the purpose
  A. Wins
  B. Loses
  C. Quits
V. SEQUEL
  A. New state of mind
  B. New state of affairs
  C. Link or coupling pin to next Scene
    NOTE: Remember CAUSE AND EFFECT!

Figures of Speech

Figures are not merely whipped cream on your writing. They are filet mignon, rich in muscle-building protein and oh-so-delicious! They are image makers. They involve your reader's imagination, cause him to react emotionally, and thus help him to live more fully. Your reader will remember you and love you for your really good, really original figures of speech (remember, he has heard all the old ones and is apt to turn you off before you finish those). Fresh figures are fun to imagine and fun to read. They can be the lasso with which you catch and hold your reader while you tie him in emotional knots.

Strunk and White give an appropriate warning: "Use figures of speech sparingly. . . . The reader can't be expected to compare everything with something else." Also they remind us: "When you use metaphor, do not mix it up."[3]

Simile—A comparison of one thing with another. Not all comparisons are similes, however. The things compared are essentially different except for one or two qualities. Similes are tagged by the words: "like," "as . . . as," and "so . . . as."

Metaphor—Says one thing is another that, literally, it is not. A simile claims resemblance. Metaphor claims identity.

Personification—Gives to an inanimate object or force of nature human attributes, emotions, or powers. Our innate interest in people can be transferred to anything by describing it as a person and giving it human characteristics.

Sarcasm—The literal meaning of the words is exactly the opposite from the meaning you intend to convey. Most useful in dialogue for characterizing your villain. Sarcasm is biting, sharp, bitter.

Irony—Like sarcasm, the implication is the opposite of the literal meaning of the words. Sarcasm is for villains. Irony is for heroes. Irony is gentle and often witty.

Metonymy—From two root words meaning "change" and "name." Puts one word in place of another that it may be expected to suggest. Valuable for its brevity, pungency, and instant image-making effect. Example: "The next moment there was a roaring, mane-shaking lion in the room. 'Father!'

[3] New York: Macmillan Co., 1979.

implored Ann, 'Calm yourself. Remember your blood pressure!'"

Hyperbole — Excessive exaggeration, not literally true but often giving a truer impression than the truth could.

Paradox — A statement that is contradictory or even nonsensical if taken at face value but with deeper meaning than is readily apparent. Not for lazy writers.

Onomatopoeia — Fits the sound of the word to its meaning. Example: "Her scolding words clacked and clattered in my ear." Frequent in poetry, but just as useful for prose.

When You Revise, You Are the Teacher

A first draft is like talking. In includes "sort of," "I think," dashes and dots and the handiest words possible. In revising, take nothing for granted. Assume that you must explain if you are to be understood. Find the exact word that matches what you mean. Check, check, check.

Writing a good sentence of description is like taking a motion picture. Start with a long shot and gradually narrow your focus to close in on details. Give details in logical order. Specify by addition, moving in on the details that are necessary for your reader to notice.

Emphasize by accurate word choice and sentence structure, not by exclamation marks or underlining. Use comparison, contrast, or a planned series. For example: "That government of the people, by the people, and for the people . . ." Use repetition, but make it cumulative — it should gather added meaning or emotion as it rolls along.

WAYS OF PRESENTING CHARACTER

A. DIRECT — A character may reveal himself through
  1. Action
  2. Speech
  3. Effect on others
  4. Effect of others on him
B. INDIRECT — The author reveals his characters through
  1. Exposition — explaining traits and motives
  2. Description (dynamic in preference to static)
  3. Psychological analysis (usually a form of exposition)
  4. Quoting what other characters say

WHAT MAKES CHARACTERS TICK?

A. TRAITS
1. Human
2. Typical
3. Social or moral
4. Individual

B. TAGS OF IDENTIFICATION
1. Appearance
2. Gesture or mannerism
3. Speech
4. Habit of mind

C. ABILITY or CAPACITY
D. TOOL or WEAPON

SHORT POEM PATTERNS

HAIKU — Three lines only, seventeen syllables as follows:
    Line 1 — five syllables
    Line 2 — seven syllables
    Line 3 — five syllables
Meaning is suggested
Closely related to the world of nature
Usually mentions or suggests the seasons
Usually employs no rhyme
Usually in present tense
Presents a clear sensory image in lines one and two
Awakens an emotion
Points reader toward some insight or universal truth

EPITAPH — A short poem about a person to be inscribed on his tomb, or a playful imitation of such lines. May extol faults or virtues.[4]

TANKA — Five-line poem containing thirty-one syllables:
    Lines 1 and 3 — five syllables
    Lines 2, 4, and 5 — seven syllables
Closely related to haiku in inspiration and content — a nature poem usually, but need not be.

LIMERICK — Usually humorous or nonsense verse, five lines:
    Lines 1, 2, and 5 — long
    Lines 3 and 4 — short
Rhyme pattern: aabba

Example: There was a young lady of Lynn
    Who was so excessively thin
    That when she essayed
    To drink lemonade
    She slipped through the straw and fell in.
                  — *Anonymous*

Typical beginning:
    There was a ——— ——— of ———

---

[4] See *Comic Epitaphs* (Mt. Vernon, N.Y.: Peter Pauper Press, 1957).

CINQUAIN—A form invented by Adelaide Crapsey: five lines, twenty-two syllables, although the syllable count is not considered essential:
Lines 1 and 5 (two syllables)—Noun subject
Line 2 (four syllables)—Two adjectives
Line 3 (six syllables)—Three verbs ("ing" form preferably)
Line 4 (eight syllables)—Statement about noun subject; an insight statement
Line 5 (two syllables)—A synonym or symbol for the noun subject. If all else fails, noun subject may be repeated.

CLERIHEW—A characterizing form invented by Edmund Clerihew Bentley:
Uses the character's name in Line 1
Four lines in two couplets, rhymed aa, bb
Name of the character provides one of the rhymes

Yardstick for Revising Poetry

Every writer must become his own judge and jury. The number of drafts and rewrites does not count. The author's question must be, how close have I come to achieving my purpose in the most effective way possible? Next, he reminds himself that all good writing is rewriting. Measuring by the following yardstick may help:

1. Does this poem have an emotional impact? Did I intend one?
2. Is it the emotion I aimed at?
3. Is every word essential? (If not, cut those that carry no emotion, those that a reader can be depended on to supply for himself, those that disrupt the mood.)
4. Have I chosen the best form for this particular poem?
5. Do my key words carry the right connotation?
6. Does the poem make a single, unified impression?
7. Does it have design—does the beginning predict the end?
8. Do pace and tone feel right? Is it unified by a single mood?
9. Did I settle for the first words I thought of, or can I find

words with more precise meaning, more fitting emotional impact, more appropriate sound and rhythm?

10. Have I placed words I want to emphasize at the beginning or end of a line, giving them a strong chance to make their impression?

11. Have I said too much—failed to trust my reader to participate?

12. Does this poem sound right when read aloud?

Prose Plan and Presentation Checklist

1. Does enough depend on my story problem?

2. Obstacles—does enough stand in the way of my character accomplishing his purpose?

3. Does my final complication contain a hidden solution?

4. Am I saying something that I honestly believe to be true? Does this story offer the reader an observation or conclusion about life that I myself have reached through my own experience?

5. Beginning—have I quickly brought to life my characters and their problems to be solved by this story?

6. Middle—does everything move toward solving the story problem, but still not succeed?

7. End—are all loose ends tied off? Will this ending leave the reader feeling satisfied? Does it end the way it had to?

8. Scenes—do they contain all five steps? Do I use cross-purpose? Are my sequels clear?

9. Transitions—are my changes in time and place well defined?

10. Point of view—have I stayed in one character, looking at and telling the story through his eyes? If not, are my changes in point of view intentional or by accident? If intentional, have I prepared my reader for the shift?

11. Unity—is this one story or three?

12. Cutting—have I developed into scenes parts of the story that do not require that much space? Can I transpose these scenes into narrative and achieve the emphasis I intended while saving space?

13. Do my characters seem like real people? If not, why? How can I bring them to life?

14. Style—have I used figures of speech, sense impression, too many adjectives, any adverbs that I can do without, specific nouns, strong action verbs?

15. Description—have I stopped my story for static descriptions, or have I described dynamically while getting on with the story?

Know Your Material

One reason we fail to get along with different peoples is that we do not know each other. Students of any ethnic background can further understanding and the causes of their own people by helping others to get acquainted with their grandmothers, grandfathers, uncles, mothers—with representatives of their culture. In fact, poems and character stories about family members are among the best pieces of writing our students have produced. One problem always threatens to defeat us in this area—students do not know their relatives and friends well enough.

Interviewing is a rather formal label for visiting, but visiting, for our purposes, should follow a plan. One delightful by-product of writing is to be found in the heightened mutual respect that results from a student honestly wanting to know what members of his family or tribe can tell him about their own experience. This is a real and immediate way to close the generation and culture gap. Everybody benefits.

When interviewing, be sure you get what you go after. To do this, go with a plan and take notes, or else take a mighty good memory.

Note taking can be distracting and even frightening to the person being interviewed or visited. It is usually possible to remember in great detail for a little while (provided you make a point of having your senses turned on during the interview). As soon as the visit is over, find a quiet place and write fast, in the Here and Now manner. Almost anyone can get very good at observing and remembering, but it requires practice and discipline. It is often possible to use a tape recorder without disturbing the free flow of talk; however, a tape recorder cannot see. For a successful visit that will give you the material you need for writing, learn to pay close, senses-awake attention to the following:

Examine Possessions

Possessions reveal taste, social status, and character. For instance: a Navajo who digs up and saves an ancient piece of Pueblo pottery that he finds while herding sheep reveals that he is not especially superstitious. If he takes the pot home and sets it in a prominent place, we can assume that he is proud of his find or pleased by its line and color. He has an eye for beauty and pride in the history of his land. If he takes it home and hangs it on a post in the corral, perhaps he is showing his regard for someone else in his family who might cringe and call it "a devil bowl."

Ask Questions and Listen

Listen to remembrances—things that stick in people's minds, even though trivial, usually have human interest and are, therefore, valuable to the writer. Listen to anecdotes, legends, beliefs, customs, feelings, attitudes, and desires.

Observe Details of People

Observe with your eyes the person being interviewed and, also, any others who are in range. Details of appearance set each one apart—a wart on the left ear, a tic in the right eye, an inverted curve in an eyebrow. Is the person fat or skinny, does he have outsize feet, hairy ears, or whatever else you can see with your eyes? Size, shape, and wrinkles have a great deal to do with personality and experience.

Observe with your ears. Listen to the manner of speaking. Is it quick, jerky, filled with big words, mistakes in grammar? Is the speech pattern sarcastic, too soft to be heard, bombastic, or what? Listen especially for bywords and favorite ways of putting things. These set one person apart from another very sharply in dialogue.

Observe habit of mind or personal outlook on life. Is it optimistic, paranoiac, selfish, openhanded, pessimistic, miserly, egotistic . . . ?

Observe body movements. Does this person walk with a limp, twiddle his thumbs, gulp his food, walk erect or stooped, sit on his neck, kick off his shoes at every opportunity?

Observe Details of Setting

Observe the character of the land—distant views, near views, the immediate vicinity (neat or messy?), livestock, garden, corral, woodpile, means of transportation, and so forth.

Observe the home—outside, inside. Does it reveal ingenuity or bursts of extravagance, good or poor taste, anything else? Is the person who lives here happy with what he has, does he want to get away and live in a different style, is he struggling to make improvements in his setting? If he is struggling, are his plans realistic, is he making real progress, or is he daydreaming?

It pays to observe a few
LAWS OF WRITING
not because Congress has passed them but because readers are so made that they can understand your meaning or experience the emotional response that you intend only when they are approached in certain ways. These ways have been discovered by studying people, not by studying writing. It is a little late for us to change human response patterns, so, instead, let us use the laws of response to our advantage in these ways:

1. Write about people, things, and facts—in that order. Remember, people are interested in people. Human beings, life for human beings—that is our universal subject. It is the subject of the readers' universal search.

2. Write as you would talk. Use contractions. Use idioms. Say it on paper the way you would say it face-to-face.

3. Write in the first person. Change it to third person later, if you wish. Present tense, which you may wish later to change to past tense, is a good way to give a first draft the feel of its really happening. Writing will retain some of the immediacy after it is transposed to past tense.

4. Quote exactly what was said. To do this, listen. Dialogue must sound like "talk," not like "writing."

5. Put yourself in the reader's shoes. Do not hurt his feelings. Do not overestimate or underestimate him.

6. Do not generalize. Write a blow-by-blow account. Give your reader sensory details and he will build his own experience.

7. Select what you tell according to the effect you want to have on your reader. Do not tell him anything he does not need to know. On the other hand, your reader needs to know whatever the other characters in your story know. If you do not tell him, he will hold it against you (exception: the guilty character in a mystery knows who did it). The reader and the other characters should have access to the same facts.

8. Plan a beginning, body, and end. When you depart from your plan, have a good reason. Remember that, if you change the end as you planned it, you will need to change the beginning.

9. Go from the rule to the exception, from the familiar to the new, from size to shape to details of appearance.

10. Use the active voice and a personal subject.

11. Prefer verbs, then nouns, then adjectives when necessary. Adverbs are dirty words to be used only under extreme provocation.

12. Keep your sentences short. Keep your paragraphs short. Overlap paragraphs when you can naturally. Your writing will be easy to read, and its appearance on the page will beckon you to read.

13. Remember cause and effect. One sentence causes the next, one paragraph causes and overlaps the next. The beginning causes the end. Character causes the solution of the story problem. The writer causes the reader to read; he does not read far in a story simply because he has nothing better to do. The writer catches him and keeps him there, reading, reading, reading to the end.

Book 2

EXPERIMENTS THAT WORKED

or

DIDN'T WORK BUT MIGHT

13. Teacher Exchange

After five years of teaching at IAIA, I resigned and began traveling to schools scattered from Alaska to Mississippi and from the West Coast to the top of North Dakota; to Cherokee, North Carolina; and back across Oklahoma, New Mexico, Arizona, Utah, and California. I found no schoolroom as spacious as the Written Arts Studio I had set up at Santa Fe. I found equipment, library facilities, administrative support both better and worse than I had known. My students had been Indian, Eskimo, and Aleut in the high school grades. Many used English as a second language; some used English in its crudest, most utilitarian forms.

When I began to travel, I worked with teachers and students of every ethnic background. In time, I worked with students from kindergarten to the university level. I found teachers in crowded classrooms, dealing with grammar texts, workbooks, complicated language labs, school schedules, state requirements, and supervisors and administrators in all stages of development. Our students were Indian, Eskimo, Aleut, Caucasian, black, Spanish, Mexican, Oriental. I met teachers who were either frustrated or stimulated by their teaching conditions. I met administrators who considered me an intruder. I met others who welcomed me with open arms and a willingness to turn everything upside down and take whatever chances offered any hope of improving their schools' teaching and learning in language skills.

I worked with teachers and administrators primarily, but I did that largely in the classroom, using students to show instead of tell. I did my best to get teachers and administrators inducted into the writing-as-a-means-of-learning pattern. Many of them tried it enough themselves to be convinced that they would like to try it with their students. Together then, in individual classrooms, each teacher and I began to teach his or her students from the top down—from writing into grammar, spelling, syntax, and all the rest.

As more and more schools invited themselves into our project, I used skilled teachers as consultants who sometimes traveled to schools with or without me, spreading the gospel. John Povey, professor of English as a second language in the University of California at Los Angeles, was one of these. Ronald Rogers had begun his writing career with me at age fifteen in that Writing Studio at IAIA. He had, by now, completed college and was ready to help. Anne Cathcart, then a junior at the University of California at Santa Cruz, wanted fieldwork experience. I was able to send her to one school in North Dakota for six months as a teaching intern. Lois Starnes, our administrative assistant for the project, helped us all in everything and more than earned the title given her by one workshop member who referred to her as "Mrs. Starnes, that Right-Hand Saint."

For two summers my teachers were brought together for a two-week workshop, during which we called in other teachers and language arts specialists. We expanded our means of communicating through the use of drama and of cameras—always with an emphasis on writing, reading, and effective English usage.

We conducted yearlong writing contests and were able, with the help of Mary Lois Mamer and the Kehoe-Mamer Foundation to publish prize-winning stories and poems and, toward the end, jacket cover paintings. These hardcover contest volumes provided students with the ultimate encouragement and reward for their writing efforts—publication. These books are now on proud display in hogans, longhouses, wickiups, and dwellings of every kind throughout most of the states.

Because of the commercial quality of our students' work, the first four of these books have been combined into a paperback, *Arrows Four*.[1]

Students receive all the royalties from the sale of this book. These writings and those in *Arrow V* and *Arrow VI* (which

---

[1] New York: Washington Square Press, 1974.

have not been commercially reprinted) are in constant demand for use in textbooks and anthologies. Student authors receive the permission fees that reprint publishers gladly pay.

Students involved in our project learned how to use the English language to serve their purposes. Of even more value, they developed self-confidence and self-respect. They stand tall. Teachers who entered fully into this project were no longer frustrated and fumbling. When they found themselves short on ideas or know-how, they wrote to me. Frequently I could put them in touch with another teacher in another part of the country who was solving the same problem that had them baffled. Soon, we began a teacher exchange of ideas. When I was not on the road and marking student papers until two o'clock in the morning, I read and clipped the teaching journals and searched the new books for additional ideas.

We were not the only ones who had discovered the upside-down method of teaching English. Most notable and the most like our approach was that of the Teachers and Writers Collaborative in New York City. Individual teachers, here and there, were writing books and appearing on television with methods similar to ours.

Our project's teacher exchange became a monthly mail-out. Believe me, it was not just another stack of paper to be filed in the wastebasket. Our teachers let us know what was happening in their classrooms. They used, five days a week, ideas they found in our exchange. They were like happy converts, (some more than others, of course) sharing the excitement of a new way to teach. "Kids can write!" they all but shouted from the rooftops. "I can hardly wait to get to school each morning to see what my students have written," I was told repeatedly in different words.

In the hope that our delight-filled successes and our tries-that-didn't-work will encourage you to attempt our kinds of experiments, this section of this book is comprised of selected excerpts from our teacher exchange that we called "Let's Talk Writing" or merely "Let's Talk."

Space does not permit reprinting all issues. It is impossible to give everyone the credit due. I am using the names of some of our teachers as they appeared in our mimeographed monthly. The list would be ten times as long if I included everyone who helped, and it would have to include the names of all the students who responded with such enthusiasm that they kept us inspired and going. Those teachers in the project whose names are not included (we had 144 schools when our government funds were withdrawn) will understand. They had their fun, too, and their rewards.

Our project covered enough territory and included an ethnic mix broad enough to do something good, not merely for hundreds of teachers and students but for the United States. Students were discovering daily that they could use our national language with enjoyment and effect. Many used their ethnic languages at home and retained a proper pride in their language heritage. They were not, however, seeking to organize expensive and divisive school programs around their home languages. They could use two or more languages, but they were united in their use of English. Our *Arrow* books went into and were enjoyed in homes of every background. They exerted a unifying influence.

In *Smithsonian Magazine,* September, 1980, S. Dillon Ripley wrote of the Fourteenth Annual Festival of American Folklife and inadvertently described the kinds of national benefits that we were beginning to see as a result of our project.

> It is possible that folklife fests such as we helped pioneer may be open to misinterpretation. Our land is one of opportunity for folk from all over the world. It has welcomed immigrants since earliest times (since the Ice Ages, in fact, if we include the native peoples who first immigrated to this continent). It has welcomed every kind and condition of people, as Emma Lazarus' lines inscribed on the Statue of Liberty make clear.... In the world today exaggerated ethnicity is becoming divisive. We see it in the divisiveness plaguing many countries, in separatist movements, in the revival of theocratic regimes bent on bringing everyone under one religious cloak. That is not what America is all about. We are created from many strains, braided together, no matter what our backgrounds or ethnic roots may imply.
>
> Never have the words on the Statue of Liberty had more relevance than they do today, for in the past few years refugees have been streaming to our shores in unbelievable numbers. We must respect their ethnic diversity—and indeed our nation can benefit from this rich cultural infusion—but at the same time we must offer the newly arrived the opportunity to assimi-

late, to become American. To do otherwise would be to misinterpret our heritage, which is one of togetherness for better or worse.

All of us (including Indians) come from somewhere originally, as Ripley points out, and "the discovery . . . of rootedness is a matter of need." We do not need, in our opinion, complex and astronomically costly new school systems for teaching dozens of languages in an officially English-using nation.

Our teachers asked for no new classrooms and equipment. They found little use for the expensive language labs someone had sold their schools. They simply turned on students of every ethnic background and let them write in English until they taught themselves skills and, through reading, understanding.

We believe this is the kind of unifying influence our schools should be fostering if our nation is not to be divided rather than strengthened by the heavy pressures of inflowing language groups. History, from early times in this country, is on our side. Language unified our beginnings. We believe that we proved, in our small way, that it can do it again, given an imaginative chance.

14. Writing Teachers Write

Because I tried to get teachers themselves involved in writing, I always talked with them and demonstrated, when I first began work in a school, how a writer thinks. Usually, we had a teachers' meeting in which I let them listen, feel, smell, taste, and really examine a stem of headed wheat in Oklahoma, a colored leaf in Utah, a sandstone rock in Arizona, a sheet from a tablet in Alaska in the wintertime. When I asked teachers to write, using their five senses, most of them tried it. A few continued to write. Most, after that first try, found all their time occupied with writing comments on student papers. We all tried to get days expanded to thirty-six hours but were only half successful.

Our teacher exchange includes the story of one teacher-involvement project that I wish we had been able to carry out in each school. It just so happened that my travel schedule one spring would not allow me a return visit to Mount Edgecumbe School early enough to miss the year-end round of parties, proms, and graduation activities. Bureau of Indian Affairs teachers, however, work a twelve-month year. None of the Mount Edgecumbe teachers had planned to start vacations for a month or so after school closed. So we set up a writing workshop for teachers and administrators—all of the teachers, that is, since instructors in any subject must deal with English language usage. Following is our report of that workshop from *Let's Talk Writing*.

Mount Edgecumbe Workshop

Most of the students at Mount Edgecumbe had returned to their village homes (see Ethel Patkotak's account in *Arrow II*) by the time I arrived last May A few stragglers were awaiting transportation and kept dashing to the dock whenever long, rusty freighters or chunky, white fishing boats plowed up the waterway between us and Sitka. For the most part, only teachers and administrators were left, and we had a week-long picnic.

Officially we called it a Writing Workshop. All available faculty members were invited to attend. Well, I know and you know, I'm sure, that learning in every area can be sparked and reinforced through writing. I confess, however, that I was both pleased and surprised to have twenty-five teachers and administrators show up Monday morning for our Writing Workshop.

No one had twisted any arms. Eighteen to twenty-five attended each session, morning and afternoon, six to seven hours a day for the full week. Those who were forced to miss a session scurried around for notes as if they were afraid of failing a final exam. Workshop members who couldn't wait used up my lunch hours and crowded around for an hour after we closed the group session each day.

We talked writing during each coffee break. Virginia Powell manned the coffee percolator, bless her. We even talked writing on the days when we had Ollie Merriott's spicy, nut-crunchy cookies.

Our aim was to dispel the mystery and fear of writing that paralyzes and strikes dumb so many teachers and students. Our method was *Writing*. I'm not sure that twenty-five would have appeared had they known that in advance. Writing does scare a great many people. Teachers and students share a sense of awe in the presence of good writing. Once they begin to practice some of the basic techniques used by authors, however, the fear evaporates. Respect remains to supply incentive. I seldom have to convince anyone that to be able to write well is a desirable goal.

The first morning of our workshop, we made up a list: WHAT WE WANT TO COVER IN THIS WORKSHOP. The last thing Friday afternoon, we went over the list and agreed that we'd pretty well covered each item—certainly not thoroughly and finally, but we'd learned enough about each problem to begin practicing with some sense of assurance. Monday morning's utter bafflement and fright were gone, and all agreed that writing had been fun.

Our Rough-Draft List:

1. How can teachers qualify themselves in writing? How help students with techniques in writing that we don't know? How criticize student work?

2. How can we convince students that they have something to say? That what they have to say is significant?

3. Poetry: Where does it come from? How recognize? The mechanics of poetry—we don't know that much about it.

4. Stories: How do you get a subject? How plot or plan? How present it? What is style and where does it come from?
5. Experience and imagination — how to get into the creative area.
6. How to develop simple exercises in writing into works of art.
7. Fiction, non-fiction, reports, journalism: Emphasis on each — differences, likenesses.
8. Editing — to do or not to do.
9. Markets — outlets for student work.
10. Total school image through outlets for student work — can we use this means of reversing an unfavorable image in the community?
11. Forms of "be" — names and uses.
12. How to criticize a manuscript.
13. Description — static and dynamic.
14. Scene development; use in total story plan.
15. Unity in writing — ways to achieve.
16. Using a model; plagiarizing.
17. What makes writing real and believable?
18. Preparing manuscripts for submission.

A few samples of writing will serve to show how members of the workshop answered their questions and wrote away their fears.

"The full moon hung low, sharpening the mountain's stark silhouette. Mrs. Brown could almost taste the beauty of the spring night as it came quietly down. She had been young and in love too and the taste of first love was heavy on her tongue."

—*Helen Williams*

"Across the street two girls, one on roller skates, chased each other in figure eight patterns on the grass. Their laughter was accented with a scream of delight as a puff of powdery stuff shot from one little hand, just missing the shoulder of the brown-coated lass. The pursuer veered instantly to the right.

"A cyclist entered the scene like a giant electric egg beater...."

—*Marcia Strand*

"Above the village, piercing the fog and rain, the great mountain dominated the landscape. Rocky cliffs, sharp boulders and perpendicular granite terminated in a rugged peak. Snow, black rock and dark timber added to its mystery and awe.

"Cloud formations at the base made Wolf Foot realize the mountain's height and majesty. Below him on the rocky trail an owl hooted his warnings of bad luck.

"What other omens had he encountered? He retraced his journey in his thoughts. Should he go on? Was the answer on the looming peak?"

—Allan Crain

"Spending an evening alone studying a driver's manual is the dullest of the dull. The black cat stretches its white legs and grins at me as if to say, 'I have no homework.'

"I ensconce myself on the bed and feel the smoothing warmth of the electric blanket as it ticks its warming melody. This is no atmosphere for study. Bright laughter of children seeps through the technicalities of drunken driving and parallel parking. Danny growls at Charlie, 'No, you can't. Come in now.' To which Charlie responds stubbornly, 'I'm goin' to sail my boat on the big ocean.'

"Let's see, licenses may be suspended for sailing recklessly—no, driving—Oh, go on in, Charlie!

"The fog horn sounds ominous in the far echoes of the throbbing ocean. What about horns? Oh, yes, you may sound your horn as you pass a car. A plane zooms up, roaring into the wild blue overhead. At least, he has no roadway or slippery shoulders off which to dive—Oops, my head has dived onto the pillow and I have committed the worst of driving offenses—falling asleep at the wheel!"

—Cleta Moorhead

"Jane sat in the dock shack waiting for the shoreboat. She was conscious of the fishy smell of the water mingling with the acrid odor of smoke and the tingling smell of tar. The sun shone on the water making bright paths along the dancing waves. Across the channel were the forbidding black rocks. Farther on, oil tanks and tumbledown shacks peeped through the needle-like leaves of the spruce. High in the sky the seagulls flew and wheeled in huge circles.

"Jane felt the cold of the bench penetrating her clothes while the wind circled around her unbooted ankles. A motor boat chugged by, its echo returning long after the boat was gone. . . . At last, Jane heard water swishing around the dock shack. Lights on the water. The shoreboat had arrived!"

—Ollie S. Merriott

"Rebecca stood with her nose pressed against the glass in the hospital's nursery. Her breath steamed up the window and she pulled away. . . .

"Now she was aware of the tiny wiggling newborn in front of her. She couldn't seem to see the baby exactly right, either by standing on her tiptoes or scooching down below the crossbar of the window.

"Random thoughts raced through her mind. Were all babies' fingers so long at birth? Were the hands always such a pale blue color in contrast to the deep rose-blue of the head? The black fuzz on the baby's head came to a peak at the forehead. She wanted to see all of the baby. It seemed more cocoon of pink and yellow than baby. 'Hi, baby,' she wanted to say."

—A. Lancaster

These authors were in guidance, social studies, science, language arts and administration. They experimented with poetry as well as prose and used the simplest student-incentive forms to discover new depths within themselves. No students were ever more pleased with themselves. Students pleased with themselves is all it takes to keep them experimenting with different forms, trying out their new-found abilities to express in words what they feel.

Cinquain may serve as little more than grammar review — a pleasant kind of review. In our workshop we found that it can also serve as a vehicle for emotion and conviction.

Bloodshed
Loathsome, abhorrent
Conflicting, demanding, annihilating
Scourge of mankind
War!

Guitar
Stringy, ungainly
Erupting, vibrating, imploring
Pent emotions released from within
Youth

—Donna Carr

Childhood
Bewildered, lonely
Reaching, yearning, defeated
The outer fringe is a lonely place
Outcast.

—Kathleen Hannafioux

Naturally, we spent time on sense awareness. This is the basic lesson for writers. Once a potential writer (and who isn't?) has all five senses turned on, he, like Shakespeare, "finds tongues in trees, books in the running brooks, sermons in stones, and good in everything." All members of the workshop, once started on writing, wrote each evening and, I hope, are still at it. Glen Morehead was one who always arrived in the morning with his night-before poem, and we all enjoyed each one. Here is a sample:

NOW I CAN SEE

What we write must come from senses,
And first we write in present tenses;
It's here and now not what is past
What we perceive, and write it fast.

So let's get started, little pen,
Remember, this is due at ten.
Flow down my arm, clear to my toe
Lord, turn me on and let me go!

I look about—what do I see?
Were I to name it, a noun 'twould be.
Come! Come! You're straying, make it fun.
Keep to the present, or you're done.

I close my eyes and grope about
To bring within those things without
Now other senses I employ,
Much as a child a brand new toy.

At first there's darkness . . . but soon aware
Of things around me, I listen. There,
The buzzing clock upon the wall,
And someone walking down the hall.

Outside the din of welcome noise
Of giggling girls and boisterous boys
In life's rough game they seek a place
As members of the human race.

Then the tingling scent of pine
Wafts through the breeze, I make it mine;
Mixed with the fish smell of the sea,
Skunk cabbage, muskeg, and Russian Tea

My wife just made. She bids me take
A fresh baked cooky, or some cake.
With eyes yet closed, I feel my way
Across the room where goodies stay.

The high-backed chair falls in my grasp,
My shins are barked, but my repast
Awaits the eating. It's used as bait—
She's unconcerned about my weight.

With steaming cup within my hand
I sense it's tang, then let it stand
To cool, and reach in confidence to take
A generous slice of luscious cake.

In fact, I take a second piece
To please my wife, not so obese.
So, filled with food, now quite content
Back to my window I am bent.

With eyes now open wide I see
First roads, roofs, shrub and tree,
The fog arising, birds in flight
Across the bay within my sight.

Far out, appears a ship at sea,
Tall peaks in quiet majesty
Stand rigid, clothed in mantles white
Of snow and ice in lofty height.

Beyond . . . who knows? But God is there
Always he shows us loving care.
So thanks to all the powers that be
For life is full for those who see.

—Glen E. Morehead

Glen loved to rhyme, you see, so we let him do his thing, and he kept us all entertained and challenged with the lilt and imagery from his fecund pen.

This, then, is a brief picture of our Mount Edgecumbe Workshop. We all had fun. We were all sorry when the week ended. Some members of the group had written before, of course. A few had written a great deal. I am sure I can safely say that all were writing with more assurance and greater enjoyment when the week was over. We had all proved, as John Keats said, "Nothing ever becomes real till it is experienced—even a proverb is no proverb to you till your life has illustrated it." Writing is real and possible now for Mount Edgecumbe students because their teachers have experienced it themselves.

If you, as a teacher in your school, are inclined to doubt that your students have something significant to say or that they can say it effectively, try proving it to yourself by writing along with them. Test your assignments by trying them yourself. Make assignments or avoid them on the basis of whether or not you could write with enthusiasm on the subjects proposed. The only way to be aware of this is to write and keep writing.

During our first summer workshop for teachers from all our project schools, we wrote and published a small volume of teacher writings. I quote from the follow-up issue of *Let's Talk Writing*:

> Workshop members will recall that you were asked to forget your role as teacher for a time and simply enter into the writing, acting, picture-making experience. Our workshop publication, "Reporting to Crazy Horse," is something of a record and an evaluation of your living a new role for two weeks. I'm sure you all agree that the experiment proved valuable.
>
> So, how about taking time out repeatedly, even for a few minutes at a time, for putting ourselves in our students' shoes? I say "our" because I plan to join you in this. I want us all to write and keep writing through this year. Write what?
>
> Poetry? Yes, some every day, if you can. I'm sure that if you are brave enough to share your attempts at poetry with your students—to let them criticize yours as you criticize theirs—you'll find a hundred gains in class response and rapport. (I'm willing to bet that, as a by-product, you'll solve virtually all of your plagiarism problems, too. Students can see that you don't lose face when you write something less than a William Stafford treasure, and they can then face their own shallow attempts.)
>
> Write or at least outline drama scenes and picture sequences. Keep a daily journal. Write your life story, and then look at it objectively, picking out emotions, incidents, and turning points to use as the bases for finished pieces of writing.
>
> For our project purposes, please, Please, PLEASE write about your classes and share these writings with us. A one-sentence success story jotted down in two minutes between classes can start a chain reaction in twenty schools. Five lines at night before you close your weary eyes can save a hundred other teachers from making a freezing comment on five hundred students' poems.
>
> What approach did you use today that resulted in sparking one or a roomful of students to life? How did you fall on your face?
>
> During the workshop we all learned a good deal about honesty and openness. We found that the blue sky never fell into the redwoods if our words read by a class proved less than deathless. The ocean still stopped at the shore, even though we never pulled our "white light" down into our too-full stomachs. The sun still continued to burn off the breakfast-time fog, in

spite of ruthless cameras exhibiting all our bumps and wrinkles.

So now that we know that honesty isn't fatal, let's make a habit of facing squarely what happens in our classrooms. If you have a tape recorder, it can facilitate your keeping a daily record. If you don't have a recorder, daily notes are significant for several reasons that you will discover if you ever skip for two weeks and try to catch up. After two weeks, we generalize. If we write every day, we put down the details that can be truly revealing and helpful to someone else or to ourselves. Don't leave out the color, bits of action, facial expressions, tone of voice, and body language. These provide the material you need for changing things as needed. The note taking, the clear observation provide their own bonus. They show you the way toward happier, more productive teaching. They also train you to write and show you what to look for in student writings.

During one of our summer workshop classes, a thought struck me what I assumed then was a glancing blow. I find since then that I still have a bump from that blow that I cannot quite ignore.

The thought was that we talk and talk about interaction between teacher and student. We honestly struggle to bring that interaction nearer some ideal of attitude and method; and yet, all too often, we as teachers go on teaching, and our students go on not learning in the same old stubborn patterns.

During the time I have worked with teachers, something very like a religious conversion has happened to some. I am fascinated when this happens because I have always been a bit skeptical about dating and timing the exact moment of religious conversion. Still, I can almost date and time to the minute the academic conversion that has happened to some of you. Immediately afterwards, I begin to hear "Hallelujah!" in the tone of your letters and in your classroom vibrations when I visit.

We can analyze and do in-depth studies forever and never get beyond mere intellectual acceptance of many educational theories. Conversion, on the other hand, while it may be perfectly reasonable, is something more than a cool act of the intellect. It is a turning around that seems seldom to occur as a result of logic or of philosophic probing.

So what happens to turn some teachers around? Why doesn't it happen to others?

The thought that struck me is a kind of lazy-Susan idea. I dare you to get on and give it a whirl. It just might make this a whole turnaround year for you and your students.

The idea is this: If, instead of constantly saying and thinking "interaction between teacher and students," what would happen if we began to say and think "interaction between learners"?

It is no trick at all for me to accept myself as a learner with students. Students have taught me a major portion of everything I know. Even techniques of writing that I assumed (and my publishers agreed) I was well on my way to learning before I started working with students are now a thousand times clearer to me since I have been in the business of making them clear to students. That is not to mention, of course, all I have had to learn about cultures, cameras, people, poetry, drama, filmmaking, and about learning itself.

For a trial spin on my lazy-Susan idea, how about forgetting that other people call you "teacher"? Let us try thinking of ourselves as "learners," along with other learners in the classroom. I think, if we can do that one turnaround, then we will immediately talk less and listen more—really listen, I mean. Let us want to learn from our students and go into the classroom with that intention uppermost. I believe that we will find classroom interactions taking on a new tone. I think we may discover that communication can truly begin at home, within our classrooms.

15. Teacher-Student Experiments in Learning to Write

The following story struck me as especially true because it has happened, almost verbatim, to me and may have happened to you:

> A member of a visiting team of teachers stepped inside my classroom as the bell rang. A petite woman in her fifties introduced herself as an English teacher. "I teach at the tenth grade level, too. May I visit your class this period?" she asked.
> "Certainly," I replied. "This is a Writing Workshop."
> "Oh?" She hesitated. "What will the class be doing?"
> "Writing," I said.
> "Well, in that case . . . ," and she smiled brightly as she stepped again into the corridor. "Thank you anyway," she chirped, "but I want to visit a class that is doing something."

Obviously, some observers cannot tell when learning is taking place. If that observer is a teacher . . . well, I wonder.

Our Classes Are "Doing Something"

Marie Rose Voigt from White Shield School in North Dakota wrote:

> Dear Mrs. Allen:
> Your letter arrived at a very opportune time, as I have wanted to let you know how your workshop affected me and my teaching.
> Already I have put many of the ideas I gathered this summer into effect. My eighth graders have bound together a book of sequence poetry along with illustrations. I am enclosing a copy.

Some of these booklets will be put on display at our booth at the North Dakota Teachers' Convention. We also plan to distribute copies at our open house during National Education Week. With your help, we hope to publish a schoolwide booklet in the Spring—one that we can get printed and copyrighted.

My students are excited and thrilled with a production we are doing by videotape for National Education Week. The class in photography at the workshop really put me on the ball as far as filming procedures. I actually feel that I know what I'm doing with the camera. I hope you can see our finished production sometime.

I am sure that with more time we will progress even more, for your summer workshop has opened a world of ideas for me. The exposure I experienced will take me a lifetime to develop.

Sincerely yours,

Marie Rose Voigt

Marie sent a copy of her mimeographed book of sequence poetry. Her cover is as simple as can be, but very effective—bright and colorful, and I think you might want to experiment with something similar.

Her cover has an overall design in circles that bleed off the page and are made with colored crayons. Start with one color in the center and then, using short strokes out from the center, make a slightly enlarged circle in another color. One that I am looking at, for instance, begins with an orange center. It has half-inch strokes of brown around it to make a brown irregular circle. Around that is a yellow irregular circle, around that a blue, and around that a red circle that runs partly off the edge of the page. I would assume that three or four circles were drawn first and then circles added to fill the blank spaces between other circles on the page. The fill-ins are irregular.

You, of course, can use any form you wish. Circles, triangles, squares, and dozens of other design ideas will suggest themselves to you and your students. Making book covers by this hand method requires a good deal of work, of course, but students like to work as long as they are making something beautiful to enhance their writings.

These bound books are useful in many ways. They recognize superior effort and can, if the writings included are so selected, recognize the top effort of students who do not do as well. The possibility of publication provides students with strong incentive for writing and for writing well. Student books make excellent textbooks if they are used as the basis for class reading, discussion, and criticism. Finally, these are usually the most popular books in school libraries and never fail to lure reading practice.

Student books can win nationwide recognition. *Náátsíílid*, the creative writing anthology of Intermountain School, was awarded first place in the country by Columbia Press, and was commended for layout and Indian expression in poetry. Credit should be given to Clarissa Lowry, Ferrin L. Allen, and Alexa West, along with the major credit to contributing student authors and artists.

Ann Gulledge's students at Albuquerque Indian School, in New Mexico, prepared such impressive copy for a book that the superintendent scrounged up money to get it commercially printed. The students then gave an autographing party to which they invited faculty members, the student body, speakers who had talked to them about writing, and this proud project director. Their books and the autographs that authors collected from fellow authors and from visitors will remain among their prized possessions for the rest of their lives. For an hour or so they enjoyed one of the rewards of writing—namely, recognition for having written.

We strongly recommend the collection of anthologies with the dab of whipped cream on top that caps it all off—an autographing party.

In addition, we recommend individual student collections. Some of our project teachers made an outstanding success of this kind of book.

To Jim White at Wingate High School, Fort Wingate, New Mexico, we give recognition for the consistent quality and artistic merit of books he produced with individual students. His equipment was no more sophisticated than a mimeograph, and yet he managed to reproduce imaginative and beautiful covers, took great care with layout, selection of colored paper, and colorful ties.

Students who finish a year of writing with one or more books, authored by themselves and tastefully bound, will surely be inspired to keep writing and to write up to the limits of their ability. Once such a book is in his hands, the student who wrote it is bound to have a heightened opinion of himself and thus to set new goals for himself. He has documented proof that he is somebody.

Naturally the quality of the writing in these individual books will vary. Excellent writers are few and far between. In such a book, however, a student competes with himself and has no reason to feel inferior to those with more practice or more ability. In some ways the collection of writings of individuals can be expected to inspire even more and better work than the more usual class or school anthologies. Both kinds of collections are recommended.

When I visited the Albuquerque school, I was greeted in the library by a life-size poster made on pegboard. The copy said in large letters: HELP SCHOOLS BRIDGE THE GAP WITH STUDENT-MADE TEXTS.

Illustrating this caption on the poster were copies of the *Arrow* books, pictures taken by the yearbook staff, and copies of mimeographed booklets made in language arts classes. You have all heard me say many times that students enjoy reading what other students have written more than anything you can find for them to read. Writing by the peer group does more to stimulate reading and writing than anything else I have ever found by way of method or technique. Students also appreciate seeing their own writings given a place of honor among what they might call "real" books in their school library.

Margaret Chapelle, then librarian at Albuquerque, was on her toes and helping in every way possible to stimulate reading and learning.

Also at Albuquerque a beautiful tree sprang up from its roots in one classroom and grew to full size during my week's visit. Students decided to make a Poetry Tree instead of a flat bulletin board. This tree grew brown-wrapping-paper trunk and limbs and, on the end of each branch, irregular leaves on which students wrote their original poems. It is my guess that this one tree has borne even more fruit as other students in the school have been inspired to write stories or poems that may someday appear on a bulletin board or on another tree in their classrooms.

Patty Allen has sent pages and pages of haiku from her classes at Chilocco Indian School, at Chilocco, Oklahoma.

She began with a brief introduction to the haiku form which she states this way:

> Do you know what haiku is? It is a poetic expression of something beautiful. The Japanese invented this form of verse pattern. Like a Japanese painting and other Japanese art, many haiku verses are about nature.
>
> Let's study these examples of haiku which have been translated into English. (Teacher writes and marks the syllable pattern on board.) Notice the number of syllables in the first and third lines. How many? How many syllables altogether? How many lines?
>
> 1. Wonderful old tree, (5)
> 2. You gave shade all summer long; (7)
> 3. Now your leaves are gone. (5)
>
> Do you think you could describe something or express a feeling about nature in exactly 17 syllables in three lines? You'll enjoy the challenge of trying to make your thoughts fit the haiku pattern. You may want to write several verses with the rest of us.

Then Patty used some of Fayne Porter's haiku from IAIA, Santa Fe, New Mexico, and as a result she had this kind of haiku from her classes:

> Theodore Toppah
> Heap big red Indian brave
> Dances at pow-wows
>
> Fields, big and wide;
> Maybe one day I'll make it
> Taking giant strides.
>
> Run, little ones, run!
> Our generation is doomed.
> You could change the world!

There's one in every class who is not turned on by haiku. One of Patty Allen's students wrote instead: "Billions of twinkling stars shone in the cool night air. They shone from vast gulfs of space across the endless wastes of the universe. The sun was only a dot of light in the vast belt of the Milky Way."

Strictly speaking, haiku is somewhat limiting, particularly if you insist to students that it must be about nature and that it must include references to the seasons. But there is another

Japanese form identical with haiku, as far as the syllables are concerned. This is *senryu*—non-nature poems that are written on the haiku syllable-and-line pattern.

Still, not everyone enjoys counting on his fingers and it might be interesting to introduce the diamanté form. Again, this is an unrhymed poem. The diamanté has seven lines which, as the name suggests, form a diamond shape. Here is how the pattern goes:

Line 1, one noun. Line 2, two adjectives describing the noun. Line 3, three participles. Line 4, four nouns. Line 5, three participles. Line 6, two adjectives. Line 7, one noun.

The diamanté is a poem of contrasts. It begins by choosing two words that represent contrasting ideas. They can be: black-white, hot-cold, fire-water, joy-sorrow, life-death. One of these words becomes the first line of the diamanté, the other, the last line. It takes on a diamond shape on the page as a result of the number of words in each line.

The adjectives and participles in lines two and three refer to the word in line one; those in lines five and six to the word in line seven. The nouns in line four can relate to either or both of the contrasting words. If you decide to use this form in class, I suggest writing a class poem first, or two or three class poems first, to get the feel of it. Then let individuals write their own diamanté. Here are two that I found in one of the papers I got:

Love
True, fair;
Helping, sharing, giving;
Family, country, school, friends;
Fighting, hurting, killing;
Evil, violent;
Hate

Black
Dark, beautiful
Color, race, proud;
David, Calvin, Michael, Rickie;
Opportunity, intelligent, sure;
Bright, light;
White.

I personally feel that writing class poems is an excellent

way to get youngsters acquainted with a certain pattern of poetry. It is also a way of getting them started writing at all. It convinces them that they can write. There it is on the board and who can deny they did it? It is also an excellent exercise for bringing a class together.

In most of the classes I go into where we write a collaborative poem, students produce something that is at least fun. We had an especially good time with one of Ann Gulledge's classes in Albuquerque, New Mexico. We began our poem by selecting our subject, and then each student in the class contributed at least one line about the subject. Without revising the lines at all, I arranged them in time sequence and wrote them so that they looked like a poem. We duplicated the page that evening.

The next day in class, we were able to read our poem and then go back to see where we could improve it. I felt that we had a really productive session. The first day, students wrote, "I walk into the canteen called Chat and Chew." The second day, when we came back, I said, "How do you walk into the canteen?" We discussed it until we had to act it out.

With two students willing to demonstrate just how they walk into the canteen, we had a small drama going. Then we had dozens of words coming very quickly describing exactly how—giving us the picture. We went through the poem, revising on our feet, and learning in this way to give the kind of detail that makes poetry specific, personal, something special, something worth passing on to someone else. Our class poem will not live forever, we know, but I submit that it has a certain feel that is characteristic of school canteens. We came about it by the collaborative class-poem way.

CHAT AND CHEW

Seven o'clock, Sunday, and it's dark
I walk into the canteen called Chat and Chew
Walk in looking around
Music!
Good songs playing in the "jude-box"
I see boys and girls
Everyone talking and eating
Some boys playing the "ping-ball" machine
Hear it—
Ping-pong, ping-ball

> The smell of popcorn
> I can't resist
> Got to get some
> I go to the counter
> The popcorn is fresh and hot
> It smells like butter
> It tastes a little buttery
> Salty too
> It feels like little rocks
> I buy a snow cone
> Cold as ice
> The candy I eat
> Tastes like sugar cane
> It sticks to my teeth
> Potato chips take the sweet away
> And I play the "ping-ball" machine
> I'm going to drink some coke
> Something to cool you down when you're hot
> The bubbles are bursting cold in my mouth
> I feel real great
> Having lots of fun
> Here in Chat and Chew.

Hazel Constance sent *The Sandscriber*—a collection of descriptions, poems, and stories by her eleventh-grade and twelfth-grade students at Phoenix Indian High School, Phoenix, Arizona. *The Sandscriber* is a mimeographed sixty-five-page book with a beautiful student-designed cover. Most of the writings in this book are too long to quote, but I want to give you one example:

ALONE AFTER GRANDFATHER LEFT
by
Dianna Polacca

The day after Grandfather left us was like the days of the empty desert with very few mesquite trees around. It was a cool, dry day. The leaves were falling to the ground like paper airplanes being flown around. I sat there wishing he were here at home with me to see the beautiful sight.

It was a shock to me when I heard he had left us. His smiling face I could see as he sat outside his adobe home on the mesa. His appearance was neat. He was always wearing joyful colored shirts and Levi's. He was not tall nor short; he was just in-between.

I thought of all the merry times we had with him. I loved the evenings when Grandfather told us Hopi and Tewa legends of long ago. Some were funny, but most were scary. His joking around with all of us was fun. When someone was sad, he would cheer him. That is the reason that I loved him so. I also recalled frequent occasions when he played with us, like when he wrestled with my brothers. I would sit there and laugh at him, because he would make funny faces while he was fighting. I would really miss his rollicking with us, as well as his kindness to us.

I sat at home alone with my baby sister. I felt sorry for her because she was too young to know what she missed. It was still and quiet in the house. The baby's breathing was like the wind whispering as it went by. The fire in the woodstove was crackling away merrily, while I sat there lonely and still. Never in my life had I been so lonely for someone I loved.

The baby started crying, but to me the sound was far off. I let her cry; then finally she fell asleep, while I sat there gazing at the dark clouds which seemed as lonely as I.

But now I know Grandfather is somewhere in a quiet and peaceful place, while I long for his existence once again.

16. Grading—That Required Abomination

Grading is a necessary evil—school systems being as they are. Still, none of us feels competent to grade students on their writing. I think it is to our credit that we feel incompetent to say this is good and that is poor. Writing is a method of learning, and the mere process of doing it is good. Surely this is one area in which effort counts. Even so, at some point— the end of nine weeks, six weeks, a semester, or whenever an accounting is required—we know we will be forced into giving a grade. Mae Schense wrote:

> Do you know that my main problem with creative writing is determining what is good. . . . I grade creative writing with: Good, Very Good, Excellent, or Let's Try Again.
> One day I gave a boy "Good" and he said, "I think my poem is better than that." After inquiring why he thought this, he said, "I copied it out of a book but I changed some of the words to make it my own." Oh, well, live and read a lot!
> Many times students have said that they thought their writing was better than the mark I gave them. So now I say that if one's not satisfied with a grade, he should write why and turn his writing in again. It works.
> P.S. One student told me, "All those spelling, usage, and grammatical errors are mine." I'm right with him.

Anne Cathcart wrote: "I'm handing out their folders in class next week. I'm going to have them choose their favorite of what they've written and write an evaluation sheet on it— their own opinion and one other student's opinion. This should help me with grading."

Once a week, how would you feel about asking each student to write in a sentence or two "my creative contribution for the week." I have never tried this. It is an idea I picked up at a conference, and I do not know whose idea it was originally. I honestly do not know whether students will do it. If they will, they may get a fresh idea of what we are trying to do. To evaluate themselves in terms of creativity will, at least, make them stop and think. At best, it may give them a forward jolt. Also if at the end of a nine-week period, for example, you had nine such evaluations from each student, I am sure you would find them most helpful in deciding on a letter grade.

"Norty" Benner was as bothered as the rest of us about the necessity of giving grades in writing. When I talked with her, she gave as her grade basis: 1. Did the student try? 2. Did he complete the assignments? 3. Was the communication clear?

Then I visited Phoenix Indian High School and started reading some of the papers Norty had marked. I was struck by streaks of sunshine here and there. Well, yes, this is Phoenix, I thought, but I was soon imagining pupils' mouths turning up in an imitation of Norty's omnipresent happy face. Hers were bright, gay markings alongside the students' well-selected, sensory words and phrases. Down, down, down the page they led me, looking for the goodies. I asked Norty to tell us about her system.

> You asked for a brief statement on two ideas I have used and how they were introduced to classes. Last spring our English Department chairman listed Creative Writing as a six-week elective in the English curriculum, open to tenth- eleventh- and twelfth-grade students. During registration three sections of Creative Writing were established and I was assigned to have two sections.
>
> Essentially, students in writing classes do not create rapidly, whether they are Indian or non-Indian. With this in mind, my immediate approach during the first week was to level with them and find out why they were in class and, since they were, what goals would we set?
>
> All assignments were spontaneous during the first two weeks, using their five senses and attempting to have them overcome the fear of writing on paper their sensory happenings. I was unsuccessful with any form of oral discussion about what they had written. At the end of the third week (mid-term) I asked if I might read all folders and, perhaps, help them unlock some of their tenseness.
>
> With their permission I took all the folders home and read, using my yellow liner (a study habit I used in college classes).

I lined all words that had impact and described any of the senses. Red-penciled margins turn me off and I react much the same as any student—after a first glance, the paper is tossed into the wastebasket or filed in a folder and forgotten.

When students opened their folders on Monday and saw the yellow lines, their curiosity was aroused and they asked what the yellow marks meant. I told them the more yellow lines the more sensory details they had used and that these made a clearer picture for the reader. After that Monday morning, they began looking for the yellow-lined words and discussing them within their groups. Something was happening.

By the end of the six-week period, members of the English Department decided to extend our course to nine weeks. Student involvement is popular and I decided to suggest to the classes that we select a Student Review Committee. A committee of five members seemed most likely to function well.

We decided that the committee would solicit permission from each class member to read his folder. Committee members were to use class time, and after-school time if necessary, to review, make constructive criticism, and agree on a grade for each assignment. Individual conferences were suggested between the committee members and other students. The purpose of this type of review was to encourage peer interaction and to eliminate the teacher supremacy within an unstructured classroom situation. I also wanted to hear some oral discussion.

One section adopted the idea (the other one has not as yet), five students (three girls and two boys) volunteered, and all were approved by the entire class. Reading and discussion of the contents of the folders were done in regular class time. Comments were made on a separate sheet of paper by the reviewer, and in all cases I found most of the criticism very realistic and honest. None of us felt any resentment from any of the students but, to the contrary, most of the students reflected attitudes that they should try harder and write more.[1]

The Student Review Committee hopes to select, edit, and publish a book of the "golden words" sometime before the end of the first semester. This will necessarily be an after-school project, since all the students will enroll in one of the other electives during the second nine-week period.

I had a professor once who required that our papers be triple spaced. I wish I had that much authority—enough to insist on typed manuscripts and lots of space for my comments. Students are so tight with paper that a page of their

[1] I read the comments and found them always encouraging and frequently of real technical help. The committee will, of course, learn more about writing than anyone else in the class. The best way to learn is to teach.

writing practically defies us to add as much as a check mark. Norty's yellow liner is one answer. Ann Gulledge has another.

Most students, profligate as they can be with some things, are stingy about margins. I usually find too little room for comments and must run them between tight lines and sideways along the skimpy edges of a page. Then the student has no space in which to respond to suggestions made. I am sure you have the same experience each time you make notes and suggestions for revision on student papers. If this happens as often to you as it does to me, I know you will welcome Ann's solution.

She tapes a whole sheet of paper on each side of each sheet that requires a student's revision. These open fields on either side actually invite the student to fill in the missing details, to write and mark out, to jot down a whole list of possible words in his search for the right word, to flesh out thin stories or character sketches.

I believe some kind of good psychology operates on behalf of the teacher who goes through the simple act of taking the trouble to paste on side pages (like sideboards on a wagon). The act imparts to the student a sense that his teacher thinks it is important for him to have plenty of space to put down all his good words in the best order possible.

Teachers frequently say to me, "But I'm not a professional writer. I don't know, the way you do, what to look for."

My answer is, "But you're a reader. You do know what to look for because you are looking for it all the time when you read. You know what you like to read. You know what you start and toss aside as being boring or disgusting or unfunny. If you can't follow a story or a news item or a recipe, the author hasn't made it clear. If you don't believe what the author is telling you, you stop reading. Apply your own everyday tests to student writing. The student and you together can then solve the problem."

"Nothing good is ever written. It is rewritten." I am not sure who said it first, but I will be saying it to the end of time. I believe in rewriting, and students (given even minimum suggestions that make sense to them) soon see their first drafts progress through rewrites to stories and poems that are alive and effective—that is, readable. A few experiences of this kind are strong convincers.

You can give help in some of the basics of writing, even though you are not and are not expected to be a professional author. The first basic is Honesty.

Phony writing automatically self-destructs, and this usually happens for the reader long before the end of page one. You, the teacher of a student you know personally, can spot phoniness in his writing by the end of line three. How?

Ask yourself these questions: Is this student writing from personal experience? Has he been in the setting he is using? Does he personally know people in the same age group and same social strata as his characters? Has he had occasion to experience personally the emotions he is asking this reader to relive?

This is not to say that he should confine himself to writing about actual places and people (although this is not a bad idea for beginning writers). It is to say that the beginning writer, if he has grown up on the Blackfeet Reservation, for instance, has to be a genius to write a successful story based in Paris or even in Harlem. Characters from the jet set are not within his range. If he has grown up on the South Side of Chicago, he cannot successfully write a story set at Lukachukai or Kotzebue. He cannot, at least, without much research. The reason is obvious.

Authentic sights, sounds, odors, tastes, and tactile impressions are to be reexperienced by the reader. He cannot help believing what he sees, hears, smells, tastes, and feels. He also believes that the author knows what he is writing about. "This author has been there," the reader says to himself. "Otherwise, how could he possibly know that the girl's eyes were amber with an outer rim of midnight blue? Or, how else would he know that piñon smoke has that strong odor of roasting nuts about it?"

Beginning writers (the same as established professional authors) can combine settings and characters they know. Putting things together in fresh ways is at the core of creativity. A writer creates by contriving combinations from known factors—bits and pieces from his personal experience. This brings us to another basic quality that keeps readers reading.

Look for BELIEVABILITY. Maybe I should say feel for believability. You have built-in antennae that will serve you here. Ask yourself: Does this piece of writing seem real? Do

I feel comfortable enough to read through to the end, taking it at face value? Is the student telling this as it really is to him? If you do not believe what a student has written, it is unlikely that anyone else will believe it. One of two things has happened: One, the student is writing something he has not experienced and, therefore, cannot make believable; or, two, he has failed to turn on his five senses and report exact and detailed observations. If the author knows what he is writing about or has ever known it at firsthand, he can (on being reminded with a marginal note) turn on the experience immediately or in memory and record on paper the specific sensory data that will make his writing believable.

You are the expert on the third basic to look for, namely, CLARITY. This is what grammar is all about. I suggest that you read a student's paper all the way through in much the same way that you would read a poem or story printed in a magazine. Then ask yourself: Did I have to reread sentences or paragraphs to know what the writer meant? Did I come across passages that failed to say anything to me even after rereading?

If so, go back and start making marginal notes, but make them on the assumption that the student had something he wanted to say. Your job is to help him say it clearly—so clearly that the rapid reader will understand precisely. I ask a great many questions on margins: Can you make this clearer? Are you sure you've said this exactly? Will you take another look at this and try to clarify? Aren't you afraid your reader might miss your point here?

Such questions can often be resolved by going back to plain old rules of grammar. Here you, the teacher, can shine. Far more important, the writer sees for himself that the rules make sense—they can help him maneuver words into saying what he wants to say.

The handling of poetry requires a special kind of light touch, it seems to me. In the first place, I never trust myself to say anything by way of criticism after only one reading. Being obvious is not a poem's greatest virtue but neither is being obscure. I do not belong to the words-for-words'-sake school. At the same time, poetry is not for mind's sake either.

Your test may be: do these words in this order cause me to relive this student's experience? If they do on first draft, you have stumbled across a major miracle. Some experienced professionals have learned to call up and discard word after word until those first set on paper have been discerningly selected. The first draft can, on occasion, come forth full-blown and right. This is rare for a professional. For a student, it is almost impossible.

So, you ask, how can I help a student finish a poem? My answer is, "Gently!"

Yesterday's mail brought a poem from a student along with a letter in which she said:

> I am writing but I'm slow because it usually takes me months to finish a writing. After I get an idea, I write all I can and then put it away for awhile. The length of time the writing stays in my notebook depends on how deeply I feel about the subject.
>
> For instance, the enclosed poem has taken me five months to get it like I wanted it. I realize you are very busy but I'd appreciate it very much if you would read the poem and give any comments you might have.

Believe me, I am not going to take a club and beat this girl's poem to death. On the other hand, she cares so much that I shall certainly help her if I possibly can.

Her poem came in longhand. I had to type it before I could visualize how it would look on a page. I recommend this procedure to you. Part of a poem's effect is visual. In addition, while typing, it is easy to spot some weaknesses.

Unnecessary words almost hang up on your fingertips as you type—"and," "but," "the," "there is," and such. These fill-in words clutter lines and serve to obscure the shine of words filled with life and emotion. The *ly* on an adverb usually trips my fingers a little as I type. I always examine these weak, distant modifiers to see whether or not I can strengthen a verb or a noun and include the adverb's worth in one impact word.

Because the poem I received was stretched over three pages, I might have missed something that could hardly be missed when it is typed on one page—namely, the poet has not gone to enough pains to unify her poem.

Visually, the typed poem was somewhat ragged. Not fatally so, but it could do with a bit of pruning. No poem should look like an unkempt shrub, unless the poet intended that effect.

Punctuation-by-whim shows up when you type. In longhand a dash can mean almost anything. In print dashes and three or more dots take on their designated meanings and, sometimes, actually defeat the author's intention.

Finally, a typed copy can allow margins and spaces enough for comments and suggestions.

Well, what's fair for the goose . . . Do not make the mistake of thinking that evaluation and comment are one-way streets. Students, too, get their chance at us, and well they should.

After I had done my "thing" in one of Myra Martin's classes at Choctaw Central in Mississippi, an undersized freshman, bless him, really boosted my morale. I had not asked for an evaluation, thinking I had read it in excited eyes and warm smiles. Even so, one thoughtful boy, all on his own, spelled it out for me.

>   Poetry writer is her.
>   Explain all sort of ways
>   to write poem.
>   Talking out plainly
>   as she could,
>   She got most of us
>   the hang of it.

A reminder in poem form that I received one day at IAIA is the kind that teachers should frame and hang above their desks.

>   ADJUSTMENTS
>
>   I wrote a poem in class today
>   I worked very hard at it
>   The poem said, "I love you"
>   I turned it in to the instructor
>   When I got it back
>   It was all marked up.
>
>   *Ron Rogers*

17. Let's Talk Pictures

Some time ago the *New York Times* carried several articles that I would like to share verbatim with each of you. Instead, I must limit myself to a few excerpted sentences. "The illiterates of the future will be ignorant of the use of camera and pen alike." That was László Moholy-Nagy's prophecy in 1932. It is startling, not only in its accuracy but in our persistent unwillingness to take heed of its implications, despite five more decades of accumulated evidence. Photography is, inarguably, the most energizing innovation in communication since the printing press.

The article points out that photography has so pervaded Western culture that, if by some chance the materials and techniques connected with it were to vanish, our society would be instantly paralyzed. Not only does communication depend on it but nuclear physics, biochemistry, medicine, all branches of industry—these are all dependent on pictures for teaching, for transmission of knowledge, and for increasing abilities in every field.

If we concentrate on the communications media—film, books, television, magazines, newspapers—we are receiving as much of our information from the photographic image right now as we are from the written word. This means that at least 50 percent of our decisions are in some way based on photography. For instance, unless we are willing to believe that the concept of war as a romantic, glorious experience simply died out, we must admit that it was irreparably shattered by photographs of war.

We must face the fact that we are now—and will be for centuries, if we survive—living in a social system utterly dependent on the printed word and photographic image.

We can no longer teach any subject as though it had to do with a nonphotographic culture. We are the illiterates of the future that Moholy-Nagy warned us about, and unless we start teaching how to make and respond to photographs in the same sense that we teach reading and writing, our children are going to be the illiterates of an even more hopeless future.

Did I hear you say you don't have a camera?

How to Make Photos Without a Camera in an Undarkened Room

In these days of pinched budgets you may like to know how to make instant, permanent photos without a camera in an ordinary classroom with no plumbing or window shades. You need:

1. Three ten-quart plastic buckets or plastic wastepaper baskets.
2. One can of Dektol paper developer to make one gallon.
3. One packet of Kodak fixer (to make one gallon).
4. A box of Kodak Repro 8-by-10-inch negative paper.
5. Four one-gallon wine bottles in which to store the solutions.

Total outlay, even at inflated prices, should be around twenty dollars, but you will have enough equipment for one hundred students to make one big picture each.

To make a picture, experiment with different opaque and translucent objects placed on or suspended above the paper. Expose for a second or two to sunlight (or for a bit longer period to a strong artificial light).

You have already mixed the chemicals with water at room temperature, arranging the buckets in this order:

1. developer
2. fixer
3. water

Develop the paper for about one minute (or until the image

is as dark as you like), fix for three or four minutes, then wash for five minutes and hang on the line to dry.

You will get very dramatic negative pictures in which everything exposed to light goes black, everything protected from light stays white. The same materials can be used to make prints from negatives made with a camera.

How to Develop Prints Made with a Camera

You do have a camera? But you cannot afford to have pictures developed for a whole class of shutter-happy students?

1. Buy a can of Kodak Microdol-X developer to make one gallon. For use, dilute the stock solution one part of developer solution to three parts of water.
2. Use the same solution of Kodak fixer as for developing the paper.

In addition to chemicals you will need:

1. A film developing tank (plastic is inexpensive and works fine).
2. A film-changing bag.

A film-changing bag is very easy to make if you have access to a sewing machine. They can be made by hand. The bag consists of a cylinder of heavy black cloth with draw strings at each end. It is long enough so that both hands can be inserted from opposite ends and the strings tied around the upper arms so that no light gets in. Use this for separating the exposed roll of film from its backing paper and winding it into the plastic apron, which is then, in turn, placed in the developing tank. Once you get the lid on the tank, you can do everything else in daylight. If you simply cannot make a changing bag, they can be purchased at photography stores.

To develop film, the solutions should all be around 70°F. Arrange the plastic buckets in this order: 1. bucket of diluted developer, 2. bucket of clean water, 3. bucket of fixer, and 4. bucket of clean water.

Pour developer into the tank (it holds sixteen ounces). Notice the time on a clock or watch. Agitate the tank for ten seconds every minute for a total of twelve to thirteen minutes (the time depends on the type of film you buy). At the end of the time, pour out the developer. Do not reuse. Refill the tank with clean water, rinse, and pour out the water. Refill tank with fixer. Agitate every three or four minutes for a total of ten minutes. Pour the fixer back into the bucket (it can be used over and over for twenty or thirty rolls of film). Refill the tank with clean water and keep replacing water, or put it under running water for about twenty minutes. Take the lid off of the tank, remove the film from the plastic apron, hang the film up to dry in as dust free a place as you can find.

Film should dry in an hour or so, depending on air movement, temperature, and so forth. After the film is dry, you are ready to print the pictures.

To print negatives you need:

1. Sheets of 4-by-4-inch glass.
2. Sheets of very heavy 3-by-4-inch cardboard. Paint cardboard black on one side.

Make a sandwich of the glass and cardboard with a strip of masking tape as a hinge along the four-inch side. Have the black surface of the cardboard next to the glass.

Cut a piece of Repro negative paper to fit the negative. Place the paper (shiny side up) on the black surface of the cardboard. Place a negative (shiny side up) on the paper. Close the glass. Hold the sandwich under a bright light for six to ten seconds or under sunlight for two or three seconds. Take the paper out and develop in the Dektol developer. It should be ready in one and a half minutes. If it is too dark, reduce the time under the light source. If too light, increase the exposure time. Put the developed paper in fixer for ten minutes, then wash for twenty minutes. Hang up to dry, or dry between two towels.

Written directions for all this seem complicated. Try it a time or two before attempting it with a class. Better still, get a camera-nut friend to demonstrate. It is the same as with any other process—once you know how, it is easy. Results may be disappointing at first, but a little trial-and-error experience should produce satisfactory pictures. Students who take pictures (like mothers who produce babies) are not that particular, I have found.

If You Have a Polaroid Camera

I am sure no student will leave the class of Cecelia Sandoval and Cheryl Dushane, her aide, without a positive self-image. A large poster in their room at Zia Pueblo, New Mexico, has on it each student's picture (taken with a Polaroid) along with name, birthday, brothers, sisters, and likes in food, play, toys, and so forth.

If You Have a Camera for Each Student

In some schools we used inexpensive cameras as a faucet to start the words flowing. At that time we were able to get Diana cameras for a few cents and could supply them to schools long enough for a camera workshop. These cameras took rolls of film—something most students had never seen. As if it had been a new invention, they enjoyed learning how to load a camera with film on a roller. They especially enjoyed the assignment: go outside and look through the lens of your camera at everything on the school grounds. Then decide which of these things you would like to record on your film. Shoot the whole roll (sixteen exposures) and come back to class ten minutes before the period is over.

When I began a two-week project with cameras at Mount Edgecumbe school, no one in the class abused the freedom and came back to the classroom late. A few returned early. One girl returned very early saying, "I want to save some."

At Mount Edgecumbe we were especially fortunate in that we had a darkroom available. We even had faculty help that enabled us to develop each day's take that night. Prints could be given back to students the following day in class. The situation was ideal, except that we had trouble convincing our frugal student to go ahead and finish shooting an entire roll of film. She wanted us to develop the first eight and let her take the rest another day.

As students returned to the classroom, I explained that this project was experimental and that I would like to have a good record to keep. "Today," I said, "I'd appreciate your using these last ten minutes of class time to write just how it felt to be given a camera and sent outside to take pictures. Did anything happen inside you? When you've written how it felt, then I'd like to know whether things around the school grounds looked different through a lens than they usually look to you. If so, in what way?"

Students grabbed paper and pencils as if they could hardly wait. "Don't worry about how you say it or whether the words are spelled right at the moment. Just get it all down fast before you forget anything."

They wrote quickly, easily, and page after page. No one asked, "How long does it hafta be?" Several wrote through the bell that signaled the end of the school day. Some asked about developing the pictures. Could they go to the darkroom and learn how to make prints? A few volunteers were accepted. Every member of the class raced into the classroom early the following day. The room buzzed with questions: "Are our pictures ready?" "Can we see them?" "Can we take pictures again today?" "What are we going to do with them?"

Their pictures were ready. They examined the little contact prints and discussed which ones were good enough to enlarge. They showed their good ones to classmates. They loudly lamented their bum shots. They exclaimed over pictures of long familiar objects that looked better or worse when photographed.

I gave out the cameras and they loaded them again. "Today, I'd like you to look a little longer before you shoot. This time, try to shoot only those things that really interest you. Don't discuss your subjects with anyone else. Just look, searching for pictures that you really like or, possibly, something that you really hate and would like to get rid of. When you come upon something that you feel strongly about, take its picture. Come back ten minutes before the end of the period."

Students hurried back to the classroom for their ten minutes of writing. "I'd like you to write today," I suggested, "what you found out about yourself while you were taking pictures. Did you discover any likes or dislikes that you didn't know you had? Did looking through a camera lens tell you anything about you?"

The third day we decided to make illustrated books. The suggestion came from the class (if it had not, I would have made it). We gave the students the opportunity to choose whether they would make an individual book or would work in twos or threes. Only Johnny chose to work alone. The others went out with their cameras (one to a group), looking for a subject for their book. That day they wrote, when they came in, a summary of their book ideas.

One group decided they would write about litter. One decided on litter but planned (as they took pictures) to clean it up and show how much better things around the school grounds looked. One decided on mountains. Naturally one group of boys decided to make their book about girls.

Each "last ten minutes" they rushed back to the classroom to record their impressions. After they left, I typed everything they wrote, making enough carbon copies for the number in the group working together. By the end of the first week, book plans were well along, and many of the pictures to be used had been selected. Those who had helped in the darkroom responded immediately to the suggestion that they write out the procedures they were learning so they would not forget how to develop pictures. At the beginning of the second week, we pushed school desks together by fours to make small-group worktables. Pictures were everywhere. I brought out my typed copies of their last-ten-minute writings.

Casually I announced, "I have been typing the things you've written and I wondered whether you might like to include some of that writing in your books."

Dismissing hands flapped all over the room. "Naw, we don't need that."

"Well, as long as I have it here all typed," I said, "I'll just leave it on your tables. You might find something you'll want to use."

I laid a stack of neatly typed pages on each work table. Each student had his own writing. Perhaps you are not aware of the authority given almost any piece of writing by a typewriter. Those students started to push the pages off their pictures but they looked and then looked again and then started to read. I gave my lone eagle, Johnny, his typed writings and went on about my business of moving from table to table to offer assistance. Everyplace I went someone looked up from reading: "Hey, this is pretty good, Mrs. Allen." "Look what I wrote that first day, Gerry." "Why don't we put this in our book. I didn't write it, Wilma did." "Say, this is almost a poem, don't you think? I could make it a poem and put it with this picture."

One book idea was coming along pretty well when one of the small groups suggested, "This is all right, but we need something at the beginning to tell what it's all about." That group wrote an introduction.

The books were not all finished at the end of the two weeks, but each one was well on its way to completion and the students had learned how to make hardcover bindings for them. By that last Friday afternoon, Johnny had his book completed, and, as it turned out, he had no intention of letting me catch a plane Saturday morning unless his book was bound and under his arm. Johnny and I stayed after school. Johnny laid out his two cardboard tablet backs and cut cover fabric and Stitch Witchery to fit. Johnny stapled his pages together and fitted and ironed the cover on the cardboards, turning every corner down with deliberate care.

I happened to have a last-night dinner engagement at the principal's home. It was cold and rainy out. It was getting dark. I rushed things a little by cutting the end papers and the Stitch Witchery to stick them on with. Johnny wielded the iron. At last, we were finished. No book was ever more proudly held in its author's trembling hands.

I had some blocks to walk in the dark, through the rain that was turning to snow. I was going to be late for dinner.

"I'm sorry," I said, shedding umbrella and boots in the principal's front hall, "but Johnny Yahola wouldn't let me leave. He insisted that we had to finish his book."

"What did you say?" the principal asked.

I repeated as he led me to the saved place at the dinner table.

"Johnny who?" His voice clearly indicated that I, an outsider, had made a mistake in the names.

"Johnny Yahola," I repeated with a good deal of confidence. After all, I had personal knowledge that the new book, *Things I Like about Mount Edgecumbe,* was "by Johnny Yahola."

"That boy has been asleep since the beginning of the year," the principal said.

Summer had come and gone before I returned to Mount Edgecumbe. When I arrived, it was Johnny who met me at the door and opened it for me. He was no longer asleep.

At Choctaw Central in Philadelphia, Mississippi, Myra Martin and I used cameras with one of her classes. I never cease to be amazed by the amount and quality of both verbal and written response the little Diana cameras will evoke. Also, I am invariably touched by the depth of students' personal response triggered by the camera experience. I am sure you will be interested in a few samples of the writings that flowed out of our Choctaw ninth graders:

> Yesterday, I went out and took pictures of whatever I wanted to take. It was wonderful to go out and take pictures. I liked it very much. I discovered that when you look through the lens, the scene is very small. Most of all, I think the scene is beautiful when you look through the lens. I want to take one of my pictures and try to write a story for it.

> I think I'm beginning to like camera. I feel that camera is good because it take picture. I discover the building and tree. I interest in a picture of flower. I like to take picture of something green. Today is good day.

> Yesterday I had a wonderful time taking pictures of some of the persons working and children playing outside. It was a nice time to take pictures 'cause the sun was shining outside. I took pictures of some friends when school was out, and they were on their way to catch the bus and go home. It is fun to take pictures and write something about it.

> Imagine, me with a camera in my hand! And not knowing what to shoot at! To me, taking pictures was some kind of responsibility.

> It was fun taking pictures. I felt self-confident for taking pictures out at the ball field and around the school. I guess I was so excited 'cause I didn't know that we were going to take pictures.

When we started I was pretty excited. It felt pretty good going out of that door, legally. And when we got outside I felt so free. The fun part was taking pictures and I did have fun. And I was kinda glad Patrick was with me. We had fun talking, laughing and looking around us. And we took pictures that was interesting. Things like beer cans, flowers, etc.

Being outside with a camera gave me a feeling of happiness. Every shot I took I captured a scene that would never happen again. Everything will change but whenever I want to I can always look at the picture and see what had happened. I got the feeling that I was a photographer, an experienced one. I got a great thrill out of it, too.

My experience in shooting a camera was that I felt lucky. I thought we were the first English class to go out. My partner and I had a good time shooting pictures. Outside it was sort of cold, but it felt wonderful. I've never dreamed of doing something like this. Another thing I enjoy is having Mrs. Allen here for a week to teach us different things.

Yesterday when I went outside I shot pictures about the birds and the flowers. I took pictures of the woods. Just woods. And I found a baseball out there but I didn't take a shot at it. I took a picture of the bush downstairs. Leonard took pictures of the flowers surrounding the bush, and we shot the grass the way it moves when the wind pushes it.

Going out and making pictures was a real thrill for me. I enjoyed every minute of it. It was something that I wouldn't of believed doing in school. I'm not good at making pictures with a camera, so I hope to learn some things by taking pictures.

I was very self-conscious of myself at first. I didn't know what to do with the camera. There were so much to take but I couldn't decide whether they were the right ones to take or not. Somehow it was so unusual.

Yesterday it was alright getting out of class to take pictures of what I want, not of what someone told me to. It was great!

I really enjoyed taking pictures this past week. I felt nervous, then I started to enjoy it. There is always got to be a first time and that was my first time with that kind of camera. I never thought that taking pictures were fun until I started. Now, my sixth period class pass so quickly each day.

After we had been shooting for two or three days, my suggestions for the writing prompted answers to questions such as: What have you learned about yourself by looking through a lens? What really interests you? What have you decided about how you will put your pictures together in a book? Will you tell a story? Will you call attention to some problem around here that you noticed while taking pictures? Or what?

Students were eager to write—fully as eager as they were to go out with the cameras. Because we had set up the project that way, the writing was an integral part of the experience. It was the last period in the day, and Myra and I decided early that we would probably have difficulty in getting students back into the classroom for the last ten minutes of the hour. At first, I felt afraid that the edge would have come off the fun if I asked students the next morning to write about using the camera the day before. I was wrong. They practically came to class with their pencils poised. They had had fun the day before. They wanted to talk about it on paper. They wanted it recorded. No one objected that we were taking "shooting" time. No one asked, "How long's it hafta be?" They were writing because they wanted to, and what they wrote is revealing.

> I want to put in Springtime
> And a sunny day.
> Yesterday, me and my friend
> went to Home Ec
> to take pictures.
> Yesterday was a good day.
> Today is better than Yesterday.

Yesterday, Leonard and I went outside to take pictures of the woods around the school. I took pictures of the scenery of the wood. I took pictures of birds' nest and birds flying in the air. My interest in taking picture is the scenery of the woods, in the spring when flowers are out, birds are chirping, birds building nests. I think in the bushes there about million of insect and some other life in there, but you don't know it.

I would like to tell you about our school. We have a wonderful High School, Junior High school buildings and also we have wonderful teachers who teaches us to learn new things around us. We all enjoy going to our school 'cause it was made or built for us, the younger generation, so we can learn to be good leaders and to be educated.

In the camera I took picture of the things that growed in the woods. I felt good things inside me when I took pictures of the natural things. My interest is nature—the things that fly, like the birds, and flowers and the woods at a distance. My series I would take is all about the forest and the creatures who live in it.

I enjoyed both days of picture taking. There were a lot of people outside yesterday and it gave me a chance to take pictures of them. There were three of us and we each had a different idea to write a story about. I have an idea about doing something in two short subjects instead of one long one, if the pictures turn out well. The whole project is both interesting and fun.

With my pictures, I'll paste them on a card and write what impression the picture means to me—what I was thinking of when I took that picture.

My plan is to see the difference between the woods and land without trees, just buildings and all those things. In the woods it is quiet and peaceful but without any trees you just see buildings, playgrounds. You see cars, trucks in the parking lot. The woods are more beautiful than buildings and all those things.

I just took pictures of things I thought was interesting. I want my book to look like a photo album, but write a little story about it on the bottom to share interest.

It has brought to my attention the beauty of nature through the lens. I like the idea of making a book out of the pictures and creative writing.

I've discovered that I'm alive. I've seen nature through the lens. I still want to take a picture of a bird.

In the Beginning Is the Word, also in the End

Given cameras or not, ours is a writing-reading project. We will always write and will certainly continue to help students to express themselves through words on paper. This is the most definitive way to communicate. Also, words on paper are basic to other forms of communication.

All forms of drama except mime rely on words. Very few pictures carry a complete message without captions. So writing is and will continue to be the solid foundation of our project and many of you—even our workshop members who were engaged with cameras—will find that you must devote the major portion of your time and effort to helping students write logically, clearly, and honestly.

Before you are ready to branch out into drama and camera work, your students should have discovered through the act of writing that they have something to say. After that, they will quickly come to care enough about saying it clearly to others that they will gladly search for ways to make their words more and more impressive. When they feel the need to illustrate their writing, they will probably think first of using their own or a fellow student's drawings. It is at some point beyond this stage that you can expect one or two students (or possibly a whole class) ready to act out or dramatize and get others to act out their ideas. At this time, one or two other students (or a class) may be interested in taking camera shots to help emphasize their words. Then, as soon as students have begun to see the possibilities for effect in still pictures, someone is bound to begin to think in terms of picture sequences. Inevitably, some will suggest motion pictures as a means of saying what they have to say.

The English class can hardly expect to explore all channels of communication. We can open doors. Beyond that, we can trust some students (not all) to grow into artists in whichever medium or media prove to be their personal means of speaking.

Writing is a first and continuous activity—the meat and potatoes of communication, to be supplemented with mushrooms, salad, and dessert of lights, action, camera. First comes the thought in words, the sequence of action conceived and recorded in words. In the beginning is the word. In the end, again, is the word.

18. We Write to Be Read

Just as paintings are enhanced by a proper frame, so word pictures benefit from good typing and an appropriate binding. Sometimes a typed cover page and stapling are sufficient. If student writings are mimeographed and the plan is to distribute the collection throughout the school, the authors are often glad to cover the staples with a strip of tape. Masking tape will add a bit of finish and keep readers from getting scratched by the staples. At IAIA we sometimes used pressure-sensitive aluminum tape and, on occasion, fiber glass tape. Once or twice we made two small holes in our paper covers and stuck in little feathers. For some books of student writings, you may want hardcover bindings.

Examine any hardcover book for a lesson on how to bind student writings. Tablet backs may do for the "hard" of hardcover, but they are usually too limber. Glue two together for each side of your book. This will work only if the typed pages are somewhat smaller than these cardboards. A better base can be found at any stationery or art supply store: buy pebble board or poster board of a weight appropriate for book covers. For each book you need two cardboards cut approximately a half inch larger than the pages you are to bind. Staple along the backs of the pages of the book, adding one or two blank sheets of paper at the beginning and the end. If the pages are a half-inch thick when stapled, lay the cardboards a half inch apart, thus allowing for a spine the same as a commercially bound book.

We mentioned Stitch Witchery. This is an unwoven fabric that melts under the heat and pressure of an iron. All fabric stores carry it. It was invented, no doubt, as an aid in sewing—to hold tops and facings of collars and such together. For our purposes it is ideal in binding books.

Lay fabric right side down on your work table, and lay Stitch Witchery on top of that. Now add the two cardboards, leaving them as far apart as you have decided you need for the spine of the book. Cut fabric and Stitch Witchery large enough to include the spine plus a half-inch or three-quarter-inch margin all around that will be turned over the edges of the cardboards.

Turn all of this over, keeping the spine allowance, and follow directions that come with the Stitch Witchery for ironing the fabric to the outside of your covers. Next, turn the margins over the cardboards, taking care to miter the four corners. Press until they are neatly glued in place. Now you are ready to attach the book to the covers.

Endpapers hold the cover to the book. They can be of cloth or paper and they are stuck (with Stitch Witchery or a good paper glue such as Elmer's or White Bird) to the first blank sheet stapled to the writings and to the inside front cover. Attach the back cover to the writings in the same way. These endpapers cover, of course, the turned-over edges of your fabric. Your books (after a little practice) look as if they had just arrived from a professional bookbindery. Your fabrics can be plain or fancy. Watch fabric stores for remnants.

Custom binding of this kind is too slow and too costly for a large edition of a book; however, when students are making individual books, they love binding their own. If a class has produced an anthology that is to be put in the library for circulation, a good binding on the book is a great asset to its appearance and durability.

I wish I could include a copy of a book I received from Orriet Overvold, Turtle Mountain Community School, Belcourt, North Dakota. It was written and bound by her tenth graders. The book is covered in plain old natural-color burlap. But the burlap is cut on the bias, and this gives the book an especially interesting texture pattern. I am quite sure that cutting the fabric on the bias made the corners tighter and neater than they could have been if cut on the square. Then, instead of plain construction paper for endpapers, this bright group used an abstract green-and-gold print of Con-Tact brand plastic. Finally, they cut three attractive shapes from the plastic to scatter on the front of their book. The effect is little short of spectacular. I have been showing this book to students who gasped and grew misty-eyed at the thought that they, too, could make such a book. There is one trouble with showing it to students, however.

Students in our schools look at the handsome binding, and then they look inside. I am likely to say, "Pass it around the room and look at it, because we can bind the things you're writing now into a book as nice as this." Then I get on with the business of teaching and look up ten minutes later to find the book still in the hands of student number one in the front row. Of course, every teacher should have such problems. As I have been insisting for years, nothing so stimulates both writing and reading as peer-group writings. When we put them into attractive bindings, they become even more cherished.

I hesitate, as I have said before, to introduce haiku to beginning writers. The shortness of the form is deceptive. It is not an easy form to follow with any high degree of creative effect—at least, that is what I used to tell myself. Our students are about to change my mind for me, and already my hat is off to them.

NIGHT RIDER

Quiet
  city
    streets

A
  roar
    from
      the
        Harley's
      pipes

Jamming
  down
    the
      pave.

—*Greg Laverdure*

Still, quiet lone path
Covered with tall grass and moss
  No longer needed.

—*Ronnie Eschback*

Hardly believing
I suddenly blink my eyes
  I'm really alive.

                              —Brenda Charette

A fox on a rock
Did not dare to make a move
  I stood with a gun.

                              —Steve J. Azure

He reached out for me
My fingers did not touch his
  And now he is gone.

                              —Rose Parisien

Rain falls steadily
Coming out from a clear sky
  The sprinkler is on.

                              —Terry Desjarlais

These students did write in forms other than haiku, but I must give you only a taste:

Sometimes I wish that
The whole day would
  Just fade
AWAY, Away, away, a-way, a-w-a-y, a w a y !

                              —Janell Eller

What does life have for me?
It seems so cold-hearted.
It strikes as if to kill.
I have to take it on
Because it's there, but it
Pushes with its cruel ways
And then laughs at me.
Must I go on being tortured?
I can't just cast it aside.

                              —Paula Morin

Someday when the sky is blue,
Maybe you'll see something new.
Maybe notice the morning dew?
Maybe find the mystery clue.
Someday when the sky is blue

Maybe you'll see where your lifetime flew.
Someday when that sky is blue
Maybe then you'll discover you.

— *Greg Thorfinnson*

Ann Gulledge, Albuquerque Indian School, recently published the second volume of *Escape,* her students' annual anthology. (This one was awarded a fifty-dollar prize and national recognition.) Authors and artists range from the ninth to the twelfth grades, and the book as a whole is excellent. A great many photographs and drawings by students are included. I am sorry I cannot reproduce pictures, but I can give you a brief, tantalizing sample of the writings from this year's *Escape*.

COOL DAY

Today is a cool damp day
People feeling cold and gay
With little drops of rain
Falling on the windowpane.

It ain't no fun
Without the sun
But watch! You wait . . .
The rainbow won't be late.

— *Michael Lewis*
(Acoma Pueblo, Grade 9)

NO SUNSHINE

People are walking around
With their heads down
While the rain sprinkles
on everyone:
　The sad,
　　The happy,
　　　The lonely,
　　　　The good,
　　　　　The bad.
It grows dark and cold
A wet nasty day
But I see
What the night rain did . . .

It opened up
Two beautiful red hollyhocks.

— *Bennett Martine*
(Mescalero Apache, Grade 9)

Then from Intermountain School, at Brigham City, Utah, came two volumes of *Writing Diné* containing a wealth of excellent Navaho writings and drawings:

FEELING

Writing a poem
Having a feeling of how it is.
Listening to the radio,
Thinking, lying back,
Looking back to when you were at home
How it was to sit on a high rock
Looking down on your herd
Feeling it would be like this forever
But you know it won't.
Just memory can bring you back to
When you were a little boy
Now that you're all grown up,
Remember how you shared love
With your mother and father,
Sister and brother?
Now that your mother is gone,
You feel like the world
Just forgot about you,
But you know that your people
Are right behind you.
Someday, their turn will come.

— *Ted Martinez*

SIGNS OF THE TIMES

One week you see a sign about a rodeo somewhere around the reservation. You sign up for it, and in about a week, you are there. You take a look at the livestock and see the one you are going to ride.

In the afternoon you are called out to report to your chute. You take the bull rope and the flank. You put on your spurs and are ready.

The man calls you out, "Larry Matern." It's the very next ride, and you sit on the bull and that bull dances.

The bull looks like it's flying in the air, twisting, bucking, and doing all it can. Don't be afraid to ride it. Spur it!

—*Paul Leo Begay*

THE BIG DAY

I think grandpa's wagon was a lot of fun to ride in. It just felt different from a car when riding on the dirt road. I liked to smooth the palm of my hand on the wheel, and sometimes I whipped the horse to make the wagon go fast. I used to jump off and run after the wagon and try to get back on. It was such fun to go someplace with grandpa! Just being with him was a big day. I believe this was my first fun as a little kid.

—*Rose Lee Begay*

Writing on the Walls

Ronald Rogers was a senior at the University of California at Santa Cruz when he became an apprentice teacher with our project. Judging by his enthusiasm, skill, and rapport with students, I will be removing the word "apprentice" as soon as he is graduated and has done a bit more teaching.

Ron and I worked at Sherman Indian High School, Riverside, California, and, because of special circumstances there, we were given the chance to spend full days working with just one teacher, Mariana Taylor, and her students. We did not exactly write on the classroom walls. If we had, they would never let us return (after all, they have new buildings now), but we did fairly well cover all available space with poems, stories, and pictures.

Students at Sherman helped, again, to convince me that haiku is certainly not beyond their capabilities, once the content and nuances are explained along with the syllable count. We quickly rounded up some ink and some soda straws and demonstrated blown designs that seem appropriate decorations for haiku (diluted poster paint is equally effective for these abstract designs and not as hard to remove from clothing following accidents).

After two days of writing, the walls of Mariana's room and the wall of the hall outside became the all-student reading center before, during, and after classes.

SNOW

Snow falls in a thousand swirls
Light, beautiful
Bright sparkles in the sunlight
Cool . . . cold
On my wet feet and face

But,
Oh, to be there
all alone
among the swirls of my own feelings!

Calm
Peace
Joy

— *Karen Benn*

SNOW

Snow is cold
Its flakes are never the same
You can have a lot of fun in snow
skiing
   sleigh riding
      having a snowball fight

Snow falls in winter
When it's cold and windy
Plowing snow is hard work.

Still, there's
skiing
   sleigh riding
      having a snowball fight

I think snow is a good good thing
   once a year.

— *Max Taylor*

If you are wondering — no, we did not have snow in Riverside, California: We had a motion picture about snow.

Up high in the sky
A bird riding on a cloud
Then why can't I fly?

— *Ron Barton*

Rain doing its job
Wetting the dry, hot desert
Life starts waking up.

— *Earl Numkena*

Indians are dead
When their heritage is gone
Where will they go then?

— *Claude Pahona*

They may be unknown
But they're trying to succeed
Yes, the Papagos.

—*John Noriego*

Burning tree crackling
Smoke rising into the sky
Nature crying help!

—*Herbert Talahaftewa*

Some weeks after our stay at Sherman, Mariana wrote:

    Lemuel has sat here for four years and given everyone the impression he's a know-nothing. I knew different and so did you, only you tapped it and I kept trying to crack the shell rather than go gently. His whole facade has crumbled and we have a really going relationship. He has done more in the last four weeks than he has done all year. I'm never sure what he's going to come up with but, occasionally, he will plunk something on my desk and be gone. The other day I caught him at it and am sending you some samples.

    She enclosed a sheaf of writings. Here is a sample from that sheaf:

> As I look into your eyes,
>   I can see the pain and suffering
> As I hold your hand
>   I feel the strength of your youth
> As I stand near you
>   I know you are fighting to live
> As I stand there helpless
>   I know you are proud and brave
> As I stand there frightened
>   I hear your heart
> As I hear mine.

—*Lemuel Jones*

    Not the world's greatest poetry, I know, but, knowing Lem and his struggle to become himself, his poem brought tears to my eyes. No professional poet would ask for more; and Lemuel, now that he has begun writing, could more than fill the walls of his English classroom.

    Another idea for encouraging writing in the classroom comes from an article, "An Identity Thing," in *Time*. The

New York subway system was spending half a million dollars annually (before recent inflation) to clean up graffiti pollution. In Philadelphia the cost of cleaning was running over $4 million. The authorities were using handwriting experts to catch and prosecute graffiti writers, most of them teenagers. Standard punishment: several hours at hard labor, scouring walls.

But David Katzive of the Philadelphia Art Museum said, "We sense that there is a lot of creativity in these graffiti. Most interesting, the trend is away from profanity and toward simple signatures—a kind of identity thing." So the museum joined with the art department of the University of Pennsylvania to sponsor a Graffiti Alternative Workshop. Vandals were hired to candystripe a dilapidated transit-authority bus. The Penn Mutual Life Insurance Company had them decorate the plywood fence surrounding its new office.

How about a classroom border of newsprint or wrapping paper on which students are encouraged to write their original ideas, which I define as "an idea that never occurred to you before"? Or poems? Or simply names? Or drawings or cartoons? It never pays to underestimate the cleverness of our students, and one good idea frequently spawns a hundred others. The "identity thing" can certainly be better served in this way than on the washroom wall.

I would place high on the list of eligibility for a graffiti border two items gleaned from a publication of the Minneapolis elementary schools. Of course, on your border you will insist on signatures. Signatures are at the heart of this experiment. Unfortunately, these gems arrived with no credit given:

>Cramalot: The country you go to when you have to study for a test.
>
>Rules for Butterflies:
>1. Don't fly in the halls.
>2. Don't bug the teacher.

Perhaps the cryptic lines from a fourth grader at Mountain View School, Mountain View, California, belong on the graffiti border:

One Day I Was Thinking

One day I was thinking of something to do
and I thought of something to do
So I did it.

— *Ronda Brouhard*

"One Day I Was Thinking" is a good heading to put on the border, don't you think?

At the request of Tom Patterson, education specialist at the Muskogee Area Office, I went to Seneca School, Wyandotte, Oklahoma, for a brief, get-acquainted visit. I came away reluctantly and was aching to return for a longer stay. Teachers and students seemed eager to work with me, and little kids in a boarding school are, somehow, very hard to leave — especially when they have their arms around you.

I brought from there one piece of writing which proves, it seems to me, that it pays to pay attention to students' spelling, but not always in order to correct it. Does this belong on the border?

Can't
think
about
anythink!

— *Annette*

Watch in your readings for headings that may inspire students to contribute a bright idea or dispose of a gripe. How about:

If you would not be forgotten when you are dead,
Write something worth reading or
Do something worth the writing.

19. Letters Are Not Dead Yet

Letter writing is almost a lost art, but for those who would learn to write, this kind of communication is ideal. Unless you are corresponding with a computer about a bill for a leather jacket you did not buy, letters usually elicit an answer. Feedback is the survival kit every author requires: because of the opportunity of receiving answers, we used letter writing as a means of helping students learn to write. (It also provides experience in the mechanics of preparing and mailing correspondence.)

Ann Gulledge and sixty-seven tenth graders (in three sections) almost carried the Albuquerque Post Office for a while. Ann wrote:

> We studied all kinds of letters for about a week—business, friendly, formal, informal, notes, and messages of every kind. For fun, we drew names in each class and wrote each other letters for valentines. I put my name in, too. We made one rule for valentine letters: Write good things about each other or what you like about your "name" person. We all had fun.
>
> Then I told the three groups about my idea for a letter-writing project to small towns with unusual names. I gave examples such as Nome, Alaska, which got its name from the surveyor's map. He wrote "NAME?" because he didn't know the name of the town. The printers left off the question mark and wrote "Nome" for the town. Other examples were used, but this one seemed to get enough interest to send the project off to a good start.
>
> Each student selected a name from alphabetical lists in the encyclopedias. (It was the first time I'd realized that we have no state beginning with *B*.) Then we all learned to use the zip-code catalog.
>
> A sample of the form letter we composed and sent out follows:

907 Indian School Road, N. W.
Albuquerque Indian School
Albuquerque, New Mexico   87107
Date

The Postmaster
Town
State and Zip

Dear Sir:

Will you please tell me about your town?
I like the name ————————— and I hope you will tell me how the town got its unusual name, something about the town's history, and news of present interest.
Please ask several people to write to me because I enjoy reading about real places. I hope to hear from elderly people as well as boys and girls near my age.
(Insert here a paragraph telling just enough about yourself to make your reader interested—the "bait your hook" idea.)
A self-addressed, stamped envelope is enclosed for your convenience. I will appreciate hearing from you soon.

Sincerely yours,

Signature

We also decided that we should "bait" the self-addressed, return envelopes: we made the envelopes and then drew pictures in color on the backs.
So far, we have letters from:

> Bullhead City, Arizona
> Ajo, Arizona
> Show Low, Arizona
> Coldwater, Michigan
> Hungry Horse, Montana
> Eunice, New Mexico
> Tonopah, Nevada
> Dry Run, Pennsylvania
> Goodnight, Texas
> Muleshoe, Texas
> Marlboro, Vermont
> Goose Egg, Wyoming
> Egg Harbor, Wisconsin

We plan to make a large wall map showing names of towns and a scrapbook of all letters received.

Ann comments, "This idea is great! Letters and brochures are more interesting than textbooks."

We might add: letters and brochures provide excellent practice in reading, spelling, syntax, proper letter-writing forms, history, geography, biography, and on and on. In addition, this project is bound to contribute to understanding between peoples. What more could we expect from one sleepless-night idea?

Another letter-writing project was the idea of Bonnie Neil at Intermountain School. It is particularly useful with boarding-school students but could be adapted by sending the letters to any relatives who do not live with students.

Bonnie gives her students paper and asks them to leave blank the top three inches of the page. Then she says: "Write a paragraph about what you did last night. . . . Now write about something special that happened last weekend. . . . Now write about the most interesting thing you've learned at school this week."

When students have finished, she says: "All right, you have just written a letter home. Address it to your folks, add anything else you would like to tell them, and finish it properly with your signature."

One form of letter writing expects no answers because the letters are the answers. Letters in this category do provide practice in writing, and they give students a big helping of feedback. This is not an original idea with us and the source is lost. We call them "Instant Status" letters.

We ask students: What is it you want to be? Artist? Lawyer? Rodeo champion? Millionaire? Educator? President?

We suggest then: Write the letter you can daydream receiving from someone in authority. Design his stationery and write the letter for him.

At IAIA students in one class wrote the following letters:

U.S. Treasury
Internal Revenue Department
Washington, D.C. 20224

Dear Mr. Stewart:

We are sending our representative to your dormitory on Monday of next week in regard to the $256,897.73 that you owe us in back income taxes.

Sincerely yours,

Doubleday & Co., Publishers
277 Park Avenue
New York, New York   10022

Dear Mr. Rogers:

We have read the book manuscript you submitted and would like very much to contract with you now for the right to publish every word you write for the rest of your life.

Sincerely yours,

Editor-in-Chief

Metropolitan Museum of Art
Fifth Avenue at Eighty-first Street
New York, New York   10028

Dear Miss Backford:

We have obtained, quite by accident, several of your rough sketches and we are wondering whether you would be available to come to New York during your Christmas vacation to give a series of illustrated lectures to the art teachers who will be visiting the Metropolitan during the holiday season.

We will, of course, pay all of your expenses and are prepared to offer you an honorarium of $25,000.

Sincerely yours,

Curator

Paramount Studios
Hollywood, California   90028

Dear Mr. Lopez:

Our scout attended the recent performance of the Drama Department at IAIA and has recommended that we send you the enclosed seven-year acting contract. You will notice that it is drawn on a sliding scale, beginning at $100,000 per picture and reaching a ceiling at $750,000 per picture after the first year.

Will you please let us hear from you at your earliest convenience as we are delaying casting six pictures for which we think you would be ideal.

Cordially yours,

Head of Studio

Someone has said, "If you can't say it, you can't think it."

I would like to add to that, "And if you can't think it, you can't be it."

No need to think small on a project of this kind. A student can give his imagination its head and let it fly. Notice that the letterhead is important. Pick a good one and let yourself go.

Many excellent books have been written on the letter format. Also, many great books have been compiled from letters exchanged between prominent people. The letter form just may inspire one of your students as it did one of mine at IAIA.

LETTER TO BE MAILED IN THE CUPBOARD

Dear Ghost:

You stay at our house, don't you? I've heard so much about you I feel I know you. But why do you slam the cupboard doors? And you look into the windows.

Why do you stay at our house? You once lived here, didn't you? I'm sorry for what happened to your family.

Why do you bother my mother when she's sleeping? Maybe it's not you. Might be another ghost.

Once my mother told me you were trying to get into the back door. Boy, you really had my mother and my brothers scared. I'm glad I wasn't here. I know how you look, but I won't describe your face to anybody because I don't want to. You are dressed in a black suit and you're six-feet ten-inches tall.

I wonder if you ever get lonesome. If you do, you can always take walks down by the creek. That's what I do. Maybe you're walking with me sometimes and I don't even know it.

I was thinking you might play with our dogs, but you're too old for that, I guess.

If you want to come in our house, don't bang on the door, just come in. Also, if you want anything to eat, just help yourself, but don't slam the cupboard doors because it scares my mother. She is a very light sleeper. Just leave the cupboards open after you get what you want to eat. We'll understand.

And another thing, stay out of our rooms except the living room. You can sit on the couch. I hope one day I'll see you or hear you.

Very sincerely yours,

Calvin O'John

20. The Identity Thing

Woodrow Wilson said, "Originality is simply a fresh pair of eyes." If we may add, "and a fresh pair of ears, a fresh sense of smell, taste, and feeling," he validated our entire project. Even so, the student is ever in need of assurances that he is, in fact, an original, a one-of-a-kind being with something unique to share with others. He needs, as most of us do, daily doses of Me vitamins. Not that he is on an ego trip but that he must believe, deep down, that he is Somebody. Otherwise, he cannot believe that he can write. A Nobody has nothing to say.

Almost everything we did and most of the teaching techniques we have suggested are ego building. Any time a student sees words come out of him and watches them develop as he revises until they say exactly what he means, he breathes deeper and stands taller. Each time his teacher and his peers read his words with respect, his self-respect grows.

William Stafford, distinguished poet and educator, describes his way of writing as "just plain receptivity." It is like fishing, he claims. He gets out pen and paper and waits. When he gets a nibble, he goes with it, accepting any first tentative thought as a starting place. He never judges this first thought. Instead, he lets it tell him what it wants him to say about it.

For William Stafford this is none too risky. Those first nibbles have repeatedly led him into the ripples and waves of worthy poems. Our students though do not yet trust their first nibbles. They have never been paid for a poem. They have never heard the applause. They have never been invited to the Library of Congress as Poet in Residence. To bring them from insecurity and distrust of first ideas, our teachers devised and filched from other teachers some self-awareness boosters. Younger students especially responded and enjoyed these. Older students, having produced more writing and received more recognition, probably do not need such self-starters.

Peggy Jo Hall, at Sequoyah High School, Tahlequah, Oklahoma, used an assignment that is helpful in two ways: it teaches students to use metaphor and simile while asking them to look inward and discover who they are. She makes a game of it, using students' writing without their names and allowing others in the class to match up the characteristics and Guess Who. Here are a few samples:

> I am a lion with long hair
> with big ideas to spare
> With my smart brain
> covered with hair.

An aside: Thomas Alva Edison said, "The chief function of your body is to carry your brain around."

> A jackass can be stubborn when he feels like he should; he kicks when annoyed with someone that tries to push or boss him around; and gets pretty smart when he wants to show a little intelligence.

> I am like a stallion. I want to be free, depend on no one. But, with the world like it is, you almost have to depend on someone. People are always trying to break you, locking you up to suit their purpose, to use you. The wanting to be free is always stronger when you're being held against your wish.

Julian Whorton and Carol Soatikee at Concho School, in Concho, Oklahoma, had their fourth- and fifth-grade class write "About Me":

> I am Russell Jim. I am fifty-four inches tall. My favorite sport is basketball. And my favorite subject is Math. I like Math. It is fun. Sometimes it is hard but I don't care. It is almost Christmas and I don't know what I am going to get.

> I'm real mean
> I'm crazy
> Hair kind of brownish

Black eyes
Little bit freckles
Don't paint good
Don't write good
Live in El Reno.
Have three dogs
Two pups and one big dog
Go to school at Concho
Math group three
Reading group two
I'm in two groups.
One brother,
One sister, and ME.
My brother's name is Milford,
And my sister's name is Terri
We are all FLETCHERS.

— *Cheri Fletcher*

Mae Schense's eighth graders at Turtle Mountain Community School also wrote in the realm of "Who Am I?" Here are Mae's samples:

Who am I?
Am I a bird that flies through the sky?
Or am I a plane soaring through the air?
Or am I a star shining with a glare?
Or am I a dog, howling through the night?
Without knowing who I am,
I am filled with fright.

— *Denise Azure*

WHO AM I?

I am nothing in a universe of everything,
A universe that stretches so far,
I am nothing, so how far do I know it goes?
I am nothing,
Or am I a small, small speck of dust in something?
I am nothing,
Or are there other specks like me?
I am nothing. . . . No, I'm not!
I am something.
There are millions like me
So I'm something, just like you.

— *Marlon Frederick*

WHO AM I

Who am I?
  I am a green frog
  sitting in the pond all day.
  I might be a bird
  flying over the bay.

Who am I?
  I am the wind
  and the leaves blowing by
  And I'm the clouds
  and stars drifting in the sky.

Who am I?
  I am the person
  I've been and always will be.
  If you don't believe me,
  Come and see.

—Karen Weber

Mae's students loved writing "Good News and Bad News" items. Her classes write them by the hundreds. Another trick she uses with seventh graders and some of her eighth-grade classes is "Yesterday I Was . . . but Today I Am." "I could go on for days," she writes. "Almost every assignment comes in with one of these or a 'Good News—Bad News' on the back. It's great to end an assignment with a laugh." She enclosed samples from her classes:

GOOD NEWS AND BAD NEWS

Student to Mother:
  Good News: I didn't get an *F* in history today.
  Bad News: I got three *F*'s in English.

Son to Father:
  Good News: I brought the snowmobile back.
  Bad News: It's in a million pieces.

Wife to Husband:
  Good News: I drove my best today. I stayed within the speed limit and on my side of the road.
  Bad News: I hit four people, two cars, and one garage.

YESTERDAY I WAS... BUT TODAY I AM

Yesterday I was a car,
    But today I am a lemon.

Yesterday I was a chicken,
    But today I am brave.

Yesterday my parents loved me,
    But today I'm a teenager.

Cal Rollins, as a first assignment, asks a student to describe his own hand. This becomes a kind of Here and Now that is also an identity experience. First, the student establishes his stance in relation to the subject (near or far, critical or approving, outside or inside, attached or detached, acting or idle, and artistic or functional or both). Next, the teacher suggests employing images and figures of speech and writing in full detail. Finally, the first drafts are polished into finished pieces of writing.

I would like to propose that these might well be decorated with handprints or fingerprints. Use diluted poster paint or washable ink. Even carbon paper will rub off on a thumb well enough to transfer a faint print. Stamp pads work perfectly. When these identity pieces are at the stage that satisfies their authors, display them on walls or bulletin board or bind them into an anthology. Titles for such a book are easy: *File for the FBI* or *Hands Up!* or *Our Handbook.*

Ann Gulledge also has some tricks for helping students to develop a sense of self along with improving their writing skills. In her "What's in a Name" assignment, acrostics give students a chance to hang a self-portrait on the letters of their names.

M escalero
I ndian
C ool it, man
H ello,
A merican Indian
E verywhere,
L ove it or leave it.

D andy
A lways outstanding
N eeds no help
I ntelligent in
E nglish and
L ove.

F ighting
R oaring
A thlete
N ever fails at
K icking.

P ower!
A paches are all over the
U nited States
L ove Apaches!

The Identity Thing

R ebecca likes to
E njoy herself playing
B asketball with
E sther,
C arol, and
C ordy
A t AIS gym.

Ann came across an opportunity to get a large supply of birthstone rings. She grabbed the lot and uses them to reward special achievement. By this means she bolsters her student's selfhood. In effect, the student says to himself, "I am me with a special day of my own and a lovely colored stone in a ring to symbolize me."

Another of Ann's methods emphasized for the student that "I have a name and I can use it to draw something that characterizes me." Students drew cars and flowers and ducks and imaginary animals and whatever they happened to be interested in at the moment—even sport shoes. Then they made skinny or fat letters and filled the body of their outline drawings with their names disguised as markings on their ducks and horses and shoes. The teacher and that visiting teacher, Mrs. Allen, both came in for a share of the students' efforts on this one. When students initiated the idea and drew our names to give to us at the end of class, even we felt a little more the sense of I Am Somebody.

21. Luring Students to Read

At Turtle Mountain Community School, in North Dakota, I followed Florence Crouse and a loaded book cart from the library, down the hall, and into an eighth-grade class. There Florence made a lively presentation of several books, showing gay jackets and telling a bit about authors. From one book she read a few paragraphs—enough to raise questions in a reader's mind and make him want to read on to get his questions answered.

Then she gave students the opportunity to check out books for the following week. Almost everyone in the class took a book. I heard a great deal of conversation about books. Book contagion was running through the group like a happy kind of virus.

When Florence passed out small squares of bright-colored paper and asked each student to write the name of a book he especially liked and, under that, his name, I saw no one hesitate. Several asked for additional pieces of paper because they wished to recommend more than one book. By this time these enthusiastic readers had seen the large poster headed: "Recommended Reading." Under the heading, their signed choices were to be pasted at random.

Reading is a spur to writing. The almost irresistible spur is reading pieces written by the peer group, but we certainly do not want our readers to stop there. Peer-group recommendations carry a lot of weight for general reading. Written recommendations on an attractive bulletin board are great. If you can get students talking among themselves about books they enjoy, this is even greater. Word-of-mouth advertising is what all public relations firms pray for.

Zow! Pop! Wham! Or, the Day the Comic Books Came to Yale

Luring Students to Read

"Deep in the confines of Yale's Cross-Campus Library, safe from the greedy grasp of envious collectors, lies a treasure of outlandish art and flashy prose. Yes! It's a $30,000 comic book exhibit, compiled by graduate students. . . . Among other rarities, it contains early issues of Superman, Batman and the Green Lantern. Terrific!"

I have forgotten where I clipped that juicy news item, but I received the following notes on comics as a teaching aid from Dennis Writer for *Let's Talk Writing*. Dennis taught at Oglala Community School, Pine Ridge, South Dakota, while I worked there. He commented:

> There's a book called *Hooked on Books*[1] that says, "It's not what they should read, it's what they will read." Very true. You can't skip a step in a human's development without leaving something out.
>
> This past year, I thought my high school remedial-reading class would like comics. I got a whole pile, two or three hundred, from the Tipi Shop here in Pine Ridge when it folded. Out-of-date comics are easy to buy at cost because, when they don't sell, shopkeepers tear the covers off, send them in, and get their money back.
>
> Students were enthralled, reading at least twice as avidly as in the recommended reading kits they had been using. The kits went from grades four to twelve. When I checked the comics' vocabularies, I found that they also fell in that range. The stories in the comics, with some exceptions, were more exciting, more sophisticated, more in tune with our electric, atomic world, certainly more poetic, and drew a lot more interest from the kids. Sometimes my small class would double in size because of visiting students reading the new crop of comics.
>
> The comics were also given to the students to keep. It's hard telling how many eyes would look at a comic before it fell apart. I have to compare that with the sterile textbook-company kits, which get reluctantly read once a day by one kid, and the comics, which are more than willingly carried to homes and dorm and devoured.
>
> Here they liked Archie, horror comics, adventure comics,

---

[1] Daniel N. Fader and Elton B. McNeil, eds., *Hooked on Books: Program and Proof* (New York: Berkley, 1977).

love comics, and war comics. Some comics deal heavily in mythology; some are deeply into future-science. Anyway, the word lists tell the story. You just don't find *"cosmic treadmills"* in textbook-company kits.

For advanced students, some comics have critiques from readers (mostly high school age) that would put your A+ Shakespeare paper to shame. They talk about character inconsistencies, story sequences, art work, and things like that.

As for vocabulary, see the following word lists and judge for yourself:

From *The Flash* (one issue)

cosmic treadmill	inadequate	theorized
idling	assassinated	extraordinary
time barrier	disintegrator	programmed
nuclear holocaust	satellite	highly sophisticated
vaporize	vivid	electronic brain
materializing	lurk	consequences
futuristic	insanity	forestall
paradox	crusader	lethal
infinite	horrendous	molecules
periodically	counterthought	momentarily
99.7 percent probability	android	converge
unorthodox	emancipator	transfiguration
transmitting	predecessor	transpired
stifling	elongated	vivid
monarch of motion	misheard	conclusion
centrifugal force	inner space	annihilate
maneuver	diabolic	

From *Prince Namor, the Sub-Mariner* (one issue)

royal soul	Neptune's trident	question echoes
to fathom	painful throb	beckon
wandering night	dusty brown edifice	human discards
searching for a shadow	frustration	depressed
maudlin thoughts	broken flotsam	stands revealed
question plagues	becalmed	ancient tenement
petty differences	past triumphs	human heritage
agony-crazed	canisters	brethren
most ultimate of pollutions	libation	radiation
engulf	sentimental	deliverance
comrade	sanity in strength	naïve
affirmation	refuge	primal
prevailed	heritage	intruder
establishment type	corrupting carnage	quirk
alienate	sought	furnish

restless, ever-renewing sea	idealistic world	awesome
melding counterpoint	perceptible effect	leviathan
instigator	invincible	proverbial

From *Captain America* and the *Falcon*

malevolent	pentagon	ultimate
elaborate demonstration	victorious	complexities
immortal	human operatives	insurrectionist
technical experts	democracy	red tape
execute phase two	vacation	avenger
sleep	cheroot	fitful sleep
extenuating circumstances	dream which cries	surprise element
social worker	operation	private property
abandoned tenement	eject	whumf!
petty doubts and fears	the economy	out of commission
sufficiently impressed	gaining equality	snap decision
reactions and reflexes	press conference	obviously
appropriation (Congress)	maneuvers	

Batman and *Superman*

another dimensional world	colonization	mocking
fugitives	prehistoric	titanic
quarry	collapsible	earthling
invulnerable	anthropology	sinister
wooly rhinoceros	ejected	matador
speculate	terrain	unerringly
materialize	proboscis	deliberately
dynamic	transformation	emanations
mortal	uncannily	dilemma
retrieve	established	dispatched
immune	hydrants	supersensitive
menacing natives		

Archie

modest	generation	talents
donated	performing	resident
nervous	condemn	confidence
chamber of commerce	cheering	mystique
mastered	commemorative	surprise
buffoons	ability	Huckleberry Finn
sensational	Mark Twain	encore
adventures	robbery	experiencing
misfits	wobbles	deceased
unanimous		

Summer of Desire (Love Comic)

funny farm	philosophy	mental institution
greener pastures	playwright	ingrate
produced (a play)	connoisseur	exception
A Midsummer Night's Dream	tactful	different concept
Maine: the Pine Tree State	rehearsal	sincere
to love and be loved	decision	train of thought
infinite sadness	odored	frequently
have their roles customized	miserable	shred of sorrow
Maine: state flower—pinecone	jilted	correcting grammar
graduate	apology	inclined
jealous idiot	permanently	sprained tongue
engineering degree		

Speaking of comic books, when I visited Choctaw Central School, Philadelphia, Mississippi, I enjoyed the *Beowulf Comic Book* made by one of Janice Fulton's classes. Janice disclaimed any credit for an original idea (a good many manuals and magazines have suggested making a comic book), but those Choctaw students really gave it their all.

Grendel looked somewhat different on different pages of the book because each cartoonist drew his own ideas. Even so, it was easy to follow the story.

After the duel between Beowulf and Grendel, Grendel's broken arm is amputated at the elbow and gore is everywhere on the page. When his mother invades the hall and makes off with the sleeping Thane and Grendel's arm, the arm is four times as big as the man. Appropriately on the same page in the book is an ad:

> Support your local football team
> **THE WARRIORS**

The creatures in the loathsome pool where Beowulf fights Grendel's mother are a long, blue, serpentlike monster; a green, serrated-sided serpent with a spaceman head, and a triangular-topped, yellow-eyed thingamabob. Following this is a full-page ad:

> Now to put your mind at ease . . .
> **THE TEEN CENTER**
> is open 1:00–7:00
> **WELCOME!**

I found an exciting senior class project underway at Cheyenne–Eagle Butte High School, in Eagle Butte, South Dakota. It came in handy, too.

Sandra Fox told me a paperback bookstore was Bill Donovan's idea, and he started it before he transferred to Riverside Indian School, at Anadarko, Oklahoma. I neglected to ask whether he was the one who found the tiny storeroom and painted three walls brilliant red and the fourth a shocking pink, against which an oversized bee hums at book browsers and buyers.

Two turning racks, such as you see in drugstores, and two narrow shelves, running the length of this tiny store, display the books. I would guess that students shop one at a time for the most part. The store could not possibly accommodate more than three or four.

Sandra Fox selects the books, adding any special orders from students or teachers, of course. She buys through a regular book outlet, and the store makes the regular 40 percent profit. Profits are given in one-hundred-dollar scholarships to worthy seniors who need money for further education.

"We have a hard time keeping books in stock," Sandra said. "This is a reading school. Students are in here every time we can have the store open, and they really buy lots of books."

Who could resist? It was such a bright, luring place that I started looking at titles. I look at titles by the hour in airports sometimes, and I seldom find the book I want. I had been searching racks for weeks to find N. Scott Momaday's Pulitzer Prize–winning *House Made of Dawn*. Sure enough, there it was at the Cheyenne–Eagle Butte High School bookstore. Before I left that Friday, I had ruined a five-dollar bill and had my arms loaded with books (this was in 1970 before the worst of inflation and before paperbacks cost as much as they do now). By Saturday morning I was snowbound in my motel room and was not able to get out until Monday afternoon. What fun I had! Who can imagine anything better than to be snowbound with a stack of new books? I loved every minute of it, and I recommend that every high school rush to establish a school bookstore.

22. Helping Students Tell a Story

Peggy Jo Hall, at Sequoyah High School, in Tahlequah, Oklahoma, enjoys working in the realm of the short story. Many teachers find this difficult, but Peggy has written good stories and plays herself. Perhaps the response she gets from students stems from her confidence with these forms. Whatever the reason, she is willing to share her secrets with us:

> Think of a character, someone you know. If he or she has a problem, so much the better because a problem is a built-in conflict, and every plot must have a conflict. Change the characters' names, make up names, and we will develop a story plot.
> I do know how to teach plotting and I wish I could report instantaneous success, but I can't. Creative writing is sixth hour. It competes with the newspaper class for writers, and all athletes are automatically eliminated. And it's sort of a dumping ground, but no matter. I like problem students if I can once get them started to work. I had several who had not turned in the first assignment out of sixteen until a new school policy decided that failing students should report to a study hour at night. Have you ever gotten sixteen assignments at once from one student?

So, Peggy Jo had problems as all of us do in all schools. I am sure we can profit from her notes and the assignment she gives students along with a sample skeleton plot for a story. With this much help her students are able to turn out good first drafts, giving Peggy the basis for detailed, personal help on revisions. This is her handout:

THE SHORT STORY

A short story has a plot (I'll add, if I may, it has a plot or a plan before writing begins because the beginning must predict the end). In the plot a conflict develops to a climax where it is resolved, and the main character undergoes a change of attitude.

The assignment:
Write a short story, following a given plot, placing the action in a familiar setting, and using the first person point of view.

The plot:
Scene 1—Theft: The narrator tells about stealing something.
Scene 2—An Average Day: This scene describes the person in an everyday situation. Use direct quotes for conversation. This social interaction may contrast with the antisocial action in the first scene, or this scene might simply indicate the person has not been caught.
Scene 3—Caught: The person is accused of and confesses to stealing.
Scene 4—Regret: The person is sorry and decides never to steal again. The change of attitude must be motivated. Regret because of fear of being caught is not convincing, as it does not indicate a real change of attitude.

Don't Forget: A short story is fiction. Although it is not true, the short story should convince the reader that it is true. The characters must seem to be real people. Their dialogue must sound like talk, not like writing. Their actions must be motivated. Enough sensory details must be given so that the reader can see and experience what the characters in the story see and experience. One technique for making the story seem to be true is the use of the first person point of view.

Note: I certainly agree that writing in the first person is the easy way to make a story real and believable. Subtle things of which the author is not conscious as he writes creep into this kind of writing; however, if students are drawing on personal experience (and they certainly should be), they often feel too self-conscious to allow anyone but the teacher to read a story written in the first person.

An excellent, revealing exercise is to have students write in the first person with the promise that, once it is written this way, they will be allowed (even encouraged) to give the "I" character a name and change the whole thing to the third person. Students enjoy doing this, and I often take their first-person beginnings, select a name for the "I," and read their writing back to them, transposing to third person as I read. Their eyes invariably light up as they hear their own words coming back to them, sounding very much like a story in a magazine.

Another addendum regarding fiction and truth: "Fiction reveals truths that reality obscures," says Jessamyn West. Her novel, *The Life I Really Lived*,[1] perfectly exemplifies her theory, and I recommend it to all teachers of writing. The late great reviewer Robert Kirsch said in the *Los Angeles Times* (1979) of this book, "The life story within a novel displays so much craft and mastery . . . the skills and mysteries of writing . . . that only in retrospect will there be some parsing out of the sources. The key opens the double lock of sources of fiction, not only experience transmuted but imagination and fantasy."

That fiction reveals truth is the reason for writing fiction, in my opinion. In a story we have a chance to manipulate facts in such a way that they say something significant about life in general. In this sense fiction is often (and always, ideally) far more true than mere fact. Our high school students are capable of understanding this. In fact, many of our elementary students are capable of understanding it. I am sure no one would accuse me of low expectations, but even I am frequently delighted by the depth of truth in writings by fifth and sixth graders after we have pointed out to them that all writing is about the one subject, Life for Human Beings.

With some classes I have found useful a cut-and-paste project that starts students on the Story Road way of thinking. From used magazines I ask students to cut stories without words (pictures) and paste them on large sheets of paper or cardboard. Such stories need a beginning, middle, and end. They need a story problem to be solved, of course, but it need not be earthshaking. Let each student test his storytelling ability by getting other members of the class to "read" his pictures and tell him the story in words. This can be done, too, by students with cameras, "taking" their stories. Magazine cutting, however, is quicker and less expensive and is an excellent first step toward the sequential thinking necessary to story writing.

Each culture has, as a part of its treasure, stories long shaped and polished by loving tongues. Many of these have never been written. A great many have been written once,

[1] New York: Harcourt Brace Jovanovich, 1979.

twice, or a hundred times. Written before or not, these are ready-made stories waiting to be tried on by our students. The act of writing such stories offers many benefits:

1. Each writer, in reliving the story to retell it, adds new color and depth.
2. In retelling the old stories, the author learns the shape and cadence of story telling.
3. In retelling, the author learns new appreciation of his heritage and new respect for his forefathers.
4. In retelling, the story is brought nearer present experience and can be of benefit to all the cultures it now touches.
5. In retelling, the new author has at hand the bony structure of a story. He can concentrate on fleshing it out and breathing life into it in the same way his storytelling ancestors did before him. It becomes a "rooting" kind of experience.

A brother and sister, never having written together before, started talking and giggling. Soon they started to write, but they kept punctuating the words with more giggles. The result of this collaboration (after I had made some marginal notes, and they had done some revisions) was the following:

GRANDMOTHER'S MISTAKE
by
A. E. Mitchell
(For Aurelia and Barney)

To prevent youngsters from killing birds and other species, grandmothers try to teach them to respect all living creatures on the earth. Sometimes, grandmothers find their own teachings turned around on them.

Once upon a time in the hot plains country, Grandmother was set to weave her homespun, gray-and-white wool into a rug. But Bobbie and Wally, both five years old, began to disturb their grandmother.

Their behavior and disorderly conduct made her shout, "Boys, boys, boys! You are very disturbing. Go out in the country and look for your grandfather from the high hill," she said. She was thinking, "Now, I'll set back to weaving without interruptions. I'll show my husband, Hosteen, how much I've done in the days he has been gone."

Tickled to the bottom of her toes with her scheme, she sat before her loom, daydreaming. She was eager to see her two grandchildren race into the hogan, all excited with news of their grandfather's coming. So, she waited.

When she heard her grandsons running, their feet beating against the hard earth, she pretended to calm all her excitement. She heard the word *"Hosteen"* and she could hardly wait to hear about her husband approaching, riding horseback. This made her so excited that her heart began to beat faster than before.

"Grandma, Grandma," said Bobbie.

"Grandpa's . . . Grandpa's . . ." said Wally. They were all excited, too.

"Yes, I know, I know," she said, not perturbed.

"Grandma!" Bobbie and Wally both shouted at once. They were almost out of breath.

"My darling, young, beastly sons, what is it?" she asked.

"My grandfather's . . ." said Bobbie.

"Yes, our grandfather's . . ." said Wally.

They didn't finish what they were going to say.

"Yes, yes, I know," Grandmother said, smiling, hearing how excited her grandsons were.

"It's . . . it's—it's," Bobbie stuttered.

"Yes, he's—he's—he's—he's," said Wally.

"Of course, it's Grandfather," she said, grinning. Then she smoothed her hair out so when Grandfather came she would be all fixed up and her hair well groomed.

Bobbie was very annoyed now. He stepped forward to his grandmother's side and cuddled against her. Then Wally stepped forward and took hold of Grandmother's arm.

"Grandma," said Wally.

"Yes, what is it?" she asked.

"We found our poor Grandfather's body on the road a mile from here."

"And," added Bobbie, "he is dead. An automobile ran over him."

"No! No! It can't be!" Grandmother cried.

"We'll show you where he is," Bobbie said.

"No! No! I don't want to go." She burst into tears.

"Why not?" asked Wally.

"It's too horrible," she said, crying and moaning. "I remember the time we got married and went dancing in the near mountains where they were having a squaw dance. Then there was the time he called me 'Bee sugar,' and used to rock me to sleep. Such a disaster!" she said, crying much louder now.

"Come, we'll show you," said Bobbie.

"Yes, please do, before the desert buzzards see him," Wally said.

Convinced, finally, Grandmother held onto the boys' hands, and they led her to where Grandfather's body got run over by the automobile.

Before they reached the sight of the body, she closed her eyes and said, "Oh, I cannot bear to see the dreadful sight."

Still, the boys led their Grandmother until they stood before the dead body of the Grandfather, but she kept her hands over her eyes.

"See, he's all smashed," said Bobbie.

"O-o-o-h, I can't look," she said.

"But see, you must look! All of his guts are hanging out," said Wally.

"And look at his tongue between his teeth," Bobby went on.

"Horrible!" she said.

Bobby pulled at her sleeve. "Please look at our Grandfather's body," he begged.

"Oh, it's so tragic!" Grandmother wailed, standing before the body, but with her eyes closed.

"It's not that bad, so look," Wally insisted.

"No! Absolutely no!" Grandmother cried.

"Now look . . ." pleaded Bobbie.

Grandmother just peeked between her eyelashes and didn't see the sight of Grandfather's body, so she opened her eyes and asked, "Where? Where is the body?"

"It's right there on the road," Bobbie said.

"Where?" she asked, really curious now.

"Right here," said Wally pointing directly at the dead horny toad.

"How disobedient you boys are!" Grandmother scolded. She broke off a branch of the nearby greasewood to whip the boys.

She did spank Bobbie, but Wally said, "Grandmother, remember you told us the horny toad was our grandfather and to respect his presence?"

After that, she never ever taught her grandchildren to respect a living species without giving an explanation. A horned toad is called "Grandfather" so a child will remember not to hurt him. But a grandfather who is expected to come riding home on horseback is not to be confused with a run-over horny toad.

My Story of a Story

My story has to do with the story, "Mescalero Apache," by Ellen Scott. It was first published in *Arrow III*, is now available in *Arrows Four*, and has been reprinted several times in texts and anthologies. We have had many oral expressions of appreciation for this explanation of the Mountain Spirit Dance and several fan letters. One of these said that it was by far the best treatment of this particular dance that the reader had ever seen.

Ellen Scott attended Albuquerque Indian School during one school year. At that time in one of Ann Gulledge's classes she wrote the first versions of her story. Ann worked with her on it, and they showed it to me for my comments. During the following school year, Ellen attended Riverside School, at Anadarko, Oklahoma, where Bill Donovan was her teacher. At the end of that year, Ellen's story was selected by the judges of our annual contest and appeared in *Arrow III.*

I am sorry that we do not have the oral and written comments that both Ann and Bill gave Ellen during the evolution of her story. That would make a truly helpful record. Unfortunately, we have only early versions of Ellen's work and my comments. On the chance that you may find that much useful in helping students see the value of rewriting, resting time, and rewriting, here is the work as I first saw it at Albuquerque. I suggest that you read this and then reread the finished story in *Arrows Four,* page 111.

THE LEGEND OF THE APACHE MOUNTAIN GODS

Many moons ago a small settlement of Apache Indians was invaded by a neighboring tribe.

They had to flee for it was plain to see that they were going to lose.

In the band were two men, one blind and the other lame. Their relatives and friends decided it was best to keep them in a cave with provisions, as not to slow them down.

As time went on, their food supply had given out. They were awaiting for death to claim them for they no longer thought any one would come back and get them.

One day just as it was getting dark, the two men saw five grotesque figures painted black with white markings. The last figure was white. With them enter some light which some how turned into a bonfire. They danced around it. During that time the two men were huddled in a corner for the figures were frightening.

I underscored "grotesque" and wrote in the margin, "Show me." I underscored "black with white" and wrote in the margin, "Good! I can see colors." I underscored "danced" and asked in the margin, "Can you show the movements of the dance? I think you can."

On the back of the page I wrote: "Ellen, maybe you can tell

a bit more about the size of the Apache settlement and the size of the invading tribe. Were the invaders bigger people by any chance? See, you can SHOW what a tough time the Apaches are going to have. This is more impressive than merely telling that 'plain to see they were going to lose.'"

At one stage Ellen evidently decided to write this story in the form of a poem. One page of her manuscript has only:

> They danced one night,
> Many years back;
> Grotesque figures, black and white;
> Skirts of buckskin, leggings too

And then, at the bottom of the page:

> And I know just how
> the two men felt
> cold and dreary (hungry?)

Next came a much fuller version of the story with my comments and suggestions (note that I did not correct spelling and grammar in this version):

MESCALERO APACHE MOUNTAIN SPIRIT DANCERS

Many moons ago a small settlement of Apache Indians was invaded by a neighboring tribe. They had to flee for it was plain to see that they were going to lose. In the band were two men. One was blind and the other was lame. Their relatives and friends decided to keep them in a secluded mountainside cave, with provisions/as not to slow them down.

As time went on the two men sat in the cave, their food supply had long given out. Their bodys were empty and they were weak. They had given up hope of anyone coming back for them.

Then one day just as it was getting dark the two men heard strange noises outside. They were afraid for they thought the enemy had found them. Then as the noise was growing louder and louder, five strange figures entered the cave. The first four were painted black with odd symbols painted in white on their backs and breasts, they had on weird and mystical head gear. Their skirt

Ellen, some words need to be developed in sensory terms so that your reader can see what you see when you say "strange" or "odd," for example.

Margin notes (left):

> Show as much as you can — symbols, and how was headgear decorated? Can you show shape & size of the mask?
>
> KTWTBT — watch sentence structure. Reads as if the figures became the bonfire.
>
> Can you give the fear in sensory terms? Were they shaking or what?
>
> Do you mean long, fine fringe or beaded or what? Show me.
>
> Ellen, this is very good. Build up your sensory detail wherever you can. Your reader must see an exact image, hear the sounds, feel the cold, etc. Give the reader everything he needs to enjoy and suffer as if he were there. Give the details necessary and I think you can finish this story for the contest. You've done a fine revising job.
>
> Congratulations!
> J. D. A.

Margin notes (right):

> Good detail here! Can you also make me hear the chant?
>
> Just how do the gods speak? I can't hear "strange."
>
> Good detail here!
>
> I like your ending very much.

---

and leggins were of buckskin and each carried a stave in each hand. The fifth was masked and painted in white.

A mysterious light entered with the figures which eventually became a bon fire. The troup danced: stamping, chanting, as they started striking the swords at un-seen enemies.

All during that time the two men sat huddled in a corner of the cave for they had seen or heard nothing like this. They were told in the gods' strange way that they meant no harm, instead, they would drive the evil away.

The gods then led them out of the cave. The white god struck a gigantic rock. The rock split open and a new passageway was formed. The two men stepped through the passageway. Suddenly the blind man could see and the lame could walk. Each were clothed in the finest and most elaborate buckskin and bow and arrows. Then the gods were gone.

In the distance they saw a village. It was that of their own band who had just returned. They joined their people and told of the miracle which took place and showed how the gods danced.

Generations have passed since then, and the dance of the Mountain Gods has been performed to drive away sicknesses, evil, and bring good health and good fortune.

So when you see the Mountain Gods perform, look deep into the fire and think how the first men who saw them felt when they were in the cave, cold, hungry and frightened.

Well, so much for the story of a story. I believe the finished version shows how much a few good teachers along the way can help a student. Do you know of teachers who would have accepted Ellen's first draft, marked it with a bold red *C,* and returned it to her? The story would have found its way into the wastebasket, and Ellen would have learned no more about writing than she knew when she wrote the first word. By remembering that "nothing good is ever written, it is rewritten," our handling let the student learn several needed lessons in syntax through her own experience. In addition, she achieved publication and a totally new image of herself. Incidentally, she has also received a nice royalty payment from the publishers and several permission fees from reprints.

23. Using Those Beloved, Obstreperous Machines

Murphy's Law was undoubtedly inspired by audiovisual equipment gone obstinate in a classroom. Tape recorders, television receivers, video cameras, motion picture projectors, and even lowly overhead projectors will go wrong if they can go wrong. Even so, they sometimes go right. When they do, they can and do tickle the urge to write, prod students toward raising standards for their writing, provide a listening ear and a viewing eye, and enhance the total process of writing to say something to somebody. Our teachers tried out whatever equipment they could beg, borrow, or uncover in their schools' storerooms.

Alexa West at Intermountain School sought out the help of the excellent communications department there and produced "The Sounds of Silence" with words, music, and pictures correlated on tape and filmstrip.

Students who had written poems, selected poetry and chose pictures from magazines or school art that illustrated their writing. These illustrations were photographed to make a filmstrip. Students then read their own poetry, found music they liked to add to the recording, and synchronized sound tape and film.

The first attempt fell short of Alexa's high expectations, but she is a bit of a perfectionist and will undoubtedly try again. The idea certainly has merit and has in it suggestions that many teachers can use even without the sophisticated equipment available at Intermountain.

Any teacher with a tape recorder will find it a valuable aid in helping students with poetry in particular, although it can also be of help with prose. Poetry needs to flow or else it needs intentionally to stumble. Whatever the intention, the student can tell from recording and listening to his words whether or not he has succeeded.

When teaching students for whom English is a second language, we have discovered that quite often they leave out key words when writing. In speaking, however, they are apt to indicate their meaning either by filling in the missing words or by inflection. A teacher who is baffled by what he finds on the paper may discover that, if the student reads and records his writing, it all comes clear. The teacher then is in a position to help get the complete thought on paper.

Carolyn Cone from Flandreau Indian School, Flandreau, South Dakota, wrote:

> My boys and girls in Creative Writing class are just beginning to hand in poems and more poems and I can hardly find the time to copy them and display them. I wish they would write some prose. We do not have a movie camera available, but we do have a television camera and, if only they'd get busy on a script, we'd televise it.
>
> Now some of them are enjoying reading their poems, using a cassette and listening to themselves. If nothing else, this creates interest and it should help them perfect what they've written. I see such possibilities in some of this writing that I'd love to "take over" and make corrections and additions myself, but, of course, I can't do this, must not do this. It's frustrating, as you know.

Note: Can't students copy their own work for display? The actual process of copying is a stimulus to revision. If you don't believe it, try copying something of your own. If you can do it without revising as you go, you have more willpower than I have. With students the knowledge that they are copying for display should also prod them toward finding more expressive words, perfecting their spelling and punctuation, and making sure that they have said clearly what they have to say.

Peggy Jo Hall always downgrades her own efforts and results, but I am sure we can all see steps forward and perhaps some steps "backward in the right direction," as Captain Fisby says to Sakini in *Teahouse of the August Moon*.

> Thought I would write and let you know how we're doing

in Creative Writing, except I'm not sure. Some of the students have real ability, but creativity seems to be the Siamese twin to instability....

We blundered through writing the standard-plot short story. Although about half didn't finish, I think they all ended up with a pretty good idea of what a plot is. Decided the next thing to do was the play. I took one student's plot for a short story, divided the students into groups of four or five, and told them to take parts and try to act out the scenes. One student was to record.

The first day they were enthusiastic, especially when I said, yes, they could use cuss words because in experimental theater you said what you thought the character would say naturally. Recording proved a problem, of course. The writer couldn't keep up. One group tried taping, but that was even less successful.[1]

So much for experimental theater, but one person in two of the groups ended up writing the scene that night the way they thought it should be. That's something, I guess.

And another student who hasn't turned in one assignment all year wrote a scene during another class. The scenes are really sketchy, of course. Several students, with their usual drive, are hiding behind magazines.... Next challenge, putting the scenes on TV tape. B—— Y—— came out from behind his magazine long enough to get enthusiastic over working the TV camera, even at 4:00 P.M. on Monday afternoon. I find out there's no room available, so I'll have to use my classroom. Mr. P—— says TV can't be moved once it's set up. That's limiting. Somehow I had visions of all getting on the bus and going to town to tape the barroom and jail scenes. I wonder how Ingmar Bergman would react to a challenge like this....

Will close since that about covers everything except R—— C——, who really writes, and D—— B——, who does have a lot of talent, thinks he's much too talented to be criticized and is extremely obnoxious in class—but he can write. I'll endure the obnoxious part. And J—— G—— who is really trying and thinks he can write, and L—— L——, who can but won't.

Well, enough of excuses.... My English classes drew illustrations for "The Devil and Tom Walker," and we did a kind of reading with musical background while the illustrations were shown on the overhead projector. The students really enjoyed it....

One girl wrote an essay on a girl and her god-witch. It's short, simple, and they've spent three days taping it with the

---

[1] She does not say why taping did not work; however, talking and confusion in the room would, of course, be picked up by the microphone.

motorcycle sounds in the background and witch screams. She is trying to get illustrations for the overhead to go with it. They're having fun and doing some rewriting.

There is an easy way to make overhead transparencies. You do not need a camera or chemicals. All you need is a piece of clear Con-Tact brand plastic. Find a magazine picture you would like to show on the overhead in glorious color and cut it out. Place your picture on the sticky side of the clear plastic and press it on firmly. Then place the picture, plastic and all, in a bowl of water or in the sink and leave it there until the paper comes off. The ink will remain on the plastic, and there's your picture.

Later, Peggy sent this followup: "Well, the plays aren't ready. Right now I'm concentrating on unoriginality: standard or given plots, technical problems such as transition, character development, and balky equipment, classroom limitations, and a three o'clock class.

"I'm throwing in some scenes."

Her plan for setting them up may prove of value to some teachers:

SCENE	LOCALE	CHARACTERS	CONFLICT
1	Living room of Joe's house	Joe Mother Stepfather	Joe's stepfather is trying to get Joe to quit stealing and running around. Joe says you're not my father and I don't have to do what you say. Joe goes out for a walk to meet his friends.
2	A beer tavern	Joe and friends	Joe and his friends break into a beer tavern to steal money and beer.
3	At home	Joe and Stepfather	Joe's stepfather finds out about the break-in. He asks Joe where he got all the money he's been spending. Joe says to let him alone and leaves.
4	Malt shop	Joe and Larry	Joe and Larry get into a fight with a drunk man in front of malt shop and the man beats up Joe pretty bad.

This is enough to give you the idea. In the next step the scenes are put into dialogue, action, and stage business. It is as simple as that, and your class members can use the same system for writing their plays.

Have you tried cassettes instead of margins? Stephen H. Vogler of Indian Riffle Junior High School, Kettering, Ohio, reported a happy discovery of his in an article, "Grading Themes: A New Approach; A New Dimension," in the *English Journal* (January, 1971). He tells of marking student papers, correcting errors in grammar and spelling, and writing comments when he first started teaching. After running out of time every day and night and feeling that students paid little attention, he devised a new system.

He had students number the lines of their writing and, at the beginning of school, purchase one blank cassette. He filed these cassettes in a box in alphabetical order with each student's name on a tape. When he started to read a paper, he would get out the student's tape and put it in his recorder. His suggestions and criticisms and accolades go into the microphone. For example:

> Karen, I'd like to talk to you a little bit here about your theme entitled "A Regular Summer storm." Before we begin, I'd like to point out a general overview that I have of your theme—uh—I think you've done, really, Karen, just a fine job of trying to accomplish what we were talking about in class: trying to present a vivid image of a storm.
>
> You have some [long pause] strong and angry-sounding images such as "violent wind" in line two and "battled" in line two and "frantically" in line three, and all these images do a great deal to create a fine piece of writing. [Cough.] You've done it also by the use of strong verbs which we talked about in class. . . .
>
> One thing I would like to point out, Karen, is, I think you overdid a little the *ing* sound in lines six and seven. Now understand, I'm not finding fault with the image. You show a lot of imagination there. But to my way of thinking, those three *ing* words have a tendency to weaken that image. Listen: "Thunder was rumbling like the churning of an erupting volcano." Do you agree?

Mr. Vogler's students were enthusiastic about this method. They said:

"Now you can tell us everything about our themes. Most teachers just mark our papers and give us a grade. All we know is how bad it is, never how to correct it. But not anymore...."

"I love it. This way, you get more individual attention. And I think you need individual attention to know what you've done wrong and how you can correct it."

Commercially made films have long been used by teachers as a means of stimulating ideas and the urge to write. I am sure that every teacher who has tried using films in this way could report both successes and failures. I have collected a few methods and examples that may be of some worth as you try older tried-and-true films and the new ones that are being produced.

The method of presentation used by James S. Mullican at Indiana State University strikes me as being useful. He began by showing without sound a color-animation, six-minute film made by *Encyclopaedia Britannica*. The assignment was to write the narrative story line after seeing the film without sound. The particular film he was using was *A Short Vision* and he says that the visual portion is specific enough to indicate the action and yet vague enough to stimulate the imagination. Students were asked to write a first draft in class while impressions were fresh, then to revise. In later sessions they read and discuss. Then he shows the film with sound.

Discussions follow. Discussion leads to another assignment as students consider whether the film is primarily art or propaganda. Finally, each student defends his thesis on paper.

In our work with elementary and high school students we are usually looking for spin-off writing that a film incites. A silent showing, however, would certainly help students to understand story line development and teach them how to construct their own stories. Films that have little or no story pattern serve to bring forth "responding" or "going-on-from-there" kinds of writing in various forms.

During one late spring visit to Turtle Mountain Community School, at Belcourt, North Dakota, I was carrying the film *Seashore* (Pyramid Films, Santa Monica, California). We showed it to one of Mae Schense's classes and immediately gave students the opportunity to capture on paper their reactions to the film. This class was ready and eager to write because Mae had been giving them many chances to write, to share their writings with others, and to enter an all-school writing contest. These eighth graders wrote almost as naturally as they breathed, and after the film they were very quickly thrusting their papers at Mae and me, eager to hear our personal reactions or to have their writing read to the class.

Many of us, as teachers, would have been satisfied and ready to congratulate ourselves on a highly successful class session. But many of us, as teachers, are too ready to stop too soon.

A good film, properly presented, will normally evoke a response in words, spoken or written. This is fine, but we are in the business of helping students to use words well. It is after that first outpouring of words that learning to select and arrange begins. It is in the second and sixth and tenth handling of our words that we begin to make them say in a clear and striking way exactly what is inside us, struggling to speak to someone else. I am quite sure that Mae's follow-up session did far more to help her students gain language facility than the first session could have. She wrote:

> I put the narration of *Seashore* on the bulletin board and handed back what students had written. Anyone who wanted to could rewrite, redo, add to, or fix up his copy in any way he wished. Then he could mount his writing and put it on the bulletin board. Anyone who didn't want to do this could read the Scholastic comics. As it turned out, no one read the comics and we have a lovely bulletin board.

At Hallsboro High School, Hallsboro, North Carolina, I showed the film, *Portrait of a Horse*. It is a beautiful, dreamy art film produced by Pyramid Films. One student, Richard Whitley, wrote first in prose. Later, he used his first prose response to the film and wrote in the form of a poem.

> A new grand piano with strings full of rich, vibrant harmonies and soft human tears is what I most want. An instrument through which I can reproduce the pains, laughter, and images of nature found in the music of Chopin and Beethoven. It must have keys over which my fingers can glide at will, always sensitive to each nuance of emotion. I want damper pedals that dampen, sustaining pedals that sustain. When I sit on its cushioned stool and begin to play, I want the air

over that piano to be thick with ferns and palms, or still water and frozen moonlight, as the music dictates.

DREAM PIANO

Strings rich with
vibrant harmonies
Soft human tears
Keys keys keys
My fingers glide
guided by Chopin
  Beethoven
Bring to life
the jagged edge of pain
joy-rippled laughter
Pedals that dampen
Pedals that sustain
Cushioned stool
And when I play
  Keys   Pedals
the air above us
thick
with ferns and palms
still water
frozen moonlight
   magic
   music

Joey Wyche, at the same school, responded to the same film in his way:

What kind of daydream
should I write about?
What daydream
  shall I write?
Some things
  I
    at one time
thought I'd like to be
But these aren't right
  anymore
... I don't know
but even if I did
I'd probably forget
  My mind
    changes a lot
You understand that
Don't you?
    Don't you?

I picked up someplace the suggestion that a teacher might do well to tape a few class sessions and then ask himself:

1. How much was my voice heard instead of a student's?
2. How much did I question? How much did I make statements?

If your school has videotape equipment, ask for a taped session of one or more of your classes. If football teams and golfers can learn to spot their faults and correct a swing or a gait in this way, we can surely learn something too. I saw an excellent taped session with Ann Gulledge and her class on my recent trip to Albuquerque Indian School, but poor sessions are revealing, too. After all, we are in the business of educating—ourselves as well as others.

24. Ready-Made Patterns

An idea I picked up years ago and have used in my teaching since is that of using a poet or a writer of prose as a model. Why not suggest to a student who becomes interested in the writings of one poet, for example, that he read everything that poet has written? At least he can read everything available to him in your school library. Then suggest that he try writing in the style of that poet. Imitations are a perfectly sound way of learning what process a writer went through to produce his effects. The student will, in time, tire of copying or imitating and will start writing in his own way but he will have learned a great deal in the meantime and learned it from a professional.

Thelma Hanshew, Chilocco Indian School, Chilocco, Oklahoma, conducted a poetry class that she shared with us. She began by asking students to read the poem by Donald Hall called "1934." Of the assignment she says: "The poet relates his experiences as he remembers them when he was five years old. This provided me an opportunity to talk about the depression and the like. Then, I asked students to write, patterning their poems after the one we had read."

The two resulting poems Thelma sent along as examples are:

WIND OF 1971

Who has seen the wind of '71?
Neither you or I
But the weathermen themselves,
the astronots of the moon.
But who has seen the real '71?
Neither I or you,
But the people who are ready

and the year is passing through.
Of all the planets that are known
Man has only gone to the moon,
Through the great and meaningful year of '71.
But then, who has seen the wind of '71?
Neither you or I.

— *David Oksoktauck*

1971

The decade of the 60's now lies behind,
Leaving the 70's to unwind.
What, how, do we need to explore
Beside the moon and Asia and the Vietnam War?
What awaits us ahead, nobody knows,
but it includes us all, friends and foes.
What we find, I hope, is peace for all.
Then "victory" won't be nobody's call.
The world is in a mess, can't you see?
Unity is the word. Now let's all agree.

— *Carolyn Wanstall*

Peggy Jo Hall used a model as a means of helping students with writing a short story. She picked one of the truly great stories by Stephen Vincent Benét. She explains:

> We recently read "The Devil and Dan'l Webster" and I decided to have students write a folk tale patterned after the devil tales:
> 1. Person down on luck (student)
> 2. A description of the devil when he first appears to make the bargain
> 3. The effect of the bargain on the person's life, good or bad, good and bad
> 4. The return of the devil to collect
>
> They will write their stories in class, in four sessions. Once they leave class with their papers, I don't see three-fourths of them again. This class seems quite interested.

Who wouldn't be interested after having read the Benét story? We commend the use of model stories, articles, poems in this way. Do as Peggy Jo did and select excellent models. From poor ones students can only learn to write poorly. Then use the model as bones on which the student builds up the flesh of a new story or poem, thus making it his own.

The truth is that story patterns are not numerous. We were all born too late to write anything original. Many years ago Georges Polti studied Goethe and Schiller and identified thirty-six dramatic situations as the only ones available to writers. David Malcomson says that he has found "ten stories forever repeating themselves on the street and in written pages."[1] Instead of trying for originality in plot or pattern then, let us try for honesty, insight, and charm of presentation. Students are relieved of a great deal of nervousness and unnecessary delay, once they are assured that the plan of whatever they expect to write need not (cannot, in fact) be an out-of-the-blue original.

Another kind of ready-made pattern useful to students can be found in symbols. Symbols are self-contained, deep-in-the-bones nuclei that an author can surround with warm creative fluid. In this environment symbols will grow and multiply into forms the author can barely conceive.

It is not fair to students to withhold the idea that they have within them this very stuff of good writing. Symbols work for beginners as well as for experienced writers. They are especially useful for members of various cultures as they seek to speak to the inclusive audience. A good symbol takes the author by the hand and leads him forward—sometimes to greatness.

Cal Rollins returned to IAIA from our summer workshop and developed the following teaching plan:

Objective: To create a poem using symbols recognizable by non-Indians as Indian; use a single point of view (take a physical position).

Presentation:
   1. Teacher discusses the meaning of symbols.
   2. Teacher discusses emotional value of words.
   3. Teacher demonstrates loaded words: (from the poem "Miracle Hill" by Blackhorse "Barney" Mitchell)—"songs of old ones," "striped blanket," "my friend the white man."

Assignment: Write a poem using symbols immediately recognizable to a non-Indian as Indian. Do not mention the word "Indian," but create a definite impression of one's Indianness.

---

[1] David Malcomson, *Ten Heroes* (New York: Duell, Sloan and Pierce, 1941).

Results of students writing in response to this presentation:

Ready-Made Patterns

> Moccasins cover my feet
> The shawl on my shoulders
> (It is old) my grandmother wore
> In the ceremonies.
>
> It is beautiful.
>
> My hair in long braids
> Falls over my shawl;
> Pieces of leather
> Hold each braid.
>
> My shawl is beautiful.
>
> The door is open
> And I may go anywhere.
> The soil is rich
> Tipis are up everywhere;
> Young and the old live free,
> And the trees fill the land
> As I walk into my world.
>
> —*Iris Burns*

> On the shoulder
> Of Mother Earth I stand.
>
> Winds ruffle my soul
> And meadowlarks and doves
> Greet the dawn.
>
> Sun's rays pierce me,
> Narrow the gap,
> Enter my mind,
> Reveal my oneness.
>
> —*Carl Winters*

My students at IAIA used symbols with excellent effect, I thought. It was as if they reveled in pointing up ever-so-slight differences among their various cultures. And why not? They had been born and brought up, nurtured on their people's symbols. Away at boarding school the feel of symbol words on their tongues, at the tip of their fingers, relieved homesickness and bragged a little to fellow students who revered other symbols.

ONCE AGAIN

Let go of the present and death.
Go to the place nearest the stars,
gather twigs, logs;
build a small fire,
a huge angry fire.

Gather nature's skin,
wet it, stretch it,
make a hard drum,
fill it with water
to muffle the sound.

Gather dry leaves, herbs,
feed into the fire.
Let the smoke rise
up to the dark sky,
to the roundness of the sun.

Moisten your lips,
loosen your tongue,
let the chant echo
from desert, to valley, to peak—
wherever your home may be.

Remember the smoke,
the chants, the drums,
the stick grandfather held
as he spoke in the dark
of the power of his fathers?

Gather your memories
into a basket, into a pot,
into your cornhusk bag, and
Grandfather is alive
for us to see once again.

—*Liz Sohappy*

In the following poem, a matter-of-fact piece of remembering employs a symbol at the end to stab it all with significance.

MY DREAM

I remember an old man with short whiskers
about a few days' growing.
I still dream his smile that wrinkled
his lips in a pleasant, easy way.
He stands not much taller than a child's eyebrow.

Small in frame, he weighs little more than
the large sack of goods he packs home on his back.
A wide, black belt and a silver buckle
hold his worn, torn pants about his waist.
Around his ankles he folds, once or twice, his pant legs
to keep them from dragging the dirt and his shoes—
heavy, old, and cracked by weather and age.
Each morning the old man's smile awakes me
to eat his simple breakfast
of coffee and jam-toasted bread
from the flames of an open wood stove.
The fingers that twitch my ear
or tap my forehead always feel warm,
as I blink my lids slow and easy to dawn.
I crawl from my heavy quilt-blankets,
and the sun beams into the one-room shack.
I slip my sheep-wool cap over my head,
and he buttons my tattered cotton coat tight.
He hands me a sack of jelly sandwiches,
and I plod the snowy, mushy soil
to the crossroad near the highway.
My frozen fingers clutch a red-hot stone
wrapped in wrinkled newspaper.
The cold wind freezes the icy air in my head
and I ask, over and over again:
Why must I wait in this gray cold
For the white man's yellow bus?

—*Curtis Link*

Symbols can make or break a short story as well as poetry. In fact, a short story without symbols usually turns out rather thin and unnourishing broth. Here is the beginning of a story written by Ron during his first year of working with me at IAIA.

THE BIRD
by
Ronald Rogers

The bird was quiet in his palms—brown, grey speckled. It looked at him, neck twitching, wings spilled over the edges of his hands, scraping his thumbs. The boy's eyes did not reply, and the sparrow spread its wings, arched into the sky. It had trouble gaining altitude at first, but it slapped its wings against the hot summer air and shot upward, the light glinting across the easy curve in its spine.

The boy watched until the bird disappeared with a blinding

flash into the sun. In return, the sun crushed the flatness of the desert, and the land in the distance wavered from the heat.

The smooth earth was broken only by the imprints of his own boots, staggering out from the city—a sprinkling of silver patches in the blue of the distant valley. The boy had walked from there, his feet scraping the dirt, carrying him slowly, making the dirt smoke.

Now he stood looking at the sky, hoping to see the bird again, but the bird was gone. It was free and no longer his.

Nothing more to do, he thought. No reason to stay.

But he stayed just the same and watched the desert, and the desert did nothing. It gave him no reason to linger, no reason to go.

The sun pressed its massive hand into the desert, and the heat became a voice—soft and foreboding.

"Go home," it said. "Go home . . ."

His father was sitting where he always sat, in front of the television with the pale light flickering across the rough-chiseled lines of his thin face, across the narrow brown scar under his left eye, puckered and starved-looking—a scar from the last war. He looked up only briefly as Jim entered.

Jim closed the door behind him, closing out the sunlight and plunging the house again into darkness. The stuffy, gravelly dust smell hit his nostrils again and he cringed inside. It was a smell he hated, had always hated. He leaned against the plaster wall at his shoulder and waited for his eyes to adjust to the dimness of the room.

His father held his eyes on the television as he spoke. "Well?"

"Sir?" Jim said, very softly.

"Whaddya mean, 'sir?' Didya get ridda that goddamn bird?"

"Yessir," quietly.

"Awright! Get yer ma outta that bed. Tell her to make supper."

Jim stood for a moment, eyes squeezed shut, trying to kill the hate, but the hate was there. . . .

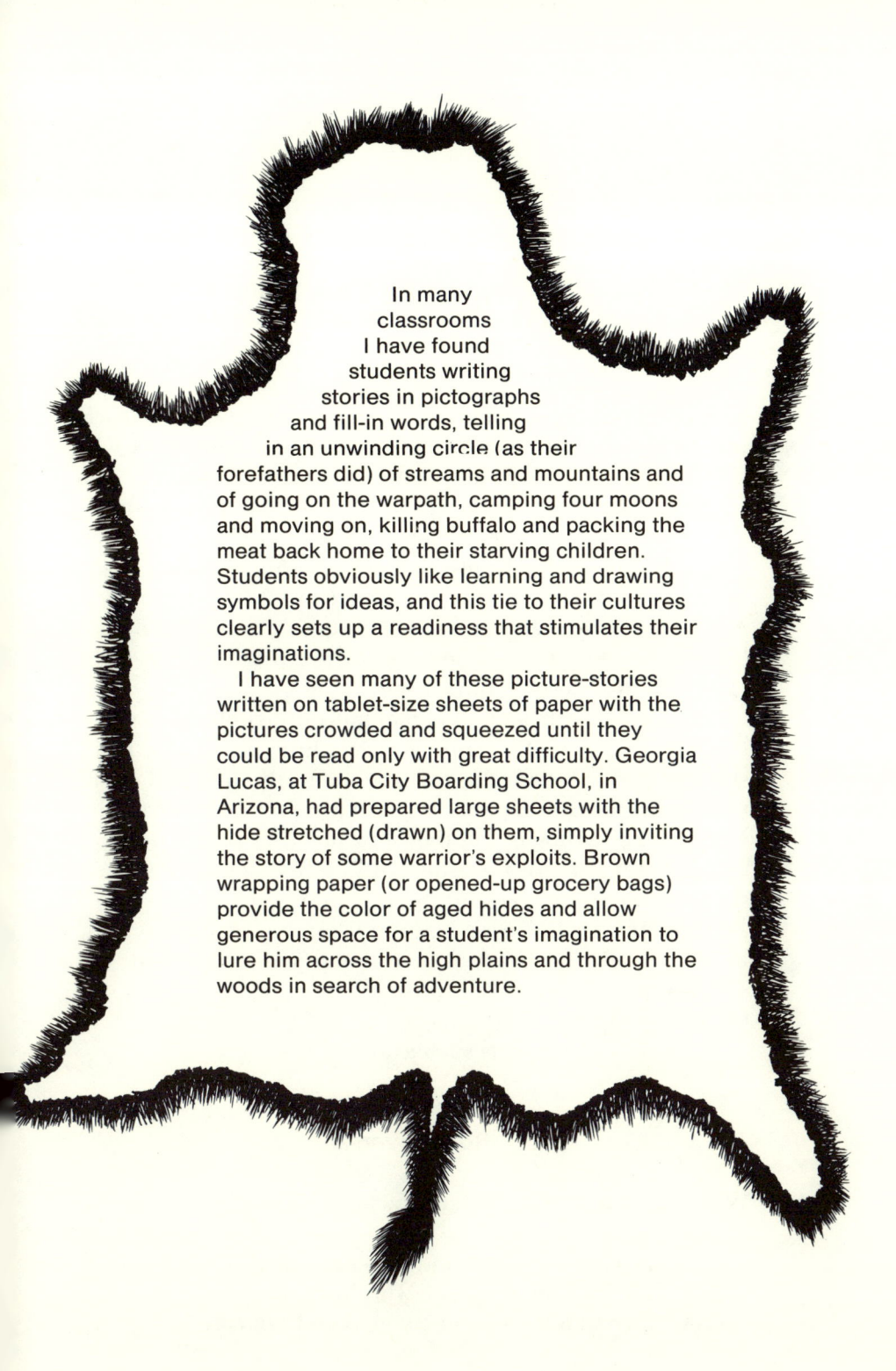

In many classrooms I have found students writing stories in pictographs and fill-in words, telling in an unwinding circle (as their forefathers did) of streams and mountains and of going on the warpath, camping four moons and moving on, killing buffalo and packing the meat back home to their starving children. Students obviously like learning and drawing symbols for ideas, and this tie to their cultures clearly sets up a readiness that stimulates their imaginations.

    I have seen many of these picture-stories written on tablet-size sheets of paper with the pictures crowded and squeezed until they could be read only with great difficulty. Georgia Lucas, at Tuba City Boarding School, in Arizona, had prepared large sheets with the hide stretched (drawn) on them, simply inviting the story of some warrior's exploits. Brown wrapping paper (or opened-up grocery bags) provide the color of aged hides and allow generous space for a student's imagination to lure him across the high plains and through the woods in search of adventure.

25. When All Else Fails

You well know from experience, even if you have been teaching no more than a week, that no approach will work with all students and that students do not always respond to your suggestions for getting started. A few of our teachers tried but were never able to persuade students to write a Life Story. I myself was unable to use that self-assignment source with some students. They simply refused to take that first step. All Navahos refused to write beyond the present. "We don't believe we should plan how the future will be," they said. "If we do, it will come out wrong."

One-to-one instruction is ideal but impossible until something is on paper. We must do something about that blank sheet of paper before the suggestions in the margins or the taped critique can happen. So here are some "if's" that have worked at one time or another for one or more of us.

If students do not respond to the self-assignment starters such as Here and Now and the Life Story . . .

If you, the teacher, get a Life Story but cannot find anything in it from which to extract a student's self-assignments . . .

If you feel that you are shirking your duty unless you make teacher-instigated assignments . . .

Then try assignments such as the following:

Role Reversal

Write three full, complete characterizations of you:

1. As if written by someone who hates you.
2. As if written by someone who loves you.
3. As if written by someone who could not care less.

Put on the other fellow's shoes. Get inside his skin. Look out through his eyes and write about You—what kind of person you are, the oddball things you do, your appearance, your drives, your ambitions and whether you will attain them—all from each of the three points of view.

Dreams

Record at least one dream—in detail. Pay particular attention to setting, whether or not the dream was in color, whether anything surprised you, and, especially, what emotions were involved. Were you in the dream or outside, looking on?

Overheard Dialogue

Record dialogue you overhear. This must be done on the spot, not remembered and recorded later. Find a place where two or more people are talking and where your note taking will not disrupt the flow of talk. Take down exactly what is said. If you have time, add the tones of voice, gestures, and so forth, but do not let this distract you from recording exact words.

Do this at three different times and in three different places.

Note: Spoken language differs materially from written language. It is supported by the nonverbal language of gesture, and behind it is an adjunct language of emotion. Eavesdrop! Listen! Get it down. While dialogue is not the same as speech, you must learn first to hear speech before you can write dialogue.

Still Strip

Using pictures collected from magazines, paste up a series of pictures or portions of pictures (without text) which communicate:

1. A story theme (a truth about life).
2. A single emotion.
3. A line of action that can become a story with a Beginning, Body or Middle, and End.

Creative Continuum

Consider yourself in the exact center of a contrived or imagined situation that is static. Regard time as a button you may press to start action forward (or backward, if you prefer). Write what happens as a result of the changed circumstance you have contrived.

For example: at twelve o'clock, midnight, on December 31, 1986, earth's gravitational pull will fail. We know this is advance. What preparations will be necessary—write them in detail.

Or, you have been the one person in the world selected to push the button, and no one else knows anything about it. Push the button and describe the results.

Or, look the other way. Suppose gravitation here has never exercised any greater pull than it does on the moon until, at noon today, it changes and we and everything around us are three times heavier than usual.

Suppose all the clocks in the world suddenly stop. Or, suppose death is suddenly eliminated. Suppose cars and all mobile machines decided to run backward instead of forward. Suppose money grew on trees, and the only work anyone would do was gardening, specializing in pruning. Suppose all food disappeared. Or that, suddenly, animals and human beings were no longer fueled by food. Would we all stay our present size without eating? Or, would we need to be fueled by something—by oil, by kelp, by sunshine, by gold nuggets, by ——— ?

Suppose for yourself whatever changed situation you will set in motion by pushing the Time Button and write fully all that happens.

Bumper Stickers, Posters

If you, the teacher, can collect a few current ones to prime students' pumps, do so. Some of these make excellent word studies along with nudging creativity. For example: "I'm neither for nor against apathy." "Some paranoiacs have real enemies."

Picture Series

Suggestions made by a series of pictures can help a student to develop his sensory awareness and to think in sequence. If your students have cameras available, the following ideas are stimulating and easy to develop. If they do not have cameras, many of these series can be found and cut from magazines. Almost all pictures require some written text. Try such series as the following:

1. Litter and a sequel on "after litter is removed."
2. Weeds and flowers.
3. Boys and girls—how we look to a camera (or a magazine photographer).
4. Eyesores on campus or in our community.
5. Eyesores we can cure.
6. Body language.
7. Textures—in general or specific, such as wood, fabric, animal fur, trees or tree bark, human skin, leather, roadways, or flower petals.
8. Long shots, close-ups, or long and close shots cut back and forth.
9. Ship designs.
10. Simple body movements taken in still sequence—of human beings or of animals, such as a horse, a dog, or a cat.
11. Bird movements as compared with those of human beings.
12. Makeup—before and after.
13. Masks and faces or faces into masks.
14. Shadows.
15. Reflections.
16. Plants growing (using one plant at different stages—possibly making a flip book that simulates the motion of growing from seed to full-blown flower).
17. Rock shapes and textures.
18. Shells.
19. Art work in progress.
20. The process of clay modeling from powder to finished sculpture.
21. Campus contrasts.

Music

Hearing music or making music will sometimes start words flowing. From a teacher at Mount Edgecumbe School I received the following:

> A boy came in after school last night and played the autoharp for about an hour. He sat in the chair, clutching that harp to him as if it were a baby and, with a dreamy expression, became oblivious to all distractions. Suddenly he stopped, tore a sheet from his notebook and began to write.
> After a few minutes, he thrust a poem at me. "What do you think of that?"
> I liked it. It was short and to the point, but he wouldn't part with it and I don't have a copy to send you.

Reactions

Record reactions to almost anything—ball games, museum trips, a motion picture, other classes, accidents, a change of seasons, and so on.

What did you see? How do you feel about it now? These are the cue questions that can start words flowing.

Robert Cable, at Cherokee Central High School, in Cherokee, North Carolina, gave his class an opportunity to write their reactions to a six-week course in drama. He received several thoughtful responses. For example, Lynnell Begay wrote:

> For the longest time I thought about my career, and one of my choices was putting makeup on movie stars. That is the reason I chose the subject of stage makeup in our drama class.
> I though it would be difficult, a lot of hard study, and, as usual, a lot of practice. Well, I found out it does take a lot of practice to become good at it, but you don't have to study hard. Most of the basics are common sense and somewhat of an understanding of facial features.
> I had a good time in this course because I didn't know any of the students before, and it gave me the opportunity to get to know some of the students in my class. It was an unusual way, because I never got to know anybody before by being in actual contact with their faces.
> Thank you, Mr. Cable, for giving me a chance to find out

the basics about this type of work. Now, I don't think I would work for a living by putting makeup on movie stars' faces because it's too gooey.

Visiting Writers

I arrived at Wingate High School, in Fort Wingate, New Mexico, immediately following a visiting poet from the Poets in the Schools Program. Sandi Gilley had asked her students to react on paper. I found their statements interesting and revealing.

>I hope to become a poet someday and learn to write my problems in words to share with others.—*Martha Ellison*
>
>I think anybody could be a Poet. The person could traveling around or stay in one place and still write many poetry.—*Sally Ann Benally.*
>
>The English in the poem is not regular English that we use or talk or write.—*Joseph Watchman*
>
>A poet is usually a person who has a lot of imagination and very creative.—*Nelson Livingston*
>
>Anyone can be a poet and actually maybe many of us are in our own ways but don't know it.—*Gary Yazzie*
>
>One thing that worries me . . . like how the sentences are written. Most of the sentences don't make sense to me. I can't get head or tail of the sentences. Most of the poets are not educated. And I guess a low standard of living. . . . I wonder if they ever make money out of it. To make a good living like other people who work hard to make a living is for me—*Glenio Billie*
>
>I think a poet should be a middle-age person who has been to quite a few place in the world or throughout the U.S. This person can compare things from big cities to small towns.—*Alfred Green*
>
>I think a poet should be old, not too old, but with greying hair so he would look more wiser. . . . A lot of poets are lonely people that keep company with themselves by writing and reading poems—*Chester Dee*
>
>My idea of being a poet is just being myself now. There's nothing with poets that are really special except the works or the poems they write.—*Raymond Hubbard*

I don't really care for poets or poems unless I really understand what it is about. — *Danny Yazzi*

Idioms

Idioms are the key to enjoyment of a second language. Bill Voron wrote from Wrangell, Alaska, that he was sending a book of English idiomatic expressions that he had found very useful (several such books are in print and can be found in inexpensive paperback editions). Bill commented:

> My students and I have had a lot of fun using this book. It has helped to fill some gaps in their conversational English. Many teachers, I've found, use a generous amount of idiomatic expressions on their students ("Knock it off," "Shape up," etc.). The student of English as a second language is at a distinct disadvantage. Alas, he cannot become a respectable class cutup; he cannot take part in the witty repartee between teacher and student that is so essential to real classroom drama.
>
> But, once armed with a handbook of idioms, he may do just battle with his idiomatic, idiotic teacher and re-establish that dialogical relationship which, as everybody knows, must be ever more meaningful today if we are to build a Pandemonium here on earth.

Here is one of Bill's class exercises. You, of course, can make up your own, simply by stopping to think about the idioms we use almost every time we open our mouths:

> Complete the Idiomatic Expressions by
> Filling in the Blanks
>
> Last Saturday the Wrangell Wolves wiped _____ the Petersburg Vikings in a hard-fought basketball game. The Wolves got off to a flying _____ with ten quick points in the first minute. Al Rinehart, who has a lot on the _____, made 6 of the 10 points. Later the Wrangell high-point man began missing too many shots. His shots were wide of the _____. By halftime the score was 48 to 48, and it was a toss _____ who would win. In the third quarter the game got rougher. One Wrangell player lost his _____ and began to argue with the referee. The Wrangell fans were up

in _____ because they felt the referee was bending
_____ to favor the
Petersburg players. Finally the referee blew his _____
_____ and threw the Wrangell player out of the
game. Petersburg quickly got 15 extra points. With three minutes left in the fourth quarter, the score was Petersburg 90 and Wrangell 75. It seemed that the Vikings had the game in the
_____. But in the last minutes of the game Wrangell pulled ahead and beat Petersburg by a score of 95 to 94.

A switch on this that I have sometimes used with students is to get them to exchange idiomatic expressions from the languages they first learned. Literal translations of these into English are often hilarious and sometimes reveal some fascinating facets of custom and culture. The exchange itself is always useful as a means of understanding the nature of language and the fickleness of words in any language.

Memory Albums

Jesse Stuart, master storyteller and former English teacher, told of memory albums as sources of writing. His was not the usual practice of memorizing poetry, formulas, prose passages, and such but that of memorizing the physical world about him:

> If you live in the country, try memorizing first houses along the highway leading to your home. After memorizing houses, go into finer details of memorizing pasture lands, meadows, streams, woodland areas—even rock cliffs, ponds, single trees along the roadside. To memorize and be able to retain what is memorized for years—and even for some for a long lifetime—is pleasurable for the individual.
> Although one can memorize while riding in a car, memorizing is best done while walking.... Not only does this practice increase one's powers of observation and provide mental pleasure, but it also allows one to travel to any time of the year, into any season, simply through recall.[1]

We all need this exercise. I recommend it to teachers and

[1] *Kappa Delta Pi Record* (April, 1972).

urge you to suggest it to students. Then provide time for students to make their albums tangible either in words or in sketches. I have an artist friend who sometimes gets caught without her drawing pen. She can remember the minutest details of tree shapes, land contours, and colors. She can because she has trained herself to remember. Most of us do not try. Students who practice this kind of remembering (following your lead, I hope) will soon write words that leap alive off the page.

Assignments According to Anne

Anne Cathcart wrote from Fort Yates, North Dakota: "You said once that you'd like a list of the assignments I made and how successful I thought they were, so here it is." I am sure that you will glean good ideas from Anne's frank reporting of her wins and losses:

Helping and Teaching Lower Grades

Did I tell you that I'm taking my ninth graders to first grade? We've been several times. We help the first graders write stories. Both classes really enjoy it. It seems to be helping the spelling and punctuation of my kids a little, because they don't want to do things wrong for the first graders. Then, too, this gives them something to write about themselves. The first-grade teacher is really happy with it too. She has been trying to get her first graders to write all year long. Now they're doing pretty well.

Note: It is also a good idea for an older group to make books of poetry or stories for younger groups. Books of this kind foster reading, of course, but they may also prod the writing bug in both groups.

Here and Now

They did o.k. once they got the idea, but I found that I had to have them write separately on each of the five senses at first. Only after this approach could they write what they observed using all of their senses.

There and Then

They didn't like this one. They said that they couldn't remember, that they didn't want to remember, and that it was none of my business. I think that if I had done these later, after I knew them better, they wouldn't have objected too strenuously. But they always did prefer to write if they could pretend that it was fiction, even if it wasn't.

Pictures

I had them choose pictures out of magazines and imagine that they were something in the picture. Then they wrote stories about themselves and the pictures. I had them remember to use the five senses. This was an amazingly successful assignment. Some of the stories were really good. One I remember was about an empty liquor bottle, and you could really feel it.

Scene

This was a bit complicated for some of the younger kids. They had trouble understanding the sequence, and had a tendency to write a story with many different pieces of scenes, instead of one complete scene. But this went over very well with some of the quicker kids and with the seniors.

Description of a Person

I had them describe a real person without naming him or her, and turn this description into a character for a story. It worked pretty well, the main attraction being that they could write about each other and then guess who they were writing about. There were problems with people being too superficial in their descriptions, and also we didn't have enough time to finish in one class session. Then, they didn't want to go back to them the next week when we met.

Diamond Poems

This was my first poetry assignment. The older kids thought it was easy, some had done it before. The younger kids had trouble because they didn't know what nouns, verbs, adjectives, and phrases were. Once that was straightened out, they loved it. One of the eighth-grade boys wrote practically nothing else the rest of the year.

Sound and Color Poems

I had them write about sounds and colors because no one could think up anything to write about on their own. I had them write in any form they wanted to in order to show what they thought a poem was. I got lots of rhymes, but more free verse than I expected. By the time we did this, they had pretty well mastered the idea of the five senses, and they did use it.

Ideas One, Two, and Three

These were dittos with about sixteen different ideas for topics on each one. They ranged from limericks to essays on drugs or religion to stories of various kinds. They had said that they wanted a choice because they never felt like doing what I assigned, so I gave them a choice. They liked it and it got some of my more reluctant writers going. Some of them got off on tangents and started thinking up their own topics. Fairly successful.

Collages

This was the first thing I did with the eighth graders. It broke the ice. I had them choose poems out of various student publications (from the other schools in our project) and illustrate them with collages. It started them thinking about poetry, and a lot of times they were surprised that kids had written the poems they liked. Collages were a great success and cheered up the classroom when we put them up with copies of the poems.

Study of the Ways a Poem Can Look and Why

Discussion on what makes poems different from prose and what makes them look different from each other. I used e. e. cummings's poem about a leaf falling off a tree for an example. They tried writing poems that looked like what they were writing about. Then we wrote short one-line descriptions, using one of the five senses and made them look like poems. Fairly successful. Fun.

Word Squares

Squares with letters in which you can find various words—across, backwards, upside down, diagonally. They loved them. I made them up on various themes having to do with creative writing. Sometimes I used strange words they had to look up in the dictionary. Good for vocabulary. They were so addicted to these that I used them as rewards. These also filled in time when they thought they didn't want to work or when some finished what they were writing before the end of the period. I got tired of them, but students never did.

Repetition in Poetry

Students liked this. We talked about different ways in which poets use repetition of sounds and words or groups of words to emphasize things. We talked about songs and then wrote poems that used repetition for emphasis. They are getting much better at thinking up subjects to write about.

Sessions with First Grade

When we started working on stories with the first grade, we wrote about pictures. The second time, about balloons. My students had the little kids use the five senses and imagine that they were the person in the picture or the balloons. They tried to get feelings and emotions. Afterward we wrote letters to the first graders and evaluations of what they had done and what they had learned. Very successful.

Science Fiction Stories

We read and wrote them. Great! The boys especially loved them.

Plays

They had some trouble remembering to use dialogue. Their plays kept turning into narratives. But there were some good story lines with good conclusions.

Balloons

Did this with the eighth grade. Mostly a review of the five senses. They liked it because they got two balloons, one to keep and one to pop. A couple of nice poems.

Characters from Pictures

Pictures of people. They had to put themselves in the place of the person in the picture and write a story or something else in the first person. Most interesting results, especially from the ones who had pictures of soldiers.

Group Stories

They love working in groups, and the stories they turned out were very good and original. This prompted the first spontaneous revising and rewriting all year, except in a few individual cases. Later, we used this same technique for poetry with lots of success. They preferred to work in groups of three or four rather than as a class.

Photography

We did this mostly out of class. Tried to do a class portrait series, showing the "real" personalities of the members of the class with poetry to go along with the pictures. They made all kinds of weird faces to express their personalities. But it never turned out because we couldn't get flash cubes to work, and the weather was too crummy to go outside. So, we wasted some film and flash cubes trying to make it work. But they had the planning experience, if not the results. We did a few short sequences —one on a fight, one about basketball, one on details. They loved to take pictures, so it was worth it.

Literary Magazines

Great! Fantastic! About 95 percent of the students at the school contributed something. Lots of participation in helping with the typing, stapling, running off, and so forth. Students loved reading their books. This also softened the administrators toward creative writing. Good public relations.

Anne's was a truly massive bookmaking project which resulted in four fat mimeographed books. These were distributed to students just before Anne left Fort Yates to return for her spring quarter at the University of California at Santa Cruz. Her books won a great deal of attention from the Fort Yates Area Office and were on display later at the North Dakota State Teachers' Meeting.

So, as Linus Pauling says, "The best way to have a good idea is to have lots of ideas." When some of those ideas have worked to bring forth writings, perhaps the best idea of all is to bind them into books. In that way we can be assured that even the lowliest first grader in the schools we have touched can say with Hilaire Belloc:

> When I am dead, I hope it may be said:
> "His sins were scarlet, but his books were read."

26. For Teachers Only

> If we take men only as they are, we make them worse than they are; but if we treat them as though they were what they ought to be, we raise them as high as they can be raised.
>
> — *Goethe*

I met Mark Van Doren only once in my life, and I talked with him for perhaps three minutes. Even so, I felt a deep sense of loss when I heard of his death. Charles Simmons, writing in the *New York Times,* December 31, 1972, came close to telling me why I cared.

Simmons tells how hard he worked on his Shakespeare term paper in Van Doren's class at Columbia University. He received no special recognition for the paper, but he did answer one question on the final exam that no one else in the class had gotten right. Van Doren explained that the question was in the final to satisfy his own curiosity and that "it changed nobody's mark, except that of the one person in class who got it right. It changed his considerably." Simmons's mark was A-minus.

Then, Van Doren took a leave of absence and turned the class over for the following semester to another professor, Raymond Weaver. Simmons wrote:

> That was about all, except for the applause. How long did it go on? Five minutes? Ten minutes? I looked around. Students were crying, from loss and exaltation. . . .
>
> Most of us were there one more semester. As for Raymond Weaver, no teacher or other public person ever took over under worse circumstances. Not L.B.J. after Kennedy. And yet within a week, with an entirely different style, Weaver had us in his hand. . . . For that one time in its long history Columbia turned out as many writers as Harvard, probably more. I won't try to name them all; I'd leave out half a dozen. They're all the sons of Mark Van Doren, who took them seriously, and Raymond Weaver, who tested them terribly. . . .

An epilogue. A few years ago, I did a review of three books for *The Times*. One of them was a reissue of Van Doren's *Introduction to Poetry,* and I mentioned that I had taken his Shakespeare course 25 years before. He wrote me, praised the review, and said he had looked up my mark. He was changing it to an *A*. Van Doren was retired and living in Cornwall; he had kept his class records with him as if they were love letters. Are there any teachers like that out there now?

Columnists, educators, concerned parents—Sydney J. Harris, Jacques Barzun, you, perhaps, and many others—speak frequently of the insight, humor, and passion required by a good teacher and bemoan the number of "artificial" teachers in our schools. Sidney J. Harris, for example, recently begged for "authenticity" in teachers. Not "authority" he specified, but "authenticity" that comes from the "realness, presence, and aura" that come from the depth of the personality. He continued: "The few teachers who meant the most to me in my school life were not necessarily those who knew the most, but those who gave out of the fullness of themselves; who confronted me face to face, as it were, with a humanhood that awoke and lured my own small and trembling soul and called me to take hold of my own existence with my two hands."

Many of those who wrote of these things insist that good teachers are born not made. I have seen many teachers transformed. I know from personal experience that just-getting-by teachers can change into "authentic" teachers. The writing experience—that of their students and that of their own—has brought about this miracle. I devoutly believe that it can happen to you.

My direct, schoolroom work with over two hundred teachers has convinced me that no teacher who cares about anything beyond his salary can help a student to express himself in words without coming to respect both the words and the student. I put respect and caring at the heart of good teaching.

At Tuba City Boarding School, Tuba City, Arizona, I found posted in Georgia Lucas's 8*b* classroom the following Bills of Rights. I do not know the original author of these, and perhaps you would like to prepare your own such declaration. The point is that rapport grows out of understanding. A clear statement in clear sight may help to set the stage for understanding and respect.

STUDENTS' BILL OF RIGHTS

1. Every student has the right to make a mistake without being laughed at.
2. Every student has the right to study undisturbed by his classmates.
3. Every student has the right to expect good manners from others.
4. Every student has the right to be heard when it is his turn to speak.
5. Every student has the right to be excused in an emergency.

TEACHERS' BILL OF RIGHTS

1. Every teacher has the right to expect students to work hard.
2. Every teacher has the right to detain the entire class for more study if one student interrupts the learning process.
3. Every teacher has the right to expect good manners from the student.
4. Every teacher has the right to expect homework finished when due.
5. Every teacher has the right to enjoy a happy working relationship with the students so that all students will achieve success, pride, and happiness.

Conditions under which learning can happen are the responsibility of many people—school board members, administrators, supervisors, as well as the classroom teacher. Given walls and windows, however, the air in a classroom is first breathed out by the teacher. It will be "caught" (like measles) as students are made susceptible to humor, respect, and high expectations.

The writing experience sets up ideal conditions for a classroom epidemic of mutual growth, transmitted from teacher to student, from student to student, and from student to teacher. The chain is fragile, however, and it is up to the teacher to keep it intact. To do this, may I offer one warning?

This suggestion is one that grows out of my visits to schools when I was demonstrating to teachers in their own classrooms. Because of hundreds of these class sessions, I feel that I must set down a firm reminder: Teachers, please do not disturb students once they have begun writing.

I know that no teacher does this intentionally. Still, sometimes when I am demonstrating, I work for half the period to nudge and prod students into writing and, bless'em, they almost always get with it, heads down, brows furrowed, pens scratching. Then frequently the regular teacher relaxes and starts moving around the room, watering houseplants, straightening cupboards, and doing janitorial work. Even more disturbing, teachers sometimes take this as a time to talk to me or an aide or a visiting supervisor.

Teachers probably are sick and tired of my pleading with them to do the assignment with their students, but this is great for the soul, and it is also the best way I know to keep the writing urge in the room intact and unified. When you get students writing, it is just as important as when I do it that you give students every chance to maintain a writing mood for as long as it will last.

If a workshop atmosphere has grown up in your classroom, you can probably type without disturbing anyone. Typing is a kind of non-noise humming, an "Everybody's Working" kind of song. Some classes like music to write by, and you can help set the character of the music they will find helpful. (I had a class at IAIA that decided they did not like words with their music when they were writing.)

The thing is, when a class is writing, write along with them if you possibly can. In any case:

Don't talk to visitors.
Don't open and shut desk drawers.
Don't tiptoe around the room.
Don't wad up waste paper.
Don't grade papers from another class.
Don't prepare tomorrow's lesson plan.
Don't look over students' shoulders.

Not disturbing someone is a sign of respect for that person and for what he has to say. In an atmosphere of respect and consideration your student can write.

Do write with your students.
Do be available to answer questions.
Do read instantly when a student shoves a paper at you.
Do find something to commend.
Do make positive suggestions.
Do share your writing efforts with students.

Now for a bit of relaxation and a tongue-in-cheek look at ourselves that I enjoy and am afraid you may have missed when it first appeared in *College English* published by the National Council of Teachers of English.

GRAMESIS[1]
By *Pauline Erickson*

1. In the beginning my English Teacher created nouns and verbs.

2. And the verbs were without form, and voice; and darkness was upon the face of the deep—my Teacher. And her shadow moved across the face of her pupils.

3. And she said, Let there be grammar; and there was grammar.

4. And Teacher saw the verbs, and laughed, and said that it was good: and she divided the bright students from those who remained in darkness.

5. And Teacher gave the bright students *A*'s and kept the others after school. And the homework and the bell were the first day.

6. And Teacher said, Let there be a sentence in the midst of the words, and let it divide the nouns from the verbs.

7. And Teacher made the sentence, and diagramed it on the board: I looked and saw that it was so.

8. And the Teacher called the sentence declarative. And the capital and the period were the second day.

9. And Teacher said, Let the noun words in the sentence be gathered together unto one place, and let the verb words appear: and it was so.

10. And Teacher called the verb words predicate; and the gathering together of noun words called she the subject: and Teacher saw that it was good.

11. And Teacher said let the predicate bring forth modifiers, the transitive verbs yielding objects, and the intransitive verbs yielding complements after their own kind, whose place is in itself, within the predicate: and it was so.

12. And the predicate brought forth modifiers, and transitive

[1] Reprinted by permission from *College English*.

verbs yielding objects after their own kind, and intransitive verbs yielding complements whose place was in itself, after their own kind: the Teacher saw that it was good and confusing.

13. And the active and the passive were the third day.

14. And Teacher said, Let there be modifiers in the firmament of the subject to further confuse and divide the students in the classroom; and let them be for proper nouns, concrete nouns, mass nouns, collective nouns, pronouns, and abstract nouns.

15. And let them be for to give meaning in the subject and to enhance the predicate: and it was so . . . . . . confusing.

16. And Teacher made two great words: the greatest word—adjective—to rule the noun, and the lesser word—adverb—to rule the verb: she made the conjunction also.

17. And Teacher set them in the sentence in order to make it difficult to diagram.

18. And to make it easier for her to divide the bright students from those who remained in darkness: and Teacher saw that her system was good.

19. And the phrase and the clause were the fourth day.

20. And Teacher said, Let the verbs bring forth abundantly the many verb forms—the gerunds, infinitives, and participles; the subjunctives; the auxiliary verbs, the linking verbs, and the phrasal verbs.

21. And Teacher created mood for every living creature that moveth, and tense for all time, and voice after their kind: and Teacher saw that it was indeed good.

22. And Teacher blessed them saying, Be fruitful, and multiply in complexity, and fill young minds with bewilderment, and let the bewilderment multiply into chaos in their minds.

23. And the lecture and the English test were the fifth day.

24. And Teacher said, Let the nouns and verbs bring forth living sentences after their own kind, book reports, essay questions, and English themes for the students to write: and it was very so.

25. And Teacher made all these things for the freshman English students to do, and everything that creepeth into her mind she gave them to do: and Teacher saw to it that it was good.

26. And Teacher said, Let us make one project in our image,

after our likeness: and let the project have dominion over the other projects, and over every subject of the college student.

27. So Teacher created the research paper in her own image, in the image of Teacher created she it; boring and difficult created she it.

28. And Teacher blessed it, and Teacher said unto the research paper, Be fruitful, and multiply, and replenish the supply of dropouts, and subdue the remainder of the college students; and have dominion over the other projects, and over the other subjects, and over every single grade that the student receives.

29. And Teacher said, Behold, I have given you every lesson on English grammar, which will help you in preparing your paper, and every lesson on English usage which will help you to get a passing grade on your paper; to you it hath all been given.

30. And to every beast of the earth, and to every fowl of the air, and to every thing that creepeth into the classroom, wherein there is life, I have given every rule and the principle for good English: and it was so.

31. And Teacher saw everything that she had made, and behold it was very good. And the Bib cards and the final draft were the sixth day.

Chapter 2

1. Thus the verbs and the nouns were finished, and everything had its purpose.

2. And on the seventh day Teacher ended her work, which she had made; and she rested on the seventh day from all her work.

3. And Teacher blessed the seventh day, and sanctified it: and all the students who had worked also, rested from their work.

4. And on the seventh day Teacher sat down on a nearby stone to begin the drudgery of correcting the freshman research papers: and the freshman students saw that it was so, and they smiled. It was very good.

As for our upside-down approach to English usage, we have stacks of praise by reviewers of our books—"All who write here are saying something important, not only for Indians but for all of us. This is a voice for youth, beautifully modulated because the writers have visions of truth." ". . . human emotions expressed in clean, fresh, and incisive English."

Our methods and results are praised by educators:

> We have made good use of the three copies of the *Arrow* books which you provided for us. Because our teachers have found the books so appealing to our students, they would like to purchase a dozen or twenty additional copies so that we may use them for small group study of current writing by Indian students. Such material is not available elsewhere—at least, we have not discovered it.[2]

> For teachers who complain that minority students can't write or that their students hate to write, *Arrows Four* could provide the liberating direction, the inspiration and encouragement, the basic first lesson in helping students "to discover themselves as people with something to say."[3]

Far more confirming and gratifying are comments from students who worked with us, those willing to go along with our topsy-turvy incursions into their safe world of grammar-rule repetition from grades one through college freshman English.

"Will there be an *Arrow III*? *Arrow II* is really great! I sincerely hope they will continue. I want more students to have the satisfaction of being published. Thanks to you and the others who made *Arrow I* and *Arrow II* possible, I have a feeling of accomplishment that I will never forget."

That was from Sherry Hampton and she also wrote: "I received your note with Ginn and Company's check." When I had sent on the request for permission to quote her poem "The Gift" Sherry wrote: "The chance of being published again makes me very happy. Although I may never be published after this, I'll continue writing. It is one way in which I can express myself. As you once said, 'Any work of writing confers its first benefit upon its author,' and it's true. Thank you for all the help and encouragement you have given me."

This week a letter arrived from Ronald Rogers: "Do you remember Ted Palmanteer? Greenfield Review Press pub-

---

[2]From the coordinator of language arts, Tucson Public Schools, Tucson, Arizona.
[3]Lou Kelly, *Iowa English Bulletin*, University of Iowa (Fall, 1979).

lished an anthology of poems, stories, essays for us this year. Release date is this month. . . . It looks nice and there's some good reading in it. It's called *Man Spirit*. They gave us the center spread in the catalogue."

Indeed I do remember Ted and his story "Man Spirit" that we worked on long and hard at IAIA in that old Writing Studio. Sometimes the letters are not so fluent, even yet, and seldom do they announce the publication of a book. Sometimes they merely say, Thanks for the chance I had to write, I'm moving on, head up, into life:

Dear Mrs. Allen,

I certainly thank you very much for taking part in my story, "Writing in the Wind." I'm glad it was published in *Arrow IV*. I'm so happy for you and Mrs. Gulledge of helping me win the story for *Arrow IV*.

Ever since the story was entered for the contest, Mrs. Gulledge was so positive that it was going to win and sure enough it did. I was not only anxious for the story to win, but along with it the memories of my beloved uncle kept coming back.

As you have known, it was on that particular day as it was when the funeral was underway that I wrote the story first. I guess we all have memories that we will always remember and think about. So I hope to continue writing, for I have some true stories told to me by my grandfather and poems I have wrote when I'm herding sheep alone.

As you have know, I wrote "Writing in the Wind" during my Senior year, last year. Now I've been home for one year. I didn't went back to school, cause of illness in the family. So I stayed and help until things got well, but I decided to stay for the winter.

Now I wished I had left back for school, for I'm going through such hardships. For example, now our sheep are lambing and we have to check at the corral every night and it's so cold with snow on the ground.

My mom tells me I'll never regret it, which I know is true, but I sure miss going to school. Now I'm anxious for fall to come. That's when I'll be going back to school which is at N. A. U.

I'll be mighty happy to correspond with you and again Thank you very much.

Sincerely,

Martha John

Index

Abstractions: 20, 55, 58, 66; ladder of, 66ff.
Acoma Pueblo: 176
Active voice: 56, 123
"Adjustments": 158
Albuquerque Indian School, Albuquerque, N.Mex.: 27, 144, 176, 183, 217
Aleuts: 6, 127
Alexander, Libby: 80
Allen, Ferrin L.: 144
Allen, Patty: 145-46
"Alone after Grandfather Left": 149-50
American Indians: 49, 52, 64, 70, 127
Antoghame, Grace: 25, 29
Apache, Mescalero: 176, 205ff.
Arrow (books): 128, 130, 145, 205-206, 246-47
Assignment: 41, 43ff., 138, 152, 183ff., 189; with camera, 163, 192, 200ff., 211, 214, 220, 226ff., 236, 242; when Life Story fails, 226ff., 234ff.; *see* life story
Athapaskan: 13
Auden, W. H.: 72
Autographing student books: 69, 144
Azure, Denise: 190
Azure, Steve J.: 174

Baby lesson: 20ff., 75
Backford, Alexandra: 186
Barton, Ron: 179
Beethoven, Ludwig van: 215
Begay, Lynnell: 230
Begay, Paul Leo: 177
Begay, Rose Lee: 178
Beilenson, Peter: 81
Belloc, Hilaire: 238
Benally, Sally Ann: 231
Benét, Stephen Vincent: 219
Benn, Karen: 179
Benner, "Norty": 152-53
Bergman, Ingmar: 211
Biemens, Leland: 86
"Big Day, The": 177

Bilingual education: 12, 131
Billie, Glenio: 231
Bills of Rights: students' and teachers', 241
"Bird, The": 223-24
Blackfeet Reservation: 155
Boyce, George A.: 6, 47
Bradley, Jodi: 85
Brouhard, Ronda: 182
Browning, Elizabeth Barrett: 78
Bureau of Indian Affairs (BIA), Department of the Interior, U.S. Government: 5, 6, 12, 16
Burns, Iris: 221

Cable, Robert: 230
Cameras: 140ff.; developing prints in classroom, 161ff.; Polaroid, 163; Diana, 163ff., 167ff., 229, 237; *see* demonstration teaching; *see also* camera-writing workshops; *see also* photographic supplies
Camera-writing workshops: at Mount Edgecumbe, 163ff.; at Choctaw Central, 167ff.
Campbell, Walter S.: 108
'Camping": 86
Carr, Donna: 136
Cathcart, Anne: 42, 128, 151, 234ff.
Cause and effect: 79, 101, 108, 123
Chapelle, Margaret: 145
Characters Make Your Story: 106
Character sketch: 19, 52, 237
Charette, Brenda: 174
"Chat and Chew": 148-49
Cherokee Central High School, Cherokee, N.C.: 230
Cheyenne-Eagle Butte High School, Eagle Butte, S.Dak.: 199
Chilocco Indian School, Chilocco, Okla.: 145, 218
Choctaw Central School, Philadelphia, Miss.: 158, 167, 198

249

Chopin, Frédéric François: 215
Ciardi, John: 71
Cochiti, N.Mex.: 81
Cohoe, Grey: 33, 35, 86
Collins, Marva: 4
Columbia University, New York, N.Y.: 239
Comic books: 195ff.
Concho School, Concho, Okla.: 189
Cone, Carolyn: 210
Connotation: 18, 36, 57, 63, 65
Constance, Hazel: 149
Con-Tact brand plastic: 173
"Cool Day": 176
Coriz, Eunice Jane: 27, 29
Crain, Allan: 135

Dee, Chester: 231
Demonstration teaching: 127ff., 132ff.; group writing, 77, 81ff., 83ff., 148–49, 241–42; *see* cameras; *see also* camera-writing workshops
Description: 113, 235; *see* five senses; *see also* sensory detail; *see also* five doors and "baby lesson"
Desjarlais, Terry: 175
"Devil and Dan'l Webster, The": 219
Dialogue: 112, 121; overheard, 227
Dickinson, Emily: 74
Dramatic action: 112; *see* scene

Edison, Thomas Alva: 189
Egavik, Alaska: 84
Elements of Style, The: 110
Eller, Janell: 175
Ellison, Martha: 231
Elwood, Maren: 106
Encyclopaedia Britannica: 214
English, as second language: 4, 5, 6, 12, 16, 17, 29, 55, 129–30, 210, 232
English, standard usage: 5, 11, 13–14, 16, 19, 29, 48
Erickson, Pauline: 243
Eschback, Ronnie: 174
Eskimos: 49, 52, 70, 127
Evans, Bergen: 68
Exaltation of Larks, An: 63
Experience, writing from: 14–15, 25, 30ff., 41ff., 71, 155; shared, 62, 77; foreign to students, 72; memories, 74; frustrations, 74; emotions, 75, 177; ready-made stories, 203

"Fallen Leaf": 28
Figures of speech: 18, 50, 115, 192; personification, 28–29; listed and described, 115–16

Finger exercises: 18, 30; *see also* assignment
First draft: 26, 48–50, 59–60, 74, 83, 102, 116, 206ff., 215
First person: 31, 36, 45, 201
Five doors: 20, 22, 24, 27, 35, 55, 61, 75–77, 83, 87
Five senses: 20, 26ff., 31, 36, 43, 46, 47, 59, 77–79, 85, 87, 152, 188, 235, 237
Flandreau Indian School, Flandreau, S.Dak.: 210
Fletcher, Cheri: 190
Forms of Poetry: *see* poetic forms
Fort Yates Area Office (BIA), Fort Yates, N.Dak.: 238
Fox, Sandra: 199
Frederick, Marlon: 190
Fulton, Janice: 198

Games: *see* word games
Gilley, Sandi: 231
Ginn and Company (publishers): 246
Goethe, Johann Wolfgang von: 202, 239
"Good News and Bad News": 191
Grades: 37, 151ff., 193; *see also* marginal markings
Graffiti: 181
"Gramesis": 243–45
Grammar, rules: 13–14, 18–19, 29–30, 102, 110, 235, 246; standards, 16; punctuation-by-whim, 158
"Grandmother's Mistake": 203ff.
Grandparents, as subject: 38, 45, 52, 84, 120, 203ff., 247
Graves, Robert: 76
Green, Alfred: 231
Greenfield Review Press (publishers): 247
Gulledge, Ann: 27, 144, 153, 176, 183, 192, 217, 247

Haiku: 61, 77, 80ff., 146, 174–75, 179–80; decorated, 178
Hall, Anne Cathcart: *see* Cathcart
Hall, Donald: 218
Hall, Peggy Jo: 42, 189, 200ff., 210ff., 219ff.
Hallsboro High School, Hallsboro, N.C.: 85, 215
Hampton, Sherry: 246
Hannafioux, Kathleen: 136
Hanshew, Thelma: 218
Hanson, Susan: 83
Harris, Sydney J.: 240
Haugen, Mike: 83–84
Henderson, Harold G.: 81
Here and now: 30ff., 45, 48, 226, 234
Hooked on Books: 195

Hopkins, Gerard Manly: 64
House Made of Dawn: 199
"How long's it hafta be?": 41, 43, 164, 169
"How to Eat a Bean": 86
Hubbard, Elbert: 42
Hubbard, Raymond: 231

"Identity Thing, An": 180-81
"I'm Only Going to Tell You Once": 74
Indiana State University, Terre Haute, Ind.: 214
Indians: *see* American Indians
Individuality, development of: 3-4, 15-16, 38-39, 171, 180ff., 185ff., 217, 220-21, 226, 239ff.; as source of writing, 5-6, 13-14, 18-19, 43, 45, 62, 73, 75, 77, 102, 110, 120; sense of self, 4, 129, 145
Instant writers: 21ff.
Institute of American Indian Arts (IAIA): 6, 24, 29, 32, 85, 128, 146, 185, 221, 223, 242, 247
Intensive Journal Workshop: 42-43
Intermountain School, Brigham City, Utah: 24, 144, 177, 185, 209
Interview: 59, 120ff.
Irving, Patricia: 33, 35

Jim, Russell: 189
John, Martha: 247
Jones, Lemuel: 180

Karate: 73
Katongan, Gordon: 84
Katzive, David: 181
Kaufman, George: 99
Keats, John: 71
Keene, Donald: 81
Kehoe-Mamer Foundation: 128
Kirsch, Robert: 202
Koto: 73
Kotzebue, Alaska: 155
Kramer, Rita: 20

Lancaster, A.: 136
Laverdure, Greg: 174
Laws of writing: 122-23, 156
Lazarus, Emma: 130
"Legend of the Apache Mountain Gods": 206
"Let's Talk Writing": 129, 139
"Letter to Be Mailed in the Cupboard": 187
Letters: 29, 183ff., 237; "instant status"; 185ff.

Lewis, Michael: 176
Library of Congress: 188
Life for human beings: *see* one subject
Life I Really Lived, The: 202
Life story: 41ff., 48, 75, 139; privacy for, 44; as subject sources, 73, 226
Link, Virgil Curtis: 34, 223
Lipton, James: 63
Literary allusions: 67
Livingston, Nelson: 231
Lopez, Alonzo: 186
Los Angeles Times: 42, 202
Lowry, Clarissa: 144
Lucas, Georgia: 240
Lukachukai, Ariz.: 155

Mamer, Mary Lois: 128
"Man Spirit": 247
Marginal markings: 47, 50ff., 74, 83, 154, 156, 157, 203, 207ff., 226; "ktwtbt," 53; cassettes, 213
Martin, Myra: 158, 167
Martine, Bennett: 176
Martinez, Ted: 177
Merriott, Ollie "Sassy": 133, 135
Mescalero Apache, "Mountain Spirit Dancers": 205ff.
Millay, Edna St. Vincent: 74
Milne, A. A.: 71
Minneapolis, Minn.: 181
Miracle Hill, The Story of a Navaho Boy: 4n., 12, 27
Mitchell, Aurelia: 203
Mitchell, Blackhorse "Barney": 27, 29, 203
Moholy-Nagy, László: 159-60
Momaday, N. Scott: 199
Morehead, Cleta: 24ff., 135
Morehead, Glen E.: 79, 138
Morin, Paula: 175
Motion pictures: 211ff.; commercially made, 214; videotape, 217
Mountain View School, Mountain View, Calif.: 181
Mount Edgecumbe School, Mount Edgecumbe, Alaska: 24, 79; workshop, 132ff., 163ff.
Mullican, James S.: 214
"Murphy's Law": 209
Muskogee Area Office (BIA), Muskogee, Okla.: 182
"My Dream": 222

Náátsíílid: 144
Nanouk, Karen: 86
Narzun, Jacques: 240
National Council of Teachers of English: 243

National Education Week: 143
Navaho: 12, 85, 121, 226
Neil, Bonnie: 185
Neologism: 63
Newman, Edwin: 68
New York Times: 20, 159, 239
"Night Rider": 174
Nome, Alaska: 183
Noriego, John: 180
North Dakota State Teachers' Meeting: 238
"No Sunshine": 176
"Now I Can See": 137
Numkena, Earl: 179

Oglala Community School, Pine Ridge, S.Dak.: 195
O'John, Calvin: 75, 187
Oksoktauck, David: 219
"Once Again": 222
"One Day I Was Thinking": 182
One subject (life for human beings): 5, 13, 39–40, 202; *see* assignment; *see also* life story
Overhead transparencies, how to make: 212
Overvold, Orriet: 173

Paganini, Niccoló: 72, 77, 102
Pahona, Claude: 179
Palmanteer, Ted D. (Tomeo-Palmanteer): 247
Paper, lined or tablet: 24ff., 77
Parisien, Rose: 175
Patkotak, Ethel: 132
Patterson, Tom: 182
Pauling, Linus: 238
Penn Mutual Life Insurance Company: 181
Philadelphia Art Museum: 181
Phoenix Indian High School, Phoenix, Ariz.: 152
Photographic supplies for classroom developing: 160ff.
Photography, as communication: 159; developing prints, 161ff.; Polaroid, 163; Diana cameras, 163ff.; Mount Edgecumbe camera workshop, 163ff.; Choctaw Central camera workshop, 167ff.
Picasso, Pablo: 103
Pictures without cameras: 160–61
"Poem: A Reminder": 76
Poetic patterns: 19, 61, 76, 87, 117–18, 236; cinquain, 78ff.; diamanté, 80, 147, 235; haiku, 80–81, 117, 146; limerick, 117; senryu, 147
Poetry tree: 145

"Poetry writer is her": 158
Poets in the Schools Program: 231
Point of view: 57, 119, 227
Polacca, Dianna: 149
Polti, Georges: 220
Porter, Fayne: 146
"Portrait of a Horse" (movie): 215
Povey, John F.: 128
Powell, Virginia: 133
Pratt, Agnes T.: 74
Present tense: 31, 36, 45, 201
Progoff, Ira: 42
Prose patterns: 88, 103
Publication, trade: 16, 134, 143, 246–47
Pyramid Films, Santa Monica, Calif.: 214

Read Magazine: 66
Readers' Digest Magazine: 67
Record player: 7, 73
Red ink: 18, 49
"Reporting to Crazy Horse": 139
Revision: 29, 36, 49, 55, 116, 123, 154, 188, 203, 208, 214, 237
Rhyme: 76, 82, 138, 235
Riffle Junior High School, Kettering, Ohio: 213
Ripley, Dillon: 130–31
Riverside Indian School, Anadarko, Okla.: 199
Rogers, Ronald: 158, 178, 186, 223, 246
Rollins, Cal: 192, 220
Royalties: 128

Samuels, Madelyn: 34
Sandscriber, The: 149
Scene: 52, 88ff., 104–105, 211ff., 235; five steps of, 89ff., 114
Schense, Mae: 151, 190, 214
Schiller, Johann Christoph Friedrich von: 220
School bookstore: 199
Scott, Ellen: 205ff.
"Sea Is Melancholy, The": 74
"Seashore": 214–15
Seed pods: 24, 26
Selye, Hans: 14
Seneca School, Wyandotte, Okla.: 182
Sensory detail: 47, 79, 83, 107, 201, 229
Sequoyah High School, Tahlequah, Okla.: 189, 200
Shakespeare, William: 136
Sherman Indian High School, Riverside, Calif.: 178, 180
Short story: 19, 60–61, 76, 200–202, 211, 219ff.; *see also* story as generic term
"Signs of the Times": 177
Simmons, Charles: 239

Simon & Schuster (publishers): 208
Smithsonian Magazine: 130
Snortum, Neil: 58
"Snow": 178, 179
Soatikee, Carol: 189
Sohappy, Liz: 222
Stafford, William: 71, 188
Starnes, Lois: 128
Statue of Liberty: 130
Stern, Isaac: 72
Stewart, Evan: 185
Stitch Witchery: 166, 172ff.
Stoppers: 18, 242–43
Story, as generic term: 88, 103ff., 202ff.
Strand, Marcia: 134
Strunk, William, Jr.: 110
Stuart, Jesse: 233
Student books: 68–69, 238; covers for, 143–45, 149, 166, 172ff.
Student Review Committee: 153
Style: 31, 42, 46, 54, 120, 218
Subjects: *see* individuality; *see also* life story
Symbol (symbolic action): 62, 220ff.

Talahaftewa, Herbert: 180
Tape recording: 7, 120, 140, 209, 211, 217; cassettes for marginal markings, 213
Taylor, Mariana: 178, 180
Taylor, Max: 179
Teachers and Writers Collaborative: 129
"Teahouse of the August Moon": 210
There and then: 36, 234
Thesaurus: 58, 67
Thorfinnson, Greg: 176
Transitions: 99ff.
Tuba City Boarding School, Tuba City, Ariz.: 240
Turtle Mountain Community School, Belcourt, N.Dak.: 173, 190, 214

Unalakleet, Alaska: 83
University of California, at Los Angeles, Calif.: 128; at Santa Cruz, 128, 178, 238
University of Pennsylvania, Philadelphia, Pa.: 181
Upside-down teaching: 5, 8, 129, 245

Van Doren, Mark: 239–40
Vincenti, Carl: 27–29
Vocabulary: 18, 36, 64ff., 195ff.
Vogler, Stephen H.: 213
Voigt, Marie Rose: 142–43
Voron, Bill: 232

Wanstall, Carolyn: 219
Watchman, Joseph: 231
Weaver, Raymond: 239
Weber, Karen: 191
West, Alexa: 144, 209
West, Jessamyn: 202
"What Shall I Write about Today?": 75
White, E. B.: 110
White, Jim: 144
White Shield School, White Shield, N.Dak.: 142
Whitley, Richard: 215
Whitman, Walt: 78
Whorton, Julian: 189
Williams, Helen: 134
Wilson, Woodrow: 188
Wingate High School, Fort Wingate, N.Mex.: 144, 231
Winters, Carl: 221
Word games: 63ff.; connotated categories, 63; neologism, 63; onomatopoeia, 64; language blending, 64; telescoped sounds, 64; Royalty word game, 64; Scrabble word game, 64, 70; Password word game, 65; word associations, 65; ladder of abstraction, 66; ladder of specifics, 66; *Reader's Digest*'s "It Pays to Increase Your Word Power" and "Toward More Picturesque Speech," 67; word origins, 67; poetry as, 70ff.; *see* graffiti
Wrangell, Alaska: 232
Writer, Dennis: 195ff.
Writing, as stimulus to reading: 3–5, 16, 68–69, 110, 145, 174, 194ff.
"Writing in the Wind": 247
Wyche, Joey: 216

Yahola, Johnny: 166–67
Yale University, New Haven, Conn.: 195
Yazzie, Danny: 233
Yazzie, Gary: 231

Writing To Create Ourselves, designed by Edward Shaw and Terry Bernardy, with special calligraphy by Patsy Willcox, was set by the University of Oklahoma Press in eleven-point Baskerline, an Alphatype version of traditional Baskerville type. The book was printed offset on Warren's #66 Antique, a permanized sheet, with presswork and binding by Halliday Lithograph Corporation.